The Honey Bee

THE HONEY BEE

James L. Gould

Carol Grant Gould

SCIENTIFIC AMERICAN LIBRARY

A division of HPHLP
New York

Library of Congress Cataloging-in-Publication Data

Gould, James L., 1945–
   The honey bee / James L. Gould, Carol Grant Gould.
     p.   cm.
   Bibliography: p.
   Includes index.
   ISBN 0-7167-5023-6
   1. Honeybee. I. Gould, Carol Grant. II. Title.
QL568.A6G68 1988   88-10084
595.79′9—dc19   CIP

Printed in the United States of America

Scientific American Library
A division of HPHLP
New York

Distributed by W. H. Freeman and Company,
41 Madison Avenue, New York, New York 10010
20 Beaumont Street, Oxford OX1 2NQ, England

2 3 4 5 6 7 8 9 0 KP 6 5 4 3 2 1 0 8 9

This book is number 25 of a series.

To Grant and Clare

Contents

Preface

It is an unalloyed pleasure to be allowed to share with the subscribers to the Scientific American Library the fascinating story of honey bees. The diminutive members of this one species have been the subject of more research and scientific papers than the other 2 million species of insects combined, and for good reason. At first bees were special because they provided that rarest of prehistoric commodities, sugar. In the process of learning how to keep bees and harvest honey (a problem not effectively solved until 1851), humans acquired a vast store of knowledge, lore, and superstition about honey bees. Their apparently harmonious and well-organized colonies of tens of thousands of individuals—the ultimate socialist state, with complete selflessness and redistribution of income—has attracted admiration and well-meaning philosophical comment since Aristotle's day.

The ease with which a hive can be kept year round to supply a virtually endless series of experimental subjects made bees an early favorite with physiologists; even today, when a writer makes a generalization about the sensory abilities of insects, the discussion almost always concentrates on honey bees. The discovery more than 80 years ago that bees have senses we lack has forever altered our picture of how animals experience the world. Finally, the discovery early in this century of how to

This space on every right-hand page contains a small drawing of a bee. If you flip the pages starting from the back of the book, the bee will dance.

train forager bees to an artificial flower opened the floodgates of behavioral experimentation and led to the discovery of the most elaborate navigation and communication systems known outside our own species. The recent discovery that bees formulate plans and have mental maps assures us that these creatures have yet to show us the limits of their capabilities.

Honey bees are the most complex organism to have evolved along an evolutionary trajectory that began more than a billion years ago. At that time, a seemingly trivial but critical separation began in the animal kingdom: In one group of organisms, the egg cell repeatedly divided to create a hollow sphere of cells; one half of this sphere then collapsed into the other, creating a two-layer hemisphere; the hemisphere then grew to create a two-layer sphere, with an opening where the original folding in took place; that opening became the creature's mouth. The other group followed exactly the same pattern, but the opening became the anus instead. From the first group evolved 17 phyla, including the arthropods, of which the insects are the dominant class; from the second group evolved only four phyla, among them the vertebrates, to which we belong. Honey bees are at the top of their part of the evolutionary tree, whereas humans are the most highly evolved species on our branch. To look at honey bees, then, is to see one of the two most elegant solutions to the challenges of life on our planet. More interesting, perhaps, than the many differences are the countless eerie parallels—convergent evolutionary answers to similar problems.

Many readers will doubtless wonder why we do not refer to these paragons of invertebrate intelligence as "honeybees," the form of the common name that dominates dictionaries and, as a result, newspapers and popular magazines. The scientific convention for insects is that, if the common name correctly identifies the organism's phylogenetic group, then the name is properly divided: honey bees are bees, house flies are flies. If the common name is misleading, on the other hand, the two words are joined: dragonflies are not flies (or dragons), silverfish are not fish. Dictionaries also often misidentify the honey bee as *Apis mellifica,* whereas to scientists it is *Apis mellifera.* These egregious errors are self-perpetuating: dictionaries proudly refuse to reflect or conform to scientific usage, and most other publications mindlessly conform to dictionaries. There is a lesson here, but this book will not dwell on the failings of lexicographers; it is dedicated instead to enjoying and understanding a triumph of nature.

J L G
C G G
Princeton

The Honey Bee

CHAPTER *1*

Beekeeping

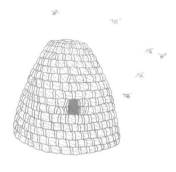

When the vast plains of the African Rift Valley were created perhaps 25 million years ago, they brought with them a totally new habitat, ripe for new species of animals and plants. Among the primates, only hominids and baboons left the security of the forests to exploit this new environment; baboons remained, like virtually all Old World primates, essentially vegetarian, while the line that led to humans began to hunt as well. Since the amino acids our species now requires are rare in nearly all vegetation, we know that the niche *Homo sapiens* filled required animal as well as plant protein. In early human societies, hunters stalked and trapped prey while gatherers harvested wild nuts, berries, roots, and honey. The antelopes they hunted had evolved from small forest-dwelling species to eat the grass of the newly formed plains, and new races of honey bees emerged to forage the wildflowers of the savannah.

Mädchen bei der Bienen *by Curt Liebich.*

A prehistoric honey gatherer has climbed a tree carrying a basket to hold honeycomb. She is reaching into the hive while angry bees fly about. Eastern Spain, 6000 B.C.

Around 10,000 years ago, humans discovered how to domesticate first animals and then plants. With domestication, the need to hunt and gather was gone; the need to live in small groups and move nomadically with the rhythm of the seasons disappeared. And the time to try to domesticate the honey bee had finally arrived.

SWEETNESS AND LIGHT

It is difficult, in our world of junk food and sugar substitutes, to appreciate the value of honey to early hominids, and thus to understand their incentive to bring the colonies that produced this precious commodity under some sort of control. The three major commercial sources of sugar today are sugar cane, sugar beet, and corn (the source of corn syrup); all are recent discoveries for the Western world. Sugar cane, for instance, was indigenous only to the Asian tropics; commercial cane sugar did not become available until Spanish and Portuguese explorers brought it back and established plantations in the New World tropics about 1600. The sugar beet was not discovered and grown commercially until 1800, and corn, of course, was restricted to the New World.

Until just 400 years ago, then, honey and fruit were the only significant sweeteners. The strong human craving for sweets (as well as the equally inconvenient and now unnecessary drive to consume fats) is an evolutionary holdover from the days when sugar and fat were in short supply, and crucial to our survival. Because our bodies require calories that were once difficult to find, our tongues are plentifully supplied with sugar receptors to enable us to recognize any source of sugar, however weak. Honey, intensely sweet and immune to spoilage (its peculiar sugars and thick texture do not support microörganisms), was to early humans a miracle of nature.

In addition to satisfying early man's craving for sweetness, honey satisfied other cravings as well. Mead, a beverage that has the inestimable value of being both sweet and intoxicating, has been made from time immemorial. From its natural 80 percent sugar, honey was diluted threefold with water (so that yeast could grow in it) and allowed to ferment for around six weeks. At the end of that time, it was flavored with herbs. Despite all the sugar that is converted to alcohol in the process, mead is still about as sweet as a soft drink, and about twice as alcoholic as most wine—four to six times as inebriating as beer.

The fatal attraction of demon mead made it a treacherous indulgence. In 946, the Slavic St. Olga is reputed to have provided unlimited mead at her son's funeral, to which she had invited her enemies. Five thousand incapacitated revelers were slain in their cups. In 1489, retreating

Russians left a huge stock of mead behind for their Tartar pursuers to find; 10,000 Tartars drank themselves into senselessness and were killed by the Russians.

Honey was also employed undiluted as a preservative. The use of honey as an embalming agent was the prerogative of the wealthy. When Alexander the Great was killed in his last campaign, his body was placed in a golden honey-filled coffin for transport home and burial. The tombs of the first four earls of Southampton were recently excavated, and the honey they were buried in nearly 400 years ago is still free flowing and fresh.

Until very recently, beeswax was also economically important. It was the only practical source of wax before the discovery of a way to extract lanolin from wool; later, journeys into the New World led to the discovery and cultivation of the wax-producing carnauba plant. (Until nearly 1700, people assumed that bees gathered their wax from plants.) Before the discovery of how to distill paraffin from oil, beeswax candles were the only alternative to tallow (rendered animal fat), and beeswax candles continue to be prized because they retain their shape in hot weather. Beeswax has also been used throughout the ages in many other ways, both practical and aesthetic. It is critical to certain forms of art and sculpture, such as lost-wax casting and batik printing, and it has been used in applications as various as wax slates for schools and as an adhesive (though it did not work very satisfactorily for Icarus).

A honey gatherer uses a rope ladder to reach a colony located in a small rock fissure. Natal, South Africa, Stone Age.

PREHISTORIC TIMES

Gathering honey before bees were kept in hives must have been a harrowing experience; that anyone would attempt it only reinforces our impression that it was an extraordinary and necessary luxury. Rock paintings from 8000 to 15,000 years old present a fascinating history of the process, and the gruelling methods shown probably predate the practice of painting pictures in temperate-zone caves by thousands if not millions of years.

The most ancient recorded method of locating a wild colony is "beelining," and it is still in use. The trick is to find a place where foragers congregate to collect something; since flowers are a diffuse resource, this something usually is water or propolis (tree sap). The hunter marks a bee and then observes which way she flies off. If she returns quickly, the hive must be close; if not, the business becomes more difficult. To find a distant hive, honey hunters capture several foraging bees and hold them in a container. After walking a fair distance in the departure direction of the marked bee, they release a forager, observe her departure, walk that

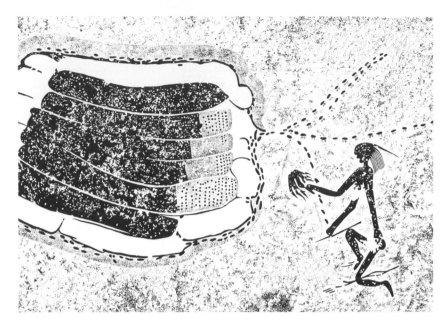

Two honey hunters use smoke to drive the bees from their colony. Left, California, twentieth century. Right, Zimbabwe, age unknown.

way for a bit, release another forager, and so on. If they walk past the tree in question, the next released forager will tell them by flying back the other way.

A popular alternative to this approach is to use one forager, feeding her honey to lure her away from a flower. She flies off to the hive, then returns for more. While she feeds, the hunter carries her in the direction she has just flown from; when she departs, he stands still, waiting. The forager seems able to relocate her mobile honey source, and the hunter slowly "walks" her to her hive in stages. The bee tells the hunter how close he is to the hive by the length of her trips there and back.

Finding the hive, though, is the easy part. Bees not only place their colonies high in trees, they also like cavities with small entrance holes. The would-be hive robber, clad in protective animal skins, must climb the tree and then break open the trunk. Guard bees are waiting and can recruit thousands of hive mates to help defend the colony. Against these odds, the prehistoric honey gatherer, like the modern beekeeper, used smoke. No one understands why smoke seems to calm some bees, but it clearly inhibits those tending eggs and larvae in the hive from flying. Some people have speculated that this may be an innate response to forest fires, others that it is an automatic behavior for dealing with low oxygen levels, and still others that it is an "artifact"—a meaningless behavior released by a totally unnatural stimulus. Whatever the cause, it has been used by beekeepers for millennia. Even so, honey collecting would have been a painful experience, potentially fatal to the allergic.

For the bees, too, the encounter may be deadly: the cavity has been breached, its value destroyed both as defense against attack and as insulation against cold. The colony must move as soon as the queen (assuming she has not been killed) can be prepared; brood, wax, and food must be abandoned. The chances that the relocated colony will be able to rebuild and resupply itself in time for winter are not very good, particularly if the raid took place in summer or autumn. In short, robbing hives is wasteful for all concerned. The goal of beekeeping is to preserve the bees and have their honey too.

THE FIRST BEEKEEPERS

From a bee's point of view, the ideal artificial cavity would have just the right volume and shape, an entrance hole of the proper size and location, and a perfect balance between ventilation and insulation. It would be dry, it would face south, and be located ten meters up. For the would-be beekeeper, the ideal cavity would be cheap and portable, located on the ground, easily opened for inspection and harvesting, and engineered so that the bees would put nothing but honey in the most accessible part of the hive. In addition, its design would allow the beekeeper to put swarms of bees directly into the hive.

The earliest recorded hives are seen in paintings and drawings on tombs and other monuments in Egypt, and the design spread and matured all around the Mediterranean; modern descendants of these first hives are still in use. The basic design was a cylinder of unbaked, hardened mud with a volume of as little as nine or ten liters; there was a hole at the bottom of the front end, but archaeological sources do not indicate whether the back could be opened. Today in the Mediterranean, several

Earliest drawing of beekeeping and honey preparation, from an Egyptian temple built about 2400 B.C. The cylindrical hives are stacked at the far left.

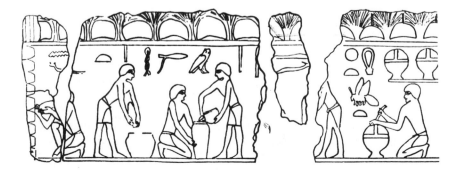

Left, in an Egyptian tomb painting. The bee-keeper works the stacked cylindrical hives from the back. Right, stacks of cylindrical hives are still used in Oman.

hundred of these hives may be stacked in a bank; the beekeeper can open the back of a cylinder in relative safety, since the guards rush out the entrance to repel the intruder and the human is hidden from view on the other side of the bank.

If the bees build their first comb near the entrance end of the cylinder, and if they choose to build it across the long axis of the hive, then they will rear brood there and store honey in new comb built nearer the other end. This is ideal for the beekeeper, since he can simply remove the sheets of comb nearest the back door. To encourage the bees, therefore, parallel grooves were scratched from side to side across the inside top of the cylinder at the entrance end; bees often take the projections between the grooves as the start of comb, and build directly down from them.

Tradition holds that some beekeepers in ancient Egypt moved their hives on rafts down the Nile, keeping pace with the progressing bloom-ing season; their modern American counterparts drive truckloads of hives north in summer and south in winter. Whether or not Eygptian beekeeping was actually migratory, it must have been quite successful: in about 1180 B.C., Ramses III was able to offer the Nile god some 14,000 kilograms of honey as a sacrifice.

A cylindrical hive in Africa fashioned from a hollowed log and hung from a branch to protect it from predators.

The Greeks inherited the Egyptian design, baking the mud into a sturdier terra cotta. Their hives (the oldest intact specimens date from about 1450 B.C.) were larger, ranging up to almost a full 25 liters. This design spread, but was adapted as local materials dictated; by Roman times, an empire-wide survey of hive designs recorded that, in addition to terra cotta, beekeepers were using hollow logs (sometimes hung from trees), cork cylinders, rectangular hives made of boards, woven wicker cylinders, fennel stems woven together into a box, and bricks. But regardless of the material, the common theme was a long, low cavity with a small entrance hole at one end and a door at the other.

BEE LORE

The experiences of beekeepers as they tried to persuade bees to remain in these man-made cavities and store large quantities of honey led to a generally accepted body of beekeeping lore. One epic formula, which illustrates the lengths to which people were willing to go, was passed from generation to generation until it was recorded, first by Vergil and then by

Florentinus. The originator is thought to be Democritus, and it requires an ox:

> Let there be a building 10 cubits high, and the same number of cubits in breadth, and of equal dimensions at all sides, and let there be one entrance, and four windows made in it, one window in each wall. Then bring into this building a bullock, two years and a half old, fleshy, and very fat. Set to work a number of young men and let them powerfully beat it, and by beating it let them kill it with their bludgeons, pervading the bones along with the flesh. But let them take care that they do not make the beast bloody (for the bee is not produced from the blood), not falling on it with so much violence with the first blows. And let all the apertures be stopped with clean white cloths dipped in pitch, as the eyes and the mouth, and such as are formed by nature for necessary evacuation. Then having scattered a good quantity of thyme, and having laid the bullock on it, let them immediately go out of the house, and let them cover the door and the windows with strong clay, that there may be no entrance or vent to the air nor to the wind.
>
> The third week it is proper to open the building on all sides, that the light and pure air may be admitted, except the side where a strong wind blows in; for, if this be the case, it is proper to keep the windows shut on this side. But when the materials seem to be animated, having attracted a sufficient portion of air, it is again proper to secure the building with clay according to the former method.
>
> Having then opened it on the eleventh day after this period, you will find it full of bees crowded in clusters on each other, and the horns and the bones and the hair and nothing else of the bullock left. They say indeed that the kings are produced from the brain, but the other bees from the flesh. Kings are also produced from the spinal marrow. But those produced from the brain are superior to the others in size, in beauty and in strength.
>
> —Florentinus *Geopontica* 15.2 (translated by J. Owen, 1805)

Implausibilities and inconsistencies in such lore led Aristotle, in about 343 B.C., to study honey bees seriously. He recorded and evaluated earlier ideas, then offered his own based on personal observation and philosophical speculation. Aristotle's word was taken as virtual law for the next 1800 years.

Aristotle focused on two knotty problems: where do bees come from, and why are there three castes (workers, drones, and queen)? Aristotle was skeptical of the prevalent theory of spontaneous generation. Various "recipes" were current for generating a swarm of bees—most, like that of Democritus, involved the corpse of some large mammal. This tradition may have had its start in chapter 14 of Judges, where Daniel is said to have discovered a swarm of bees in a lion's carcass. (This story is not totally implausible; a sufficiently old carcass might be hollow and dry enough to attract a swarm.)

For all his study, however, Aristotle had never seen an egg in the comb, and so related (with a clear note of skepticism) that some authorities said that the larvae are fetched from the flowers of reed and olive. The olive seemed particularly likely to Aristotle because there are more bees and more swarms when the olive harvest is good. He never explained how the larvae came to be in the olive flowers in the first place.

The other problem that puzzled Aristotle is why bee societies have castes. He noted that, although some authorities referred to the large ruler bee as the hive's mother, he found this singularly unlikely. Nature, he asserted, only arms males. Since the hive's ruler has a sting, Aristotle concluded that he must be the king; the defenseless drones were therefore the females, and the sting-equipped workers males. But this neat bit of philosophy runs up against Aristotle's own observations: when the hive is "kingless," only drones are produced (by, as we now know, unfertilized workers). So, he concludes, the rulers produce workers and other rulers; the workers produce the drones. It was not until 1609 that Charles Butler, in his famous book *The Feminine Monarchie,* seriously challenged the idea of king bees, and in 1670 a Dutch scientist proved his conjecture through dissection.

Aristotle perpetuated the myth that there are several rulers in each hive, as well as the still-common notion that honey is gathered directly from flowers rather than being distilled from nectar. He says nothing about the division of labor among the workers, though by Vergil's time this seems to have been common knowledge:

> *Such is their toil and such their busy pains,*
> *As exercise the bees in flowery plains,*
> *When winter past and summer scarce begun,*
> *Invites them forth to labor in the sun.*
> *Some lead their youth abroad, while some condense*
> *Their liquid store, and some in cells dispense:*
> *Some at the gate stand ready to receive*
> *The golden burden, and their friends relieve;*
> *All, with united force, combine to drive*
> *The lazy drones from the laborious hives,*
> *With envy stung they view each other's deeds;*
> *The fragrant work with diligence proceeds.*

—VERGIL *AENEID* I. 430–436
  (translated by John Dryden)

Regardless of the superstitions prevalent among the Greeks and Romans, beekeeping flourished around the Mediterranean. A tax imposed on Corsica around 180 B.C. required 90,000 kilograms of beeswax. This quantity would probably have been the full output of at least 100,000 hives.

BEEKEEPING IN NORTHERN EUROPE

Beekeeping in the forests of northern Europe took a very different course. The earliest managed colonies were not kept in artificial hives at all, but in natural cavities that beekeepers had modified to suit their needs. When a beekeeper located a bee tree, he cut a door in the back of the cavity. To harvest the honey, the beekeeper climbed a ladder and, armed with a smoker, opened the back and went to work. The oldest surviving evidence of this technique is about 2000 years old, but the practice probably dates back 4000 years.

The bees in a tree were a valuable commodity, and were often owned independently of the tree itself. Landowners were forbidden to cut down trees with colonies in them; beekeepers staked their claims by carving initials into the bark. Beekeepers also took advantage of empty cavities that were too small or had unsatisfactory entrances. After cutting a back

Left, forest beekeepers harvest honey through doors cut in the back of natural cavities in trees. Germany, 1774. Right, other than poaching, the major problem faced by forest beekeepers was bears. To deal with these creatures, the hive owners fashioned elaborate traps. When the bear climbed to rob the hive, it stepped onto the platform; its weight caused a bent branch to snap loose and hold the platform away from the tree; a trap on the platform prevented the bear from escaping before the beekeeper could kill it. Germany, 1774.

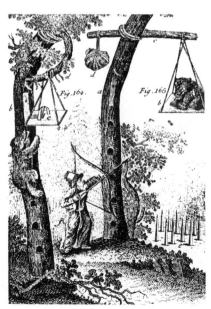

Beekeepers wearing wicker veils harvest honey from straw skeps; detail from a drawing by Pieter Breughel the elder, made in 1568.

door they could enlarge a cavity from the inside, or seal the old opening and make a new entrance that would be more appealing to the bees. At some point, beekeepers began to hang hollowed-out logs from the limbs of trees in the hope of attracting swarms. The beekeeping industry in eastern Europe was so successful that the annual parish tax for St. John's church in Novgorod in 1136 was 350,000 kilograms of beeswax—the produce of perhaps a half-million colonies.

Commercial beekeeping took a giant step when keepers brought the hives out of the trees and down to the ground. Two traditions of hive construction developed. The first used log or cork hives with no doors; instead the top was left open but covered with a plank or flat stone. The other tradition, which developed about 2000 years ago in Northern Europe, used an inverted woven basket.

The woven-basket hives were the precursors of the picturesque skep, the Western symbol of beekeeping. A true skep is woven from coiled straw and so has very thick walls; skeps are much warmer and drier than mere baskets. Kept out of the rain, a skep can last dozens of years. Unfortunately, though, harvesting honey from a skep is fatal for its bees: beekeepers either plunged the skeps into water or put their skeps into pits filled with burning sulfur. In general the heaviest colonies (those with most honey) and the lightest (those least likely to survive the winter) were chosen for harvesting; medium-weight hives were left to carry on, and the emptied skeps were set out to attract new swarms.

Straw skeps covered with snow are visible in a winter scene from the Très Riches Heures *of Jean, duke of Berry, early fifteenth century.*

Left above, the last wicker skeps in England, in Herefordshire in the 1880s. Above, driving bees—moving them from the lower skep to the upper—in the late nineteenth century. Far left, extensions could be added to skeps during peak honey production to induce the bees to build new comb and fill it exclusively with honey. The honey was harvested by removing the extensions (bell jars in the elaborate observation skep pictured here) and adding new ones. Left, an alternative way of obtaining honey-filled new comb was to add an extension at the bottom of the skep. The bees extend the existing comb down into this "eke," after which the honey is harvested by drawing a fine wire across the junction between the skep and the eke, severing the new comb from the old.

Given these disadvantages, it is surprising that skeps caught on so thoroughly, but in fact the design was frequently modified to overcome some of the problems. The most useful adumbration was an extension, either at the top or bottom, added in late spring when honey stores begin to grow rapidly. Top expansions looked like miniature skeps, and were perched on top of the skep itself, a hole having been made in the top of the hive to allow bees access to the cap. The bees would build fresh comb and stock it with honey, and then the beekeeper would remove it, harvest the wax and honey, and replace the cap in hope that the bees would fill it once more. Bottom extensions (called "ekes") raised the skeps, allowing room to extend existing comb which, the beekeeper hoped, would be filled with new honey. The eke comb was then harvested by drawing a fine wire across the junction between the eke and the rest of

Above left, to protect skeps from the elements, many houses and castles had niches, called bee boles, built into the walls or into free-standing structures, such as this one in England. Above right, skeps could also be protected by free-standing shelters. Austria, 1502.

the skep to sever the new comb from the old, and then slipping the eke out.

Protecting skeps from the elements is essential if they are not to rot, and this led to the practice of building niches called bee boles into walls to accommodate the hives. These shelters can be found in surprising numbers in houses and castles built after 1100 A.D., and some are even found in free-standing structures that have no other function. The practice of devoting entire structures to bees led to the building of bee houses, in which the hives were completely sheltered. Bee houses probably helped bees weather the northern winters better, and must certainly have offered more protection from honey-hunting predators (including bears, skunks, opossums, hedgehogs, and shrews). Again, the amount of effort and expense devoted to accommodating bees points up the value of their honey and wax in an age before modern substitutes.

MOVABLE-FRAME HIVES

In all these very different sorts of hives, the bees attach their comb to the top and sides of the cavity just as they do in the wild, making it necessary to cut out the comb to harvest the honey. As substitutes for beeswax became available, the market for the comb thus destroyed began to dwindle and the wastefulness of the system became even more obvious. Moreover, the inability to examine the combs containing larvae and

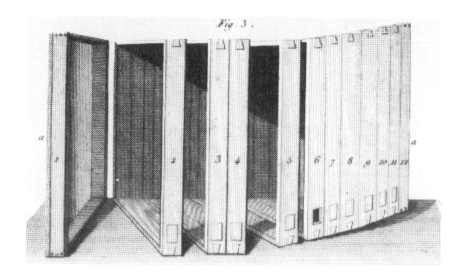

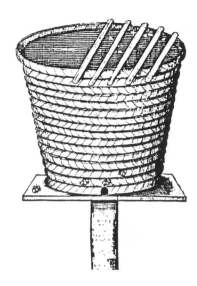

pupae made intelligent management and disease control almost impossible.

The modern hive draws inspiration from many sources. One of the first was a traditional form of Greek hive. In 1649, the Reverend William Mew in England, who had seen the Greek hives, nailed a set of parallel wooden bars across the top of the cavity to force the bees to build their comb down from it, one sheet to a bar. He also made his hive multilayered, and installed shutters to control access between the layers; the idea was to open the upper layer only when flower nectar was abundant so that only honey would be stored in it. The honey could be harvested by smoking the bees back down into the main body of the hive, closing the shutter behind them, and then removing the upper layer. Though ingenious, this hive was far too complex to be practicable.

Around 1790, the blind Swiss naturalist François Huber had a so-called "leaf hive" built for him. It consisted of twelve frames all hinged together at the back. If the frames were just the right thickness, the bees could be persuaded to build a single sheet of comb in each frame and, at the same time, not to attach one comb to the next. The end frames were covered so that, when the leaves were closed, the colony was completely enclosed; for observation, the "book" could be opened to the desired leaf, and studies made. Huber's assistant would describe what he saw, answering Huber's countless enquiries. The spacing Huber worked out was one of the key elements in the development of a practical movable-frame hive.

Left, Huber's leaf hive consisted of frames holding a single comb each. Because he judged the spacing just right, the frames could be separated and the activities of the bees observed. Right, the first top-bar hive; bees built their comb down from the bars, but attached the comb to the straw of this oddly shaped skep, so that the sheets could not be easily removed.

The secret of the Langstroth hive is the precise gap of one bee width on all sides of the frame; the bees leave these openings clear, and so the frames can be removed at will. Right, the first practical movable-frame hive.

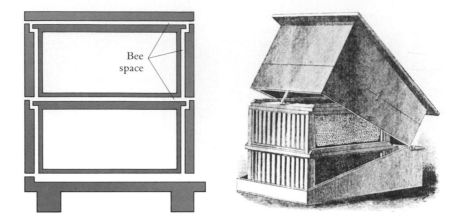

Bee space

In 1851, the Reverend L. L. Langstroth of Philadelphia analyzed why Huber's hive induced bees to leave the combs unjoined. He discovered (as others had earlier) that the spacing between the combs in a natural colony is precisely two bee diameters—about a centimeter. This allows bees on one comb to go about their business without interfering with those on the adjacent comb. But if the spacing is even slightly larger, the bees begin building cells across the gap. Huber had insisted that his frames be built a centimeter wider than the thickness of a sheet of comb.

Next, Langstroth figured out that if he built frames to go into a hive box that left a gap of a half a centimeter at the bottom and sides, the bees would leave this space as a passage one bee wide, and not build comb across the gap; a centimeter gap, on the other hand, would be filled. Finally he realized that the same gap had to be left above the frames as well so the bees would not join them to the top of the hive.

Langstroth's movable-frame hive took the world by storm, and today more than a half-billion kilos of honey are produced annually from its modern descendants. Of course, many other technical improvements have contributed: queen excluders (sets of parallel wires or zinc sheets with perforations large enough to pass workers but not the queen) keep the queen out of the upper part of the hive, with the result that only honey is stored there. Thin sheets of wax with the bases of cells already embossed result in even comb with few if any of the larger drone cells. (Beekeepers, obviously, have no use for drones; restricting their numbers results in a larger quantity of stored honey at season's end.) Hot wax-knives are now used to remove the cell caps, which are sold as beeswax, and the honey is removed from the comb by centrifuge. The empty comb can be returned to the hive to be restocked, saving the honey that would otherwise have to go to fuel the construction of new comb from scratch.

For all their efforts, though, humans have not succeeded in domesticating bees. A swarm escaping from a commercial hive has just as good a chance of surviving in the wild as a feral swarm, and the number of wild colonies living in trees still far exceeds the population living in accommodations designed for them by humans. The history of beekeeping, then, has not been a story of domestication, but rather one of humans learning how to accommodate the needs and preferences of the bees themselves.

CHAPTER 2

The Life of the Bee

The life cycle of a honey bee hive finds its parallel in the life of a single organism. It moves, feeds, reproduces, even breathes more like an animal than a community of individuals. Virtually all bees in this colonial organism are female: a single queen lays up to 2000 eggs a day, and the tens of thousands of workers in the hive are all females. Despite their sex, though, worker bees have poorly developed ovaries and cannot mate. During a portion of the year, a few hundred (in large hives perhaps as many as a few thousand) males—the drones—are reared. The drones exist only to mate; they are incompetent to work in the hive, and cannot even sting. It is the worker bees that build honeycomb, rear the young, clean the colony, feed the queen and drones, guard the hive, and collect food. In its intricately choreographed life, each worker bee serves the needs of the colony as a whole. Without her hivemates, no bee can sur-

A forager collecting pollen and nectar from a gazania (African daisy) blossom; the pollen is packed into "baskets" on the rear legs.

vive long; moreover, it is the colony that reproduces, not individual bees. The proper place to begin our story, then, is with the life of the colony, and then progress to the lives of its members.

THE HONEY BEE NICHE

Every species has a niche—a strategy for making its living that is different from those of the other species in its habitat. If each niche were not different, one of two species that were competing directly for a resource would inevitably outperform the other, however slightly, and in time the second species would be driven to extinction. Several special aspects of the honey bees' lifestyle allow them to coexist with other insects, and even with other bees. Like almost all bees, honey bees gather nectar and pollen from flowers. Wasps, from whom ants and bees evolved a hundred million years ago, generally prey on other invertebrates.

Nectar is the bees' carbohydrate source, the food that provides the energy they need; they turn it into honey by adding an enzyme (invertase) that converts the sugars to a chemical form that bacteria and many molds cannot metabolize. Worker bees fan the nectar in honeycomb cells until it is too viscous for bacteria to move in and so dry (honey has less than 20 percent water) that it dehydrates and kills yeasts and other microörganisms. In addition, bees add another class of enzymes (oxidases) that convert some of the sugar into hydrogen peroxide, a potent antibiotic. Taken together, these measures keep honey from spoiling.

Pollen is the bees' protein source, used for the most part to feed the growing young and to nurture the queen. The balance of different amino acids in pollen is precisely matched to the needs of bees, and so these vegetarian insects do not face the dietary troubles humans encounter when we attempt to forego animal protein. The pollen also contains vital lipids, vitamins, and minerals. Bees add a phytocide to the pollen they store to prevent it from germinating. Nectar and high-protein pollen are found only in insect-pollinated flowers; species that depend on wind pollination have very little nutrition to offer bees. Flowers, of course, do not provide these edible commodities out of charity, but rather to lure bees into carrying their pollen from one blossom to another; in this way, they avoid the wastefulness of scattering their pollen to the wind: though bees may take most of it back to the hive, they deliver enough to other flowers of the same species to assure cross-fertilization. Without bees to pollinate them, most flowering species would perish.

The main feature that makes honey bees special among the bees and wasps of the temperate zone is that not only are they social (a rarity in itself), but their colonies are perennial. Nearly all wasps and other bees

are solitary; each female provisions an egg with food, abandons it to develop on its own, and provisions another. Even bumble bees and paper wasps, social insects whose colonies can comprise dozens or even hundreds of members by late summer, all begin the spring in the same way as solitary queens (usually having mated the previous fall and overwintered in a protected spot). These colonies grow as the summer progresses, finally producing a burst of reproductives—queens and drones—before the first frost. Honey bees, by contrast, live in permanent colonies throughout the winter, and so begin foraging the flowers of spring and early summer in force. It is this capacity to outcompete other pollinators for a few crucial weeks—specifically, from mid-April to late June in the mid-temperate zone—that constitutes the special niche of the honey bee. During the other forty weeks of the year the colony, for all its best efforts, barely breaks even, or may even run at a loss, consuming more food than it gathers.

Everything evolves from something else, and the perennial strategy of the honey bee did not appear *de novo*. Instead, like most behavior, it grew out of a chance combination of circumstances and solutions to quite different challenges. Honey bees evolved in the tropical forests of the Old World—indeed, there are no honey bees native to the Americas; Columbus brought the first colonies. In the tropics, two species, the giant honey bee *(Apis dorsata)* and the dwarf honey bee *(Apis florea),* live in the open, suspending their honeycomb from branches and rock overhangs. The stores of honey in these combs, as well as the nutritious larvae reared in the same structures, are a strong temptation for predatory ants, wasps, birds, and a variety of mammals.

Left, dwarf honey bees (Apis florea) *suspend their single sheet of comb—about 15 centimeters across—from the branch of a tree or bush. Right, giant honey bees* (Apis dorsata) *build their sheet of comb down from a cliff or a tree trunk; their colonies can be more than a meter across.*

*The distribution of Old-World honey bees, and the
spread of* Apis mellifera.

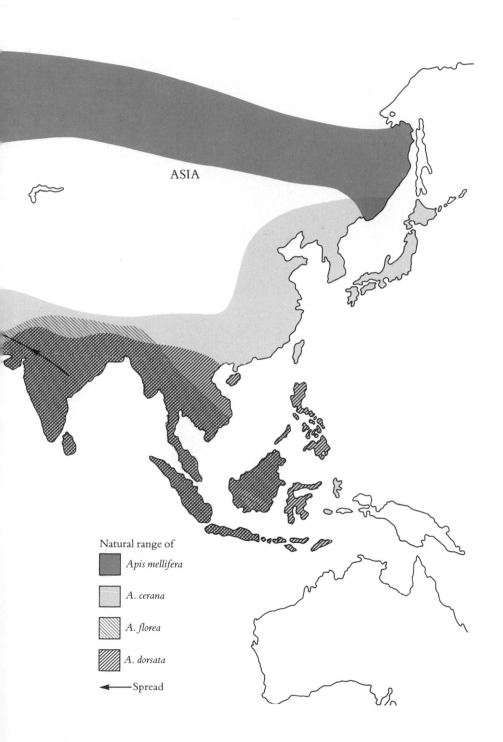

ASIA

Natural range of

Apis mellifera

A. cerana

A. florea

A. dorsata

Spread

Dwarf bees coat the branch from which their nest is suspended with propolis; four weaver ants, who might otherwise have stolen honey and recruited additional raiders, are trapped in this sticky substance.

The dwarf bees defend themselves against ants by collecting tree sap (called propolis) and creating sticky moats to trap the raiders. Their small stings provide some defense against wasps, but for the most part dwarf bees depend on going unnoticed. To this end they locate their nests in bushes, hidden on all sides by leaves. Giant honey bees, by contrast, place their enormous nests in inaccessible places and attack large intruders *en masse*. These group attacks, which may include thousands of bees, can easily kill large mammals.

The third species of tropical honey bee, the Indian bee *(Apis cerana),* has another solution: it sets up housekeeping inside a hollow cavity (usually in a tree) and defends only a small entrance hole. Many larger predators simply cannot get inside, and smaller raiders are met by a solid phalanx of stinging guards. This strategy has its problems, the most obvious of which is that heat can build up to dangerous levels inside.

Our temperate-zone honey bee *(Apis mellifera)* has put this disadvantage to good use. As it spread from the tropics into the temperate zone, not only was the heat stress of summer less of a problem, but the thousands of warm bodies in the cavity, protected from the elements, could keep the colony warm in winter. The new problem was to store enough honey during the summer to "burn" through the winter. It is the colony's drive to store honey that makes commercial beekeeping possible and profitable.

THE COLONY CYCLE

In winter, a colony of temperate-zone honey bees goes into semi-dormancy. During the coldest part of the season, tens of thousands of bees form a tight cluster over a portion of the comb containing the hive's honey and pollen stores. The queen is at the center, warmed by the nearby bees as they consume honey and generate heat by shivering their wing muscles. A typical colony will burn about 25 kilograms of honey over the course of a mid-latitude winter, producing a more-or-less steady heat output equivalent to that of a 40-watt incandescent light bulb.

While the center of a December cluster may be a comfortable 25°C, the bees at the periphery of the tightly packed mass are no warmer than the air in the cavity. The cavity is usually a good deal warmer than the outside air (perhaps by as much as 17°C), but when the temperature falls far enough, those in the outer layer are sometimes very cold indeed. On what are, for the winter, warm days, this sheet of invertebrate insulation becomes active, and these outside bees push their way toward the center of the cluster. But if a cold snap goes on too long, the outer layer finally freezes to death. This slow attrition continues until spring.

As the day length increases after the winter solstice, the bees near the queen begin to feed her a rich, highly proteinaceous secretion from glands near their mandibles. This so-called royal jelly, which is synthe-

Left: the queen bee is larger than the workers and has a shiny thorax (back); she is surrounded by nurse bees who feed and groom her. Right: when she finds a clean, empty cell, the queen inserts her long abdomen and lays a single egg at the base of the cell.

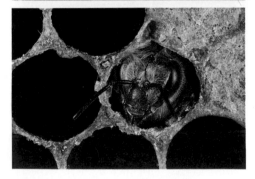

The comb (above right), which is normally covered by workers, is used to rear new bees. The three photos above show stages in the development of bees. Top, larvae, visible as white C-shaped grubs. Middle, pupae in cells capped with tan wax. Bottom, fully developed bee emerging from the cell.

sized from a diet high in pollen, provides the protein she needs to lay eggs. Slowly at first, and then more rapidly as winter draws to a close, the queen lays eggs in vacant cells in the heated portion of the comb, using cells that have been emptied of their honey or pollen during the preceding weeks. This part of the nest, which may have a thousand eggs, is now kept at 36°C, the optimum temperature for rearing new bees.

Workers feed the larvae that hatch from these eggs three days after they have been laid. At first the larvae feast on royal jelly, but, after another three days, they are weaned to honey and pollen. About ten days after hatching, a larva has grown as large as the cell itself, and it spins a cocoon in which it will metamorphose into an adult bee. The workers cap the cell with wax when the developing bee begins this pupal stage. When metamorphosis is complete, about a week later, the new bee chews through the cap and joins the swelling ranks.

Most of the new bees are workers, but a healthy hive rears a few drones as well. Exactly who determines the number of males is still not clear, for there are many levels of control in the colony. Drones develop from unfertilized eggs, a genetic curiosity unique to the order Hymenoptera, comprising the 100,000 species of ants, wasps, and bees. It would seem at first thought that the queen controls the sex of an egg by simply choosing whether to fertilize it from the store of sperm she obtained months or years earlier on her nuptial flight. However, things are not so simple. Drones require wider cells than do workers; queens will lay

Drone   Queen   Worker

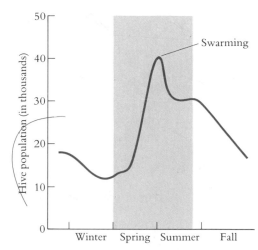

drone eggs only in wide cells. Because the cells are built by the workers, it is they who control the number of drone cells. Moreover, the drone cells are generally built only at the periphery of the comb: placing them in the center would disrupt the precise hexagonal geometry of the comb. The workers can either keep the queen away from areas of drone comb or herd her there to lay. In addition, workers regularly fill the drone cells with honey, an effective way to block laying. Even after the queen has laid an egg, the workers can eat it, or even eat the larva after it hatches.

As spring flowers begin to bloom, the bees begin foraging in earnest, rearing more and more new workers. The number of developing brood may rise to 30,000, filling almost a third of the cells in a typical hive. In mid spring, the colony grows so large that the bees begin to run out of room, and preparations for swarming begin. The workers first construct special queen cells, which hang from the bottom of the comb. The larvae that hatch in these one or two dozen queen cells are fed royal jelly for their entire larval lives; it is this continued feeding that turns an ordinary worker larva into a queen. At the same time, the queen, who is normally too large and heavy to fly, is taken off her usual rich diet and forced to thin down to about 70 percent of her normal weight in preparation for the coming event.

When the new queens begin pupation and their cells are sealed, the old queen and about half of the bees gorge themselves with honey and leave the hive in a mad, swirling rush to form a cluster on a nearby branch.

Left, the three types of adult honey bees. Right, the hive population declines slowly in the winter as some of the workers insulating the cluster perish, but begins to rise again as new workers are raised in anticipation of spring. As flowers begin to bloom, the population rises very rapidly until the overcrowded colony swarms. After swarming, the population remains roughly constant until fall approaches, when, because of the dearth of blooming flowers, new bees are no longer reared.

This swarm cluster, with the old queen somewhere in the middle, has formed near the old colony. Scouts are flying out to search for new cavities and back to report discoveries.

From this temporary perch they will move to an unoccupied cavity sometime in the next few days. Scouts search for suitable shelters, weighing their size (which should be from 10 to 30 liters), dryness, freedom from drafts, entrance size (none larger than 80 centimeters will do; below this size it can be narrowed with progressive applications of propolis until it is just right), entrance location (preferably near the bottom of the cavity, 3 meters or more off the ground, and facing south), surrounding vegetation, and so on.

The choice of a new nest site is critical for the swarm. They have abandoned a cavity that has proved its worth as a dry, warm shelter that saw the parent colony through the past winter. It went unnoticed or resisted the attacks of predators, and is full of very precious honeycomb that the swarming bees cannot take with them. Not only is the new cavity untested, but the bees will have to construct comb from scratch before they can begin raising brood. The chances that the swarm can recover from the annual setback, beginning at what is nearly the end of the season of abundant flowers, to build and stock a hive for winter, are not always good. In New York State (which is near the northern limit for winter survival), more than 90 percent of old colonies survive the winter after producing a spring swarm, but only about 25 percent of those swarms survive. No wonder then that scout bees strongly prefer cavities with abandoned comb, and spend up to a week scouring the habitat for possible nest sites. When the scouts eventually reach a consensus about which cavity is best, the swarm moves in.

Meanwhile, the first of the new queens hatches out in the parent colony. If the hive population is still large enough, she may lead another swarm—the afterswarm—out of the hive to cluster and to search for a new cavity; some colonies will produce as many as four swarms, though only the first afterswarm has much chance of surviving. When the last afterswarm has left, the next queen to hatch kills any others still in their cells, and she fights to the death any that emerge. Eventually, only a single, unmated monarch is left. The virgin queen flies forth on her own a week or so later to mate. Mating takes place in the early afternoon at special mid-air congregation areas 10 to 30 meters up. How either the drones or queens find these traditional places, which remain stable year after year, remains a mystery: drones do not live through the winter, so each new population of drones, and virgin queens as well, must somehow decide where to go to mate according to the same rules used by previous generations. These areas are usually spaced about 2 kilometers apart, and drones from many hives are found in each, since the drones from any given hive divide themselves among several nearby areas. After finding a drone-congregation area and mating with a dozen or more drones, the queen returns to the hive to take up her egg-laying duties.

The drones, which do not work, are ejected from the colony in the fall.

From this point on, the emphasis in the hive shifts from producing more workers and drones, a necessary preparation for swarming, to storing as much pollen and nectar as possible in anticipation of winter. As the swarming season ends, the workers begin to grow impatient with the now almost worthless drones. The males are still tolerated because, even after the swarming season, there may still be a queen to be mated. This eventuality arises when a laying queen dies or runs out of stored sperm (which takes, on average, about three years), and so larvae must sometimes be kept on a diet of pure royal jelly and turned into queens late in the season. But as fall arrives, even this slim need for drones wanes, and the males are unceremoniously ejected from the hive to starve. With the onset of winter, the yearly cycle of the hive is completed.

THE WORKER CYCLE

Each worker bee goes through a behavioral cycle of her own. After a worker hatches, she grooms herself and then begins cleaning cells, preparing them for eggs or food storage. Queens inspect each cell and will not lay in any that are not cleaned and polished, a fastidiousness that reduces the spread of disease among the brood. On average, 15 to 30 workers take part, in turns, in preparing a cell, which takes more than 40 minutes. As she grows older, the worker's mandibular glands mature,

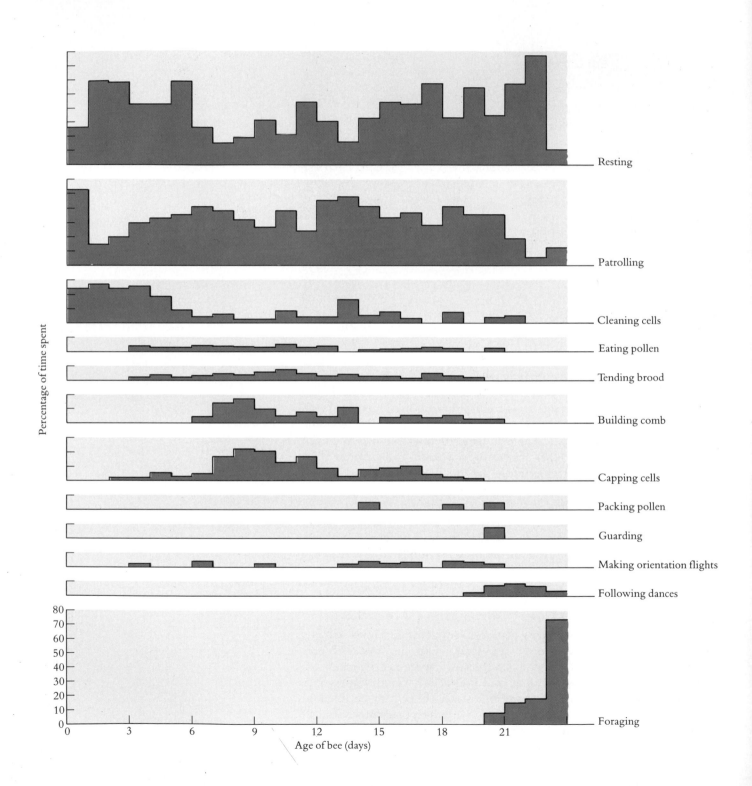

Percentage of time spent

Resting

Patrolling

Cleaning cells

Eating pollen

Tending brood

Building comb

Capping cells

Packing pollen

Guarding

Making orientation flights

Following dances

Foraging

Age of bee (days)

and she begins nursing young larvae and the queen with royal jelly. The amount of time devoted to this activity in a typical hive is astonishing: an average larva is checked by nurse bees 1300 times a day; the time devoted to each developing bee by the 2700 or so different workers that check and feed it is more than eight hours over the course of its week-long larval period.

As time passes, the worker's mandibular glands atrophy, while the eight wax-secreting glands in her abdomen mature. She then spends a few days producing wax flakes and using them to build the parallel sheets of hanging comb characteristic of honey bees, as well as to cap cells containing pupae or ripe honey. Beeswax is a fatlike substance that is metabolically expensive to produce: a kilogram of honey plus an undetermined amount of pollen is converted into only 60 grams of wax; it takes about 7 kilograms of honey to produce the comb in an average hive.

The cells are built according to a design that minimizes the use of this expensive commodity; a kilogram of wax is sufficient to work into 80,000 cells. Less social bees generally build cells on a horizontal surface; bumble bees, for instance, most often use the floor of an abandoned underground mouse nest. The cells are basically cylindrical pots arranged in a hodge-podge manner, sometimes sharing a thick wall, sometimes not. In a honey bee colony, the cells are arranged in an efficient hexagonal grid, with every cell sharing a wall with six adjacent cells. The comb hangs down vertically from the top of the cavity, and every cell shares its base with cells opening on the other side of the two-layer structure. The cells are not quite horizontal, but rather tip up 13° from their bases; this helps keep the nectar and honey from oozing out. Moreover, the cells on the two sides are offset slightly, so that the center of a base on one side is the junction of three walls on the other, an arrangement that adds greatly to the strength of the comb. The result of this architectural scheme is that the wax can be incredibly thin: the walls are only eight-hundredths of a millimeter thick, and the base (which forms the backbone of the comb) is only two-tenths. Feather light and brittle, the comb can nevertheless support many kilograms of honey. In especially hot climates, where the comb tends to soften and lose its essential rigidity, the bees mix propolis with the wax flakes during construction to create a strong alloy.

As her wax glands atrophy, the worker begins to help unload returning foragers and store the food they have collected. She "begs" from a forager by drumming her antennae on those of the newly returned bee, at the same time probing the forager's mouth with her tongue. The forager regurgitates the nectar, and the unloading bee accepts it; the forager then leaves to collect more food while the unloader searches for a cell to deposit the nectar in. The exchange of food between bees, a be-

Facing page, the typical activities of worker bees shift with age. The youngest bees clean cells, while slightly older workers tend brood, nurse the queen, and produce wax for building comb and capping cells. Eventually, workers shift to guarding the hive and foraging. Regardless of age, however, workers spend a considerable portion of their time either resting or "patrolling," an activity that allows them to monitor the hive's needs.

Top, bees frequently exchange food with one another. The worker on the left has begged food from the one on the right, who has spread her mandibles and is sharing the contents of her stomach. Returning foragers are relieved of their loads of nectar in this manner. Middle, guard bees at the hive entrance adopt a characteristic alert posture with their forelegs ready for grasping. They check the odor of all incoming bees to make sure they belong to the colony and (bottom) expel any that do not.

havior called tropholaxis, is very commonplace: in the hive, hardly a minute goes by without every bee either begging a bit of food from others it encounters, or being solicited by them. Indeed, if one bee is fed a bit of radioactive nectar, the majority of bees in the colony will carry the tracer before the day is out. In some sense, a colony has a communal stomach.

Within a few days the aging worker, now more than two weeks old, begins guarding the hive and taking short "play flights" at midday. Guards place themselves at the entrance and adopt a characteristic alert posture with head and forelegs raised. The guarding serves two purposes: first, the sentries repel the attacks of wasps, ants, birds, and mammals; second, they guard against the more constant threat of robbery by other colonies. Some foragers seem to specialize in locating other hives and attempting to sneak in and fill up: it is easier to take a full load of honey from a cell than to go through the tedious process of visiting countless flowers to collect dilute nectar, which then must be evaporated. Weak colonies are frequently stripped of their winter supplies by cadres of robbers.

Guards recognize potential robbers in two ways: first, raiders have a characteristic "guilty" flight pattern, hovering back and forth in front of the entrance looking for an opportunity to slip by the security forces. The second telltale cue is odor. Each colony takes on a unique odor, partly genetic but primarily the odor of the foodstores in the hive. Each bee is covered by waxy fur that readily absorbs this bouquet, and guards check returning bees to see if they have the proper smell. If not, they are challenged and, if they fail to take up the necessary submissive posture (curled up and motionless) while being ejected by the bouncers, they are attacked.

The defense of the hive, as nearly everyone has discovered by personal experience, depends on stinging. The barbed sting in worker honey bees is unlike anything seen in other Hymenoptera: although a bee can sting other insects with impunity, when a guard drives her sting into mammalian skin, the barbs catch and the sting cannot be easily removed. When the attacking bee flies away, its sting, venom sac, and a large part of the bee's internal anatomy remain behind, and the bee dies. The usual tendency to swat the sting or try to remove it by pinching it just serves to squeeze more venom into the wound. (A sting should be removed with a pocket knife or long fingernail by inserting the blade or nail *between* the sting and venom sac and then dragging it out.)

Because the worker dies after stinging, her threshold for losing her temper is high—at least compared with yellow jackets, hornets (both wasps), and bumble bees, whose smooth stings allow them to attack repeatedly with little personal risk. Except when opening a hive, getting

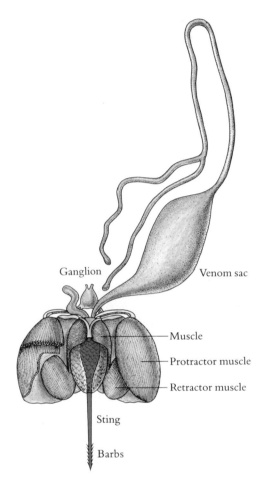

Ganglion

Venom sac

Muscle

Protractor muscle

Retractor muscle

Sting

Barbs

When a honey bee stings (right), the barbs of the sting become lodged in the victim's flesh; as a result, the entire sting apparatus (above; the apparatus includes muscles, odors that attract other guard bees, and the venom sac) tears out, fatally wounding the bee. Even after the attacking bee has departed, the muscles continue to work driving the barbs farther in and pumping venom into the wound.

in the way of incoming and departing foragers near the hive entrance, or coming near a colony that is having trouble with robbers, it is not easy to get stung by a honey bee. The evolution of the barbs was almost certainly a response to avian and mammalian predation, since the stings do not usually get stuck in wasps or other bees. The queen, by the way, has the conventional smooth sting typical of the Hymenoptera, and so runs no risk of suicide in her fights with other newly hatched queens. The drones lack stings altogether.

The purpose of play flights is not well understood. These short excursions take place at midday, when the sun is shining on the entrance. One obvious purpose early on is for the bees to relieve themselves; only a sick honey bee will discharge feces inside the hive, and for some reason a bee must be flying to unload the unwanted by-products of its metabolism. But there is clearly more going on: two-week-old bees hover in front of the hive as though studying it, land, take off again immediately, hover some more, land again, and so on. As a bee gets older, these noontime excursions become more extensive, and she may venture out 10 meters before returning. The bees are probably learning what the hive and its immediate surroundings look like, as well as coming to know something about how the sun (which is their chief landmark on early foraging flights) moves through the sky from east to west.

Finally, at perhaps three weeks of age, a worker begins foraging, making trip after trip to collect food. The physical and mental effort required to collect food is remarkable, and it forms the subject of most of the rest of this book. The forager visits familiar patches of flowers up to

A forager, with her right pollen basket already full, about to land on a crocus blossom.

10 kilometers from the hive; for us, this would correspond to a trip of about 1300 kilometers. Elaborate navigational abilities are necessary to get to a familiar patch and home again, particularly since bees have very poor vision (about 20/2000 by our standards, almost legally blind) and so must get fairly close to a target before they can recognize it. A worker is just over a centimeter long and weighs only about 60 milligrams; nevertheless, she can fly with a load heavier than herself. Even so, the nectar she collects from perhaps a hundred blossoms on a single foraging trip is often quite dilute and, when evaporated, will turn into very little honey. As many as 75 foraging trips may be necessary to produce even a gram of honey.

Workers die after about nine days of heavy foraging, or up to three weeks of light-duty food collection. The flight muscles simply wear out after about 800 kilometers, usually while the forager is *en route* to food or on the way back. A worker expiring alone in the grass of a summer field may have made 400 sorties, and will have brought back less nectar than is required to make even 7 grams of honey. If she spends part of her day gathering pollen, or if nectar is rare, the figure may be far lower. But a strong hive may have ten or even twenty thousand foragers, so the small individual contribution is magnified enormously.

VARIATIONS IN THE CYCLES

It is easy to talk about *Apis mellifera* as if all bees and all colonies were identical. We tend to see how different humans are from each other, but when we look at another species we focus on how that species is different from ours. When the difference is as large as it is between humans and honey bees, variation between individual bees and hives becomes practically invisible. Adding to this problem of perspective is the obvious fact that insects are more nearly creatures of instinct than we are, and so we expect bees to be nearly identical automatons. (Readers fond of this illusion are in for some rude shocks.) But even if every bit of behavior is genetically determined, the proper response at one season or in one climatic area may be quite inappropriate in another; we should not be too surprised to find that a species as cosmopolitan as the honey bee should be endowed with enough flexibility to make a living in both Central America and southern Canada.

One of the most obvious examples of flexibility is seen in the sequence of worker tasks. Although virtually all workers pass through the series of jobs described earlier, the needs of the colony can accelerate or delay the transitions: in a colony short of foragers, the hive jobs that normally occupy up to three weeks may be run through in perhaps six days, whereas in a hive short of nurse bees, a young worker's stint at feeding larvae may be extended from less than a week to two or three. Colonies lacking this sort of flexibility would have died out in the face of competition from those that *could* fine-tune their labor force.

On a more global scale, there are regional differences as well. As the original honey bees spread from India through the mideast and then through Africa and Europe, they encountered climates very different from the one they were well adapted to in the tropics. As a result, regional races developed, of which about twenty are now generally recognized. Their colony cycles differ in ways that either reflect differing environmental challenges or, as is often the case in animals, seem to have arisen by chance and been preserved by geographical isolation.

Examples of extreme climatic adaptation are found in the Central African races, *Apis mellifera adansonii* and *A. m. scutellata*, the so-called killer bees. Living as they do in the winterless African tropics, these races produce swarms all year and store very little honey. Their colonies are far smaller than those of more conventional races and are frequently located in the ground or even in the open. The colonies readily abscond, abandoning cavity, comb, and brood in search of a new home when conditions turn bad; more temperate races, on the other hand, tend to wait out the bad times, living on their "savings." *Adansonii* and *scutellata* workers generally refuse to forage at midday (a sensible choice, considering the heat), compensating by extending their foraging hours into the predawn and postdusk hours; they will even fly in the rain and at night when the moon is bright enough. The queens fly out much later in the afternoon to mate, again probably to avoid the heat. These behavioral preferences persist even in temperate habitats, and do not appear in temperate races moved into the tropics; they are, therefore, probably genetically programmed. Both races produce a high proportion of drones; they are smaller than the bees of temperate climates, and they rush their workers through the hive duties so they can begin foraging almost a week early.

Finally, *adansonii* and *scutellata* have very short fuses, attacking potential intruders more determinedly and with less provocation than any other race. The standard test for aggressiveness in bees is to suspend a small, dark leather ball near the hive entrance, disturb the hive by striking it, and then bob the ball. After a predetermined interval (usually 30 seconds), the ball is carried slowly away from the hive. The observer scores the delay until the first bee stings the ball, the distance at which the last sting is delivered, the total number of stings, and the time until the aggressive buzzing of the disturbed colony abates. An average colony of the familiar yellow-and-black-banded Italian honey bee (*Apis mellifera ligustica*) takes 19 seconds to begin stinging; the Africans respond in

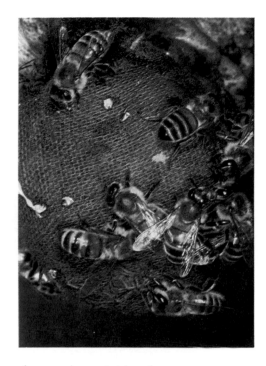

An aggressiveness test in action.

three. Italian bees put 26 stings in the ball, the African bees (limited by the space available for stinging and their preference for attacking the observer rather than the test object) only increase this measure to 64; Italian bees will follow the ball 25 meters, African bees 170 meters; Italian colonies calm down after two or three minutes, whereas African colonies require half an hour or more. Clearly these bees are well adapted to protect nests that are too readily accessible to predators.

The venom of "killer bees" is no more potent than that of other races; in fact, since the workers are generally smaller, *adansonii* and *scutellata* actually have somewhat less venom. The occasional report of someone being killed by African bees, unless another species was actually responsible (in the eastern United States, for instance, most "bee stings" are actually delivered by yellowjackets) or the individual was allergic (and so a single sting might have sufficed), are actually the result of the large *number* of stings inflicted.

As nearly everyone has heard by now, several colonies of either *scutellata* or *adansonii* (we do not know which; they were considered to be the same race back then) escaped from a research station in Brazil when a well-meaning local beekeeper removed a protective device from the entrances of their hives. These devices, known as queen excluders, generally consist of a series of parallel wires so spaced that workers can pass through them easily, but drones and queens are prevented by their girth from leaving. They have the unfortunate side effect of stripping off the pollen loads of some returning foragers, and so the visiting beekeeper took pity on the bees, which promptly absconded and "disappeared" into the Amazon. But, like the gypsy moths that disappeared into Massachusetts in 1869, they reappeared in a few years and began to spread. Because of their unusual late-afternoon mating schedule, African queens are not crossing with drones from less aggressive hives; but since African drones do begin to fly early enough to catch part of the more usual mating period, aggressive genes are spreading into other races in South and Central America. Within a few years, so-called "Africanized" bees should reach the southern United States, notwithstanding the "barrier" in Mexico planned by the U.S. Department of Agriculture. The limit to their northern expansion will be, at worst, the line of hard frost that will freeze or starve their small, poorly protected, honeyless clusters; at best, temperate races will out-compete them somewhere farther south. (There remains the worry that the USDA's plans to hybridize the African bees with Italian bees will result in aggressive colonies with good winter tolerance.)

Corresponding but opposite trends are seen in the more northerly races of Europe. The black carniolan honey bee of Germany (*Apis mellifera carnica*) insists on larger cavities, stores more honey, and maintains a larger population than even the Italian races. This is essential, of course, to accommodate longer winters: more honey will be needed to heat the cluster, so more bees are needed to harvest food, and more room to accommodate both them and the food stores. At some point, however, further increases in colony size can no longer overcome longer, colder winters, probably because, as the number of foragers scouring the countryside for flowers rises, the average distance a bee must fly to find an unexploited flower goes up. As a result, the profit per flight drops as bees take more time and use more energy to fly farther. The solitary-hibernation strategy of bumble bees permits them to make a living more than 1600 kilometers farther north than the most northerly honey bees—beyond, in fact, the Arctic circle itself.

One striking racial difference that has no obvious selective value is seen in the South African race of honey bee, *Apis mellifera capensis*. Most races of honey bees exhibit a curious behavior that puzzled even Aristotle: about a week after the queen has died, drone larvae begin to appear, long before a new queen can emerge. Indeed, in colonies that fail to rear a new queen and so are doomed to perish as their workers die, a steady stream of drones appears. What is happening is that, in the absence of the queen, the atrophied ovaries of a few workers begin to function and they lay unfertilized eggs. The presence of these laying workers is easy to spot: eggs are laid everywhere—on the walls of the cavity, the surface of the comb, the sides of cells, often several to a cell. The queen, by contrast, lays a single egg per cell, dead center on its base. Drone production by queenless colonies may be a mechanism for providing the new queen with mates during what may be a drone-poor portion of the year. For colonies that are unable to raise a queen, drones are the last chance to contribute genes to the next generation.

A curious thing about *capensis* workers is that their ovaries are much larger than those of workers in other races, and become functional much sooner after the queen dies. More unusual than this, however, is that most of the eggs that are produced by laying workers are female; a new queen can be reared directly, and an uninterrupted supply of diploid workers produced. The genetic basis of this anomaly is fairly clear: there is a failure during egg maturation that prevents the gamete from losing half its chromosomes—a step necessary, if fertilization takes place, to prevent the number of chromosomes from doubling each generation. As laying workers do not (indeed, cannot) mate, this problem does not arise. It seems possible that this quirk arose by chance, since there is nothing about the habitat that would seem to favor such a capacity especially, and the other 19 or so races lack it.

Genetically based behavioral variation is evident within races as well. A striking example comes from, of all places, studies of disease resistance. There is a bacterium, *Bacillus larvae,* that infects larvae and kills them as pupae. The condition—American foul brood, one of many social diseases of honey bees—spreads because the bacteria leave the dying or dead pupae and move through the wax into adjacent cells. About three decades ago, researchers were told of a group of colonies unusually resistant to the ravages of this widespread disease. After tests and controlled genetic crosses, they came to the surprising conclusion that the colonies' immunity was not physiological or biochemical, but behavioral: workers of resistant strains uncap and discard infected pupae before the disease can spread. Less obvious differences between colonies with regard to honey production, propolis collection, aggressiveness, and other behavioral characteristics are also well known.

ANATOMY

Many of the adaptations by which a species meets the challenges of its niche are evident in its anatomy and sensory apparatus. By the same token, anatomical features and sensory capacities inherited from earlier species can limit the evolutionary "options" available, blocking certain avenues of change. The anatomy and sensory apparatus of honey bees are as different from our own as any we might expect from an extraterrestrial life form. This makes it all the more difficult—and all the more important—for us to imagine what it must be like to be an advanced creature without a backbone.

Like all insects, honey bees have an external skeleton of chiton divided into three body segments. The head contains the brain and some glands, and on it are mounted several important structures. The compound eyes and antennae, which are sensory devices we shall touch on presently, are the most obvious; the antennae are quite long, as in all the Hymenoptera. This makes it easy to distinguish bees and wasps from the many flies that mimic them, but cannot disguise their characteristically stubby antennae. At the bottom of the head are the mandibles, which are external mouthparts used for chewing; they are especially important in building comb. Next to the mandibles is the proboscis, which is actually a set of eight body parts that unfold from where they are stored under the "chin" and refold to create a long, hollow, flexible, strawlike structure through which nectar is pumped in. Although bees seem to lap with the proboscis, they are actually just exploring with the tip, which contains taste receptors. The proboscis of a worker is quite long; drones and queens, which do not feed from flowers, have much shorter organs.

The thorax contains most of the bee's muscle mass, and mounted on it are the legs and wings. Bees, like all hymenopterans, have two pairs of

A forager drinks the nectar in flowers with her tonguelike proboscis. The hairs growing between the facets of her compound eyes monitor air movement and are important during flight. There are vibration receptors at the base of each antenna and also where the antennae bend. Near the top of the head, between the compound eyes, are three simple eyes known as ocelli.

wings, which again distinguishes them from flies, all of which have a single pair. The bee's muscles do not move its wings directly; instead, they alternately compress the thorax vertically and lengthwise. Each wing is mounted on two plates, one at the base like a rower's hand on an oar, the other just a bit farther out like an oarlock. The alternating compressions move these two parts of the wing, causing the wing to snap up and down. This indirect arrangement for moving the wings allows for a high rate of beating (250 to 300 beats per second); insects whose muscles are actually attached to their wings—butterflies and grasshoppers, for example—flap their wings more slowly and so cannot fly as fast.

Each pair of a bee's legs is different, though all have the clawlike hooks and sticky pad at the end that allow a bee to hold on to surfaces smooth or porous. The front leg has a special notch and a projection at one joint that is used to clean the antennae; the middle leg has a spine used to dislodge pollen; the hind leg has a flattened, comblike segment for brushing pollen off of the body, an anvil-like joint used to compress the pollen, and a set of long incurved hairs—the pollen basket—for trapping packed pollen. Queens and drones, logically enough, lack all the structures used for pollen collection.

The last body segment is the abdomen; it contains the crop, where nectar is stored temporarily, the organs of digestion, the wax glands (missing in queens and drones), the sting (absent in drones), a scent gland that produces an odor that attracts other bees (not present in queens and drones), the sexual organs (atrophied in workers), and the curious heart typical of insects.

THE SENSORY WORLD

Honey bees have our five senses and more, but the arrangement and architecture of their sense organs is very different. Their eyes, to take the most obvious example, are nothing like ours. Vertebrate eyes (and those of the octopus and squid) are like miniature cameras: light enters through a large lens which focusses the image on a light-sensitive "film," the retina. The nerve cells of the retina interact to sharpen the image and emphasize certain features, and the resulting picture is sent through long fibers to the brain for further analysis. In nearly all invertebrates, the eyes are compound, having many small lenses. Worker bees have about 4500 facets, or *ommatidia,* in each eye; queens (who have little use for vision) about 3500; and drones (who must spot the queen at a considerable distance if they are to win the ensuing race to be the first to mate with her) about 7500. Each facet is an independent eye aimed at a unique part of the visual world, but no image is formed in an ommatidium; instead, the

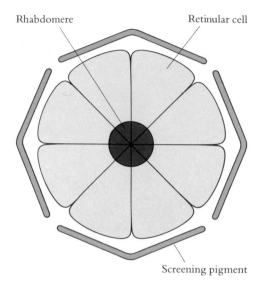

Rhabdomere   Retinular cell

Screening pigment

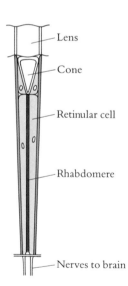

Lens

Cone

Retinular cell

Rhabdomere

Nerves to brain

Right, in a cross section view of a bee's eye the many long ommatidia are clearly visible; each looks out in a slightly different direction. Top, cross section of an ommatidium. Bottom, a single ommatidium.

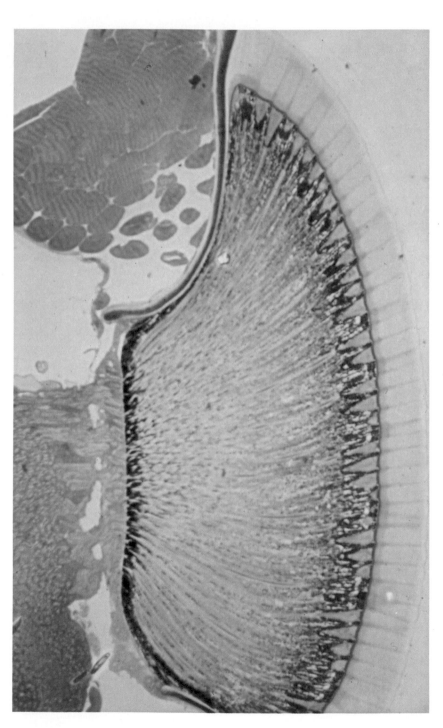

picture is pieced together from the thousands of individual ommatidia. As a result, the world for a bee must have a very grainy appearance, rather like a needlepoint canvas. For a rough comparison, the bee's brain receives about one percent as many connections as our eyes provide. But this visual economy is necessary for an animal as small as an insect; a camera eye with the resolution of the bee's compound eye would be larger and heavier than the entire bee.

In each ommatidium are nine receptor cells. Two of these are sensitive to green light, two to blue, and two to ultraviolet; two more are also set to monitor one of these three color bands, the choice depending on the part of the eye—green in the part of the eye that looks down, for example. These eight cells provide the bee with a color picture of her world, a picture that is blind to red but sensitive to ultraviolet. (We are normally blind to ultraviolet because of a faint yellowish pigment in the cornea; people who have had their corneas removed see ultraviolet light, though they experience it as blue rather than as a separate color.) The ninth cell in each ommatidium is sensitive to ultraviolet polarized light; the responses of these cells are processed separately and do not take part in form vision.

That honey bees have color vision was discovered early in this century by Karl von Frisch (who later won a Nobel Prize for his work on bees). At the time, the prevailing dogma was that only humans could see color— most mammals have predominantly black-and-white vision, and so how could "lower" animals such as insects be any better endowed? But von Frisch refused to believe that flowers, depending as they do on insects for pollination, were colorful for no better reason than to make the world pretty for our species.

When bees look at a flower, like the zinnias (left), they must see a blurred mosaic of different colors (right). Even with 8000 individual facets, the picture is far grainier than that of even a poor-quality color television screen, which may have a resolution of 50,000 to 100,000 points.

Two views of evening primrose (Denothera sp.) Top, in white light. Bottom, in ultraviolet light most bee-pollinated flowers have a striking dark spot in the center and, frequently, lines or spots called nectar guides leading from the petals to the middle of the blossom.

Though the color vision of bees came as no surprise to von Frisch, the ability to see in the ultraviolet (shared, as we now know, with some species of birds) was unexpected. Using his evolutionary logic in reverse, von Frisch wondered what there could be in the world for bees to see in the ultraviolet. He arranged to have ultraviolet photographs made, and when he looked at the snapshots of flowers he was astounded: bee-pollinated blossoms have a dark spot in the middle and, frequently, lines leading from the petals to the center; on most flowers, these marks, called nectar guides, are invisible to us. In essence, the plants are telling the bees where to look for food.

The sensitivity to polarized light, which von Frisch did not discover until the late 1940s, has its own particular use: there is an elaborate and beautiful pattern of polarized light in the sky, invisible to us, that enables bees to find their way when the sun is hidden behind clouds. An ability to see polarized light is now documented in certain fish, amphibians, reptiles, and birds.

One property of the honey bees' visual system that may help compensate for its fuzziness is its high flicker-fusion frequency. Humans see motion pictures as continuous images, but bees would see a movie as what it really is: a picture, followed by darkness, followed by the next frame, and so on. The basis of the illusion for us (the same illusion that fools us into thinking that a television image is continuous and uninterrupted and prevents us from noticing that fluorescent lights go dark 120 times a second) is the slow response of the photoreceptors in our eyes. Any event occurring faster than about twenty times a second is lost in a blur. For bees, the flicker-fusion rate is far higher, well above 100 times a second in good light. Though this is not fast enough for them to resolve the 280-per-second wingbeats of other bees, it does help them see rapidly moving objects better—other flying bees, or the ground moving past them at 7 meters per second (m/s) when they fly.

Honey bees are often said to be deaf, and it is true that they cannot hear airborne sounds as we do; this is probably an advantage, given the cacophony of buzzing in the hive; in addition, bees have little need to listen for flowers in order to find them. But bees *can* hear, and have at least three sets of organs for doing so. One set of "ears" is found inside the legs. It consists of a thin, easily vibrated membrane that is set into motion by sound in the comb. This structure listens for messages passed between the old queen and new queens still in their cells.

The other two ears are located on the antennae, one at the base and another about a third of the way out along its length, just at the point where it bends down. The antennae act like miniature tuning forks, resonating only to sounds of certain frequencies. The antenna as a whole is vibrated by nearby sounds at or below the lower limit of our hearing, which is about 20 beats per second; this frequency range corresponds to one element in the communication dance. The outer portion of the antenna, by contrast, resonates at a much higher frequency, ranging from about 250 to 300 beats per second; this frequency is also part of the dance message. By being nearly deaf to airborne sounds, then, bees are able to attend to the signals of the dancer they are nearest without being distracted by the noisy confusion of the hive as a whole. By only being sensitive to narrow ranges of sound, they are similarly enabled to shut out irrelevant noises in their busy world.

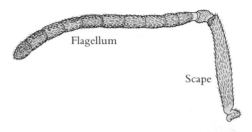

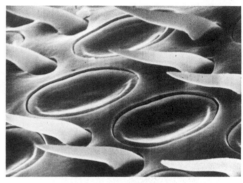

A bee's antennae are covered with sensory hairs and other structures. Some of these organs are sensitive to touch, but most respond to odors.

The honey bee's antenna is also her nose, and is covered with organs sensitive to odors. Some of the olfactory receptors respond to a single smell—odors that have special meanings for bees—but most are broadly "tuned" cells like those in our noses; they allow bees to learn and distinguish hundreds or perhaps even thousands of odors. The absolute sensitivity of bees to most odors is similar to ours (allowing for their ability to get further than we can inside a blossom to smell it), and their capacity to differentiate smells is roughly equivalent to that of a well-trained human. Bees also have special receptors, which we lack, for smelling carbon dioxide and water vapor.

Honey bees also have taste receptors, though none are in the mouth. Each foot and antenna can taste what it has stepped into or touched, and the tip of the proboscis is also able to taste. Insects in general recognize the same four basic taste categories that we do: sweet, sour, acid, and bitter. Interestingly enough, bees are less sensitive to sugar than we are, perhaps because it is advantageous for them to ignore extremely dilute nectar, which would be a waste of time to collect. Bees do not find saccharine sweet, which means that their sugar receptors are at least a bit different from those of most humans.

Bees are, of course, sensitive to touch, and also have a system for sensing body orientation. However, this sense of balance is very different from our own. Vertebrates have an elaborate set of fluid-filled rings and weights in chambers; bees, by contrast, simply measure the "sag" on various parts of their body. For example, a bee's head is balanced on a pivot joint just above its center of gravity; as a result, the bottom of the head always points down, like a plumb bob. Receptors placed around the neck determine which way the head is pointing, and thus the direction that is down. We can fool this system by adding a tiny weight to the top of the head, thus moving the center of gravity above the joint; when this happens, the bee tries to fly upside down.

One ability we lack is the capacity to sense the earth's magnetic field. Bees are more sensitive to this mysterious force than any other species that we know of. The basis of their ability lies in thousands of minute crystals of magnetite—lodestone—which develop as pupae mature.

Communication

The whole fabric of honey bee society depends on communication—on an innate ability to send and receive messages, to encode and decode information. Only by speaking the same language from the outset can a colony of as many as 60,000 short-lived individuals coordinate its efforts and avert chaos. Bees use chemical, tactile, auditory, and (at least in tropical *Apis*) visual messages. The most common communication medium among invertebrates, however, is chemical, and so it is with odors that we begin.

A pollen collector, her wings slightly spread, is performing a waggle dance that specifies the location of the food she is foraging; potential recruits crowd around to attend the dance.

PHEROMONES AND OLFACTION

Even bacteria sense chemicals, and the way they manage the task has led to the evolution of olfactory senses and chemical messages in animals. A bacterium such as the common intestinal symbiont of humans, *Esche-*

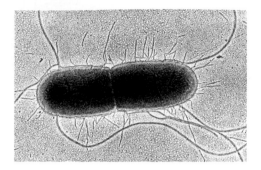

Even the bacterium E. coli *is able to taste and smell. The short projections are pilli, which are used in mating; the long curving whips are flagella, which rotate like propellers to move the organism.*

richia coli (a symbiont rather than a parasite because one of its waste products is the essential nutrient cobalamin, better known as vitamin B_{12}), can "smell" dozens of chemicals. When it encounters a smell that it likes (usually a food odor), it moves along a weaving path slowly but inexorably toward the source of the chemical; when it encounters chemicals that betoken danger, it moves away.

The bacterium senses the presence and strength of these chemicals with vast numbers of receptor proteins embedded in its surface. When a chemical encounters the corresponding receptor protein, the two substances bind to one another; this causes the end of the receptor that sticks through the surface into the bacterium to change shape. This change causes yet other changes, whose end result is to inform the bacterium of the receptor's encounter. After enough bad encounters, or a dearth of good ones, an electrical message is transmitted along the cell surface to the whiplike propulsion units, called flagella, and the course being steered is changed.

The olfactory receptors in our noses and on the antennae of insects operate in much the same way. When a chemical is encountered that fits a receptor protein in the membrane of an olfactory cell, they bind to one another. As in bacteria, the binding depends on complementary molecular contours, and also on electrical attractions between slightly positively charged regions on one molecule and corresponding negatively charged parts on the other molecule. The binding causes the receptor to change shape; the change can be in the portion that protrudes into the cell, or it can open a channel that allows a particular kind of ion to pass across the membrane; regardless of how the receptor changes, the result, directly or through some intermediate steps, is an electrical change on the cell surface. In higher animals such as bees and humans, however, this information does not cause a behavioral change on its own; it is fed into a nervous system for analysis.

Another major difference between bacteria and higher animals is that the receptors in bacteria are adapted to recognize specific small molecules, whereas in animals most binding proteins are designed to accommodate small parts of much larger molecules and to be less choosy. The limitation of the bacterial system is that, for an organism to smell something, there has to be a particular receptor devoted to that chemical; as a result, bacteria can sense about two dozen substances, but are blind to all the rest. To take a simple analogy, we could imagine that each word in the dictionary corresponds to a particular chemical, and bacteria are able to read only 24 three-letter words.

The major part of the animal strategy is much more like the way we recognize words. Each receptor binds to a part of many different mole-

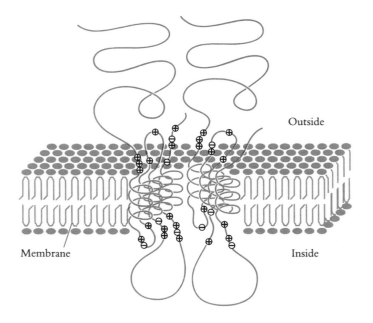

Outside

Membrane

Inside

Membrane receptors are proteins anchored in the cell membrane. They can bind to specific molecules or (as in the cross section shown here) form channels that pass them through the membrane.

cules, as if it were able to recognize the letter "b" in "bath," "isobar," "beetle," and "football"; such a receptor has no ability to recognize a particular odor. But, instead of only two dozen single-word receptors, imagine 26 receptor types, one for each letter. Now the odor corresponding to "bath" simultaneously stimulates four receptors—"a," "b," "h," and "t"—and no other odor produces that pattern. This strategy has two obvious drawbacks: First, there can be olfactory anagrams—two different molecules that cannot be distinguished because their subunits (to which the receptors bind) are the same; to return to our dictionary analogy, "meal" and "male" would be one such pair. Second, because the receptors are so unspecific, an animal must learn what different odors mean.

In fact, animals have their cake and eat it too: noses and antennae come equipped with both kinds of receptors, the general and the specific. Specialized receptors recognize (that is, bind to) odors that animals need to be able to react to before they have an opportunity to learn. Some of these important odors are produced by food, as for instance the butyric acid generated by all mammals; this by-product of our metabolism enables ticks, mosquitoes, and black flies to locate their victims; insect repellents work by exuding a special kind of olfactory anagram that binds the butyric acid receptors so strongly that the insect can no longer tell in which direction the prey odor is getting stronger.

Other odors are produced by members of an animal's own species to communicate information; these chemicals are called pheromones. Two of the best known pheromones are the sex attractants of Japanese beetles and gypsy moths—(R,Z)-5-(1-decenyl) dihydro-2(3H)-furanone and 2-methyl-7(R),8(5)-epoxy-octadecane, respectively. Females emit these scents, and the pheromone receptors of males react, informing the attached nervous system that a potential mate is upwind. If we place pheromone-baited traps (now available commercially) side by side, the beetles and moths will segregate perfectly into their respective receptacles.

There are dangers inherent in this private-odor approach to communication: other species may be using the same chemical to communicate, and some may even use it to lure hapless victims, which arrive expecting to find mates. Other predators simply follow pheromone trails to potential meals. Chemical communication systems generally perform the jobs they were designed for, though, and their very success makes the exceptions notable. One ludicrous confusion involves the truffle, a fungus much prized by humans. It grows on tree roots, and happens to emit an odor that mimics the musk scent of male pigs. Truffle hunters allow sows in heat, apparently expecting to find mates, to sniff out and excavate the truffles.

Honey bees have both sorts of receptors. Their many unspecific detectors allow them to learn and distinguish at least 700 floral scents (the largest number that has been tested) as well as many artificial odors. A unique bouquet characterizes each hive, and guard bees check for it as they "frisk" incoming foragers. The private-message receptors of honey bees include, in addition to those for several pheromones, at least three specialized detectors that do not receive messages: receptors for water vapor, carbon dioxide, and oleic acid.

The last odor, which has the aroma of decay, is given off by dead bees and releases what can only be described as undertaking behavior: the deceased insect is removed from the hive, carried away, and discarded at some distance. The behavior of undertaker bees in accomplishing their essential task provides an insight into colony life. When a bee dies in the hive (though 90 percent of all fatalities occur outside while foraging, in the height of the season there may still be a hundred corpses a day in the hive to dispose of), it is not carried directly out. For a time, in fact, it still elicits begging gestures from hungry bees. But as the oleic acid begins to be emitted, an occasional worker will pick up the dead bee, carry it a short distance, and then drop it. A minute later a second bee will happen by, notice the body, and move it some more. The bees that specialize in dealing with the dead eventually get the remains to the entrance and out, but it is not clear whether this happens by chance—as a drunken sailor's aimless wanderings eventually carry him off a cliff—or by design. What is clear is the totally innate response to this odor: if we brush a dab of oleic acid on a live bee—even the queen—she will be carried about, struggling and obviously quite alive, by the cadre of undertakers; eventually she will be ejected, but as the odor evaporates, she will be accepted back once more.

HONEY BEE PHEROMONES

The queen produces many odors, of which at least two are pheromones. The best known, (E)-9-oxo-2-decanoic acid, is secreted by her mandibular glands (the same organs that, in nurse bees, produce royal jelly). The pheromone is exuded into the air, wiped on her body for the attendants to lick off as they groom her, and passed to nurse bees in the process of feeding. It is communicated through the hive in the air, by being rubbed off onto nurse bees that then wander through the hive, and through tropholaxis, the sharing of food. Most of the dissemination of the queen's odors is by nurse bees who pick up pheromones on their bodies through physical contact. Unlike most chemical messages, decanoic acid has many different effects. First, it represses the ovaries of the workers, preventing the development of laying workers; a pheromone produced by developing brood also aids in this inhibition. Second, it attracts nurse bees to the queen and elicits their care. Third, it inhibits the production of new queens. Finally, it is the odor that attracts drones during mating flights.

The role of decanoic acid in the control of swarming reveals how order can emerge from apparently random behavior. Queen cells are built when too little decanoic acid reaches the workers that are passing through their construction phase. This can happen if the population becomes too large, so that there is not enough of the pheromone to go around. It can also occur if the hive becomes too crowded, so that the queen's attendants, having groomed and fed her and thus obtained some decanoic acid, are unable to share the pheromone widely enough. Cell builders in an overcrowded hive may never have the opportunity to exchange food with or smell the body of one of these attendants, or contact the bees she has shared food with; as a result, they will begin constructing queen cells. In either circumstance, it is important for the colony to swarm.

The actual process of queen-cell construction is a lesson in participatory democracy. Even an uncrowded, underpopulated hive will have the start of several queen cells at the bottom of a comb. The construction

Drones gather in congregation areas to await the arrival of queens; they recognize queens by detecting pheromones. Here a group of drones chases a caged queen suspended from a balloon.

process seems random: it may begin as little more than a few flakes of wax in the telltale vertical orientation, but it is there. A worker may stumble on it and tear off some of the wax, carrying it off or dropping it; the next bee may tear some more off, the next may repair it, and so on. Each bee is casting a vote for or against swarming; presumably the yeas are from bees that are short on decanoic acid. If the queen is removed, the pheromone supply vanishes, and the tide in the voting slowly turns; more bees will begin adding to cells than those tearing off bits, and in time a set of queen cells is completed.

This strategy, by which a behavior is controlled by the careful balancing of two opposite forces, is common in our own bodies. Virtually every movement of a finger or limb is tempered by muscles pulling in the opposite direction; this gives us more precise control of our actions than we would have otherwise. Some hormones circulating in the blood have antagonistic effects, and it is the balance between the two at any given moment that determines the net response. The idea that all the bees in a hive work in concert in a common effort to achieve a single goal, then, is a myth. The ambivalence of individual bees and the differences of opinion between workers is highly adaptive: it allows for faster, more flexible and finely graded control than would be possible if all acted with one mind.

Workers emit at least two alarm pheromones. The most potent is isopentyl acetate, which is released from the sting chamber when a bee is angry or whenever a sting is everted. This scent, which has the aroma of ripe bananas (sufficiently angry bees *will* respond to the odor of banana oil), attracts other bees and induces them to sting if a likely object presents itself.

From twenty years of experience, during which we have been the victims of fewer than a dozen stings, we have found that only a serious gaffe near the hive entrance is likely to cause trouble. The most potent releaser of stinging once the alarm odor is abroad is rapid movement. Unless actually stung (in which case so much alarm pheromone is released that further dissimulation is hopeless), we find that standing absolutely still and edging *very* slowly toward the nearest large object is the best course. It is as if the guards were aching for an excuse to sting but, given the effects of what is for them a kamikaze attack, want to be sure of the threat. If the object of their wrath can manage to sidle up to a nearby tree, the guards nearly always give up and leave. Running away makes sense only if there is a fairly stiff breeze to run into: honey bees fly about 7 m/s (they do a four-minute mile), which is significantly faster than a human can run across broken ground; but in the face of a 5 m/s wind they can only manage 2 m/s.

Workers also have a recruitment pheromone, which is released from the Nasinov gland at the top rear of the abdomen. When exposed, this organ releases geraniol and other less important chemicals. Geraniol is a powerful attractant to other bees, and the Nasinov gland is put to use under two sets of conditions. First, when a forager finds an extremely good source of food, water, propolis, or a desirable cavity, she may expose the gland. If it is a food source, this has the effect of attracting searching recruits from downwind; the odor lingers only as long as the forager emits it, but recruits successfully guided to the food may take up the signaling before the original forager leaves. If it is a cavity, the odor can be emitted inside the potential colony site, leaking out slowly after the scout leaves.

The other major use for the Nasinov gland pheromone is to mark the hive itself after some disturbance. When a sudden wind comes up, for example, or a heavy rain, foragers in the field may be grounded; bees will not fly in winds higher than about 7 m/s, though by flying low to the ground they may be able to find protected areas and so push that limit. During such disturbances, the rate at which foragers return to the hive drops sharply; when conditions have improved and the delayed returnees begin to arrive, they often pause in the entrance, expose their Nasinov glands, and fan their wings. Apparently, these returning foragers are attempting to guide the return of their colleagues still in the field. In addition, when the queen has departed on her nuptial flight, rows of bees surround the entrance to the hive and fan their everted scent glands, apparently attempting to guide her back safely when she has finished mating.

Workers attract other bees with a pheromone from the scent gland near the tip of the abdomen. This forager is fanning her exposed gland at the hive entrance.

AUDITORY COMMUNICATION

Bees can produce sound by vibrating their wing muscles; if the wings are kept folded, the result is a loud buzz rather than flight. The best-known example of sound communication by bees takes place before swarming. After the queen cells have been started and the queen has been put on her thin-down diet in preparation for her flight with the swarm, there is a period of waiting for the new queens to mature. Normally, swarming begins soon after the developing queens start to pupate, but poor weather may force a delay, so that new queens may near the age of emergence. As the pupating new queens mature but swarming is prevented by weather, the old queen pauses from time to time, presses her thorax against the comb, and buzzes in a particular pattern—a long,

The old queen and virgins ready to emerge communicate by means of sounds transmitted through the comb. The old queen's signal is called "tooting" and the response is known as "quacking."

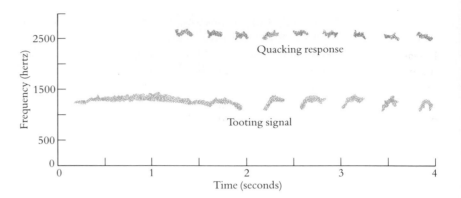

two-second pulse, followed by a train of quarter-second emissions. These sounds resonate through the comb, and all the workers on the piece of comb being vibrated freeze in place. (Playing sound directly into the comb is one way to get workers to hold still when we want to number them.)

If there is an unhatched queen old enough to respond, an answer can be felt in the comb. The reply consists of about ten short pulses, and informs the bees that this new queen must be kept forcibly in her cell. This is accomplished by means of a curious ritual: a worker stands on the cell and vigorously shakes it with an up-down vibration of her abdomen. The same signal, performed atop other workers in the hive, stimulates foraging; when administered to the old queen on the comb, it inhibits her wanderings and egg laying.

The queen-to-queen signaling is much more important after the primary swarm departs. If the colony is large enough (and most are), the first virgin to hatch will lead an afterswarm, but other new queens will be nearly ready to emerge. The tooting and piping serves to keep the unhatched queens in their cells until the coast is clear. When afterswarming is complete, the next virgin uses the same system to help locate the potential pretenders to the throne, stinging them in their cells or fighting them on the comb.

Though the auditory exchange between queens allows swarming to proceed in due course, these sounds do not trigger swarming. Swarming is actually initiated by scout bees that dash through the hive producing a peculiar buzz of their own.

There are two other sounds in the honey bee repertoire, both incorporated into the dance language.

DISCOVERY OF THE DANCE LANGUAGE

It was Aristotle who first noticed that a successful forager soon recruits many of her colleagues to a rich food source. His guess was that the forager actually led the recruits from hive to flower. In 1788, the Reverend Ernst Spitzner, observing through the glass walls of an observation hive, reported what appeared to be the initial alerting maneuver:

> When a bee comes upon a good supply of honey [nectar] anywhere, on her return home she makes this known in a peculiar way to the others. Full of joy, she twirls in circles about those in the hive, from above downwards and from below upwards, so that they shall surely notice the smell of honey on her; for many of them soon follow when she goes out once again.

In an observation hive like Spitzner's, a single sheet of comb is sandwiched between two sheets of glass, with just enough room between the comb and glass for one layer of bees. A hive like this, in which all the activities of the bees are visible, was invented earlier in the 1700s, though Pliny mentions putting small pieces of transparent horn in the walls of Roman hives to provide tiny windows for viewing. The colony in an observation hive is very small by normal standards, and has great difficulty heating itself in cool weather; its large surface area relative to its small volume causes it to lose warmth.

Using such an observation hive, N. Unhoch independently discovered the "dance" in 1823, though he failed to notice that it was performed by returning foragers and served in recruitment:

> Without warning, an individual bee will force its way suddenly in among three or four motionless ones. . . . They twist and run together in something more than a semicircle now to the right then to the left five or six times. . . . The dance mistress often repeats her dance four or five times at different places.

The idea that the forager leads the recruits to the food received a blow in 1901 when Maurice Maeterlinck, who later won the Nobel Prize in literature, was doing research for his book *The Life of the Bee*. Maeterlinck captured a forager and, while she was feeding on a drop of honey, carried her from the hive entrance to another location. After marking the forager with a paint drop, he went back to the hive and watched her return. When she reemerged Maeterlinck captured her, and then he rushed back to the food in time to see a recruit arrive without having followed the forager.

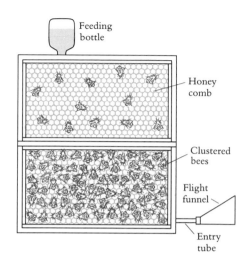

The behavior of bees can be studied with an observation hive. This colony consists of two frames, one above the other, covered with glass. The bees enter and exit through the tube and "flight funnel" to the right; the jar at the top is used to provide sugar water when there is little natural forage.

Labels in figure: Feeding bottle; Honey comb; Clustered bees; Flight funnel; Entry tube

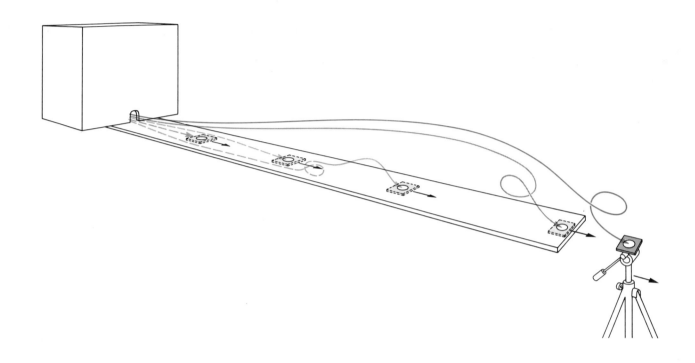

Training begins with drops of sugar water near the hive entrance leading out to a small feeder. The feeder is moved progressively farther away until the foragers begin to fly, and then it is shifted to a tripod. As the tripod-mounted feeder is moved farther away, the foragers are given individual markings.

In 1919, Karl von Frisch took up the question. Years earlier, the Austrian zoologist had discovered a way to train bees in order to test their color vision. His technique is important for understanding how such experiments are begun. First, a few drops of concentrated, scented sugar solution are placed in the hive entrance. Foragers on their way out encounter the drops (by stepping in them), consume the artificial nectar, reenter the hive to unload the unexpected find, and then return to search for more. The next drops are placed a few steps farther away. The foragers soon find them, aided by their willingness to search around a little and by their memory of the scent.

After a while, the foragers (and, by now, some recruits) are walking farther from the hive along a plank, placed against the entrance for this purpose, to a feeder large enough to accommodate several bees at once. In our lab, we paint a straight line down the center of the walkway, since otherwise the foragers often fail to maintain a straight course and fall off. By about 60 centimeters the foragers have given up walking and begin to fly to the food, learning at the same time to recognize the feeder from the air. At this point, the feeder can be moved to a tripod. This is also the

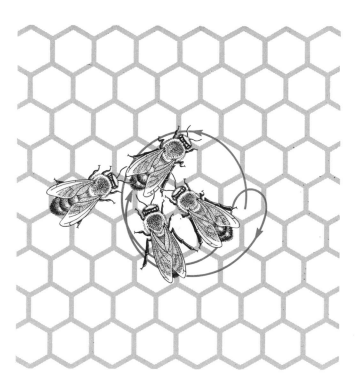

moment to mark each forager with a distinct combination of colored paint dots or to glue plastic numbers to their backs. Bees hardly notice these operations while feeding. In time, the concentrated food may be replaced with a more dilute solution lacking any scent; this reduces further recruitment once the forager force is about the right size.

Now the trick is to let each forager visit once, and then to move the feeding station farther away. The returning foragers seem to accept about 25 percent farther. From 60 centimeters, therefore, we can move it to about 75 centimeters; at 8 meters we can jump to about 10 meters; and at a thousand meters we can increase the distance to 1200 or 1250 meters. Bees have been trained by this method to about 13 kilometers, but von Frisch had no reason to go more than a few meters for his early experiments.

When von Frisch rediscovered the dances, he realized that there were two basic forms. In the round dance, the forager circles one or more times clockwise, and then counterclockwise, and so on. The other class of dance is the waggle dance, in which the forager waggles her body

Returning foragers will dance if they have found unusually good food. When the source is near by, they perform round dances; at greater distances, the dances take on a figure-eight shape and incorporate both sounds and waggling.

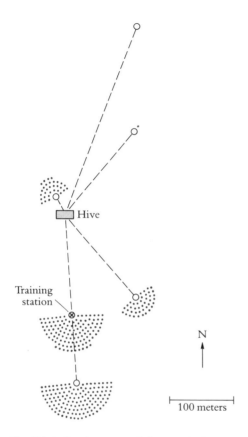

Von Frisch first demonstrated that recruits know the approximate location of the food sources advertised by dances by training foragers to collect scented food at a site 150 meters south of the hive. He then set out five plates with the same odor and counted recruit arrivals. The new bees (indicated by dots) arrived predominantly near the training station.

from side to side (about 13 times per second) while running in a straight line, then circles to the right back to the starting point, waggles again, then circles back (this time to the left), and so on. The crucial observation for von Frisch was that the foragers he trained and marked, collecting sugar solution a few meters away, performed round dances; bees with pollen on their legs, on the other hand, always used the waggle dance.

Thus von Frisch thought he had deciphered the code: a round dance meant nectar, a waggle dance meant pollen. True, some waggle dancers lacked pollen, but they might already have disposed of their loads. Von Frisch then showed that the odor of a flower clings intensely to the waxy hairs on the body of the forager, and that recruits smell this odor while they follow the dance. When a recruit goes looking for the advertised food and is offered a choice of several floral odors, von Frisch showed that they pick the one that they smelled on the body of the dancer minutes earlier. Hence, according to this olfactory theory of dance recruitment, the recruits are informed by the dance that there is a good source of food, that it is nectar or pollen, and what it smells like.

Von Frisch's original theory of recruitment was challenged almost immediately by Americans who reported having observed round dances by pollen collectors. Later, when a European colleague rejected the hypothesis for the same reason, von Frisch repeated his experiment: he trained foragers a few yards away and fed them sugar solution; they inevitably performed round dances. He then watched for pollen dancers, and they inevitably produced waggle dances.

The error in his thinking came home to him in 1943. By the mid-1930s, von Frisch had become the preeminent zoologist in Germany. His reputation protected him from the Nazis, who were displeased that he sponsored Jewish graduate students. Indeed, he became their protector, and wound up as the official advisor for theses as far removed from his own area of expertise as geology and physics. Eventually, however, his high standing in academic circles could no longer shield him, and he was sent back to his family estate in Austria for the duration of the war. There he gave a co-worker a piece of bad advice that ultimately led to the discovery of the dance language.

The associate needed to train bees about 500 meters, a longer distance than von Frisch had ever attempted. He advised her simply to train one group to a scented solution near the hive and then put out food with the same odor at the desired location; though most recruits would doubtless find the closer food station, some should chance upon the more distant one. The attempt failed.

When the co-worker, Ruth Beutler, had performed the training in the more tedious, step-by-step fashion, however, the foragers visited the distant station regularly, recruiting many new bees. But when she looked at the dancing in the hive, the real surprise came: her marked foragers were performing waggle dances. Now von Frisch repeated the training and set out food in several locations around the hive; the recruits came predominantly to the area near the one station that the trained foragers were visiting. The recruits clearly knew something definite about where the food was located.

The season ended before any further investigations could be made into the nature of the location communication, and it is easy to imagine the excitement with which the work began in 1944. The first breakthrough came when von Frisch watched the dancing of marked foragers as they were trained ever farther away. He observed that up to about 75 meters these bees performed round dances, but beyond 90 meters the waggle-dance form became evident. What is more, these first waggle dances were very brief, with perhaps only a single wag; as the training station got farther away, the tempo of the dancing slowed, and waggle runs began to incorporate additional wags. In fact, he could graph the duration of the waggle run (or the entire dance circuit, waggle run plus return) against the distance to the food and so decode the dances of bees that had visited food sources unknown to him.

Though it would certainly be helpful to know the distance to the food, a recruit must also know which direction to fly if she is to find the source efficiently. The discovery of this component of the dance language came when von Frisch had two groups of foragers trained to separate locations simultaneously. Although he had always noticed that the orientation of the waggle runs of a particular bee on the comb were consistent, different bees chose different angles. During the long-distance training he had observed that all the marked foragers visiting his feeder danced at the same angle, and now, with two stations out, he saw that the two groups danced in different directions; moreover, the difference between the two preferred dance angles was roughly equal to the difference in the directions to the two feeders.

Exploring the matter more systematically (and with mounting excitement), von Frisch learned how to decode the dance direction: when the waggle run in a dance is pointed up (the dances are performed on vertical sheets of comb), the feeding station is always in line with the sun; when the food source is directly away from the sun as viewed from the hive, the dances point down; when the food is located 80° to the left of the sun, the dance points 80° to the left of vertical. A bee attending a dance need only determine the orientation and duration of the waggle run in order to know the distance and direction of the food.

The dance communication system is called a language because it satisfies all the intuitive criteria that have been posited for a true language. When a chimpanzee points at a banana in plain view and grunts excit-

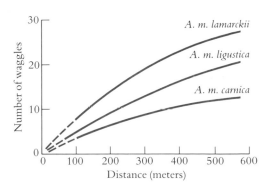

The number of waggles in the dance increases with distance; the distance codes for three different races are shown here.

The direction of the food is encoded in the angle of the waggle run of the dance: when the source is in the same direction as the sun, the dance is aimed straight up on the vertical comb; when the site is 80° to the left of the sun, the waggle run is oriented 80° to the left of vertical.

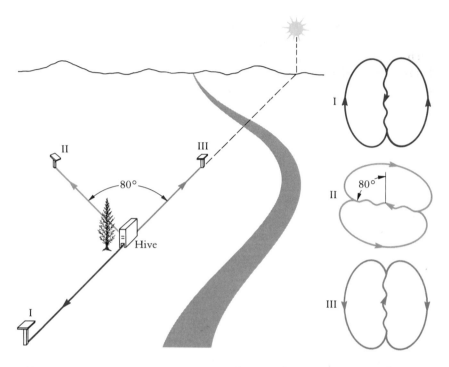

edly, it might represent a message, or be merely an expression of a passing emotional state. The dance, however, refers to subjects distant in time and space; it can refer to flowers kilometers away, that the dancing bee visited many minutes previously. Moreover, the conventions for dance communication are arbitrary: the bees interpret the direction of the sun as "up"; it could just as easily be "down" or "20° to the left of vertical," as long as both sender and receiver agree to abide by the convention. In fact, the use of the sun's direction at all is arbitrary; it could just as easily have been the direction the hive faces, or true or magnetic north.

The apparently arbitrary nature of these conventions is most compellingly illustrated by the distance code. In the race of bees von Frisch studied *(A. m. carnica)*, each waggle corresponds to about 45 meters, but in the Italian race *(A. m. ligustica)* the convention is roughly 20 meters per waggle, and the Egyptian race *(A. m. lamarckii)* pegs the conversion rate at one waggle for about 12 meters.

The existence of dialects in the bee language, however, does not mean that the language is learned: honey bees reared in isolation from dancers can perform correctly oriented dances after their first foraging discovery *and* correctly interpret the dances of others from the outset. When pupae of one race are put into a colony of another, they dance as adults using their own race's conversion factor, having learned nothing from the dances of their foster sisters; bees of different races simply misunderstand each other's dances. Anyone who considers a communication system language only if it is wholly learned will dismiss the dance language, but, as we shall see in a later chapter, the same criterion, rigorously applied, also excludes human language.

DANCE COMMUNICATION

When the dance language was discovered, it astonished one and all—indeed, many scientists believed von Frisch must be suffering from delusions. Just as we had once thought that only humans had true color vision, the idea that far and away the most complex communication system in nature other than our own is found in a mere bee was even harder to swallow. Our error, of course, is in thinking of insects as lower animals: they have been evolving just as long as vertebrates have, and where complexity has been selected for, body size and number of legs are unlikely to present insurmountable barriers. Every animal is as complex as it needs to be; supposedly "higher" vertebrates like the sloth that occupy unchallenging niches tend to be dull witted, whereas insects with complex tasks to accomplish can be remarkably resourceful.

The sophisticated language that von Frisch deciphered is more complex than he realized, however. First of all, it has an acoustic component. When a forager waggles, she produces a motorboat-like sound by moving her wing muscles (with wings folded) in short bursts about a thirtieth of a second long. Since occasional silent dances seem to arouse no interest, the sound must be essential to communication, and since it occurs simultaneously with the waggling, it correlates with distance. Why there should be two distance measures in the dance has puzzled researchers ever since the discovery of the dance sound. There is a second sound associated with the dance as well: when a dance attender wants a sample of the food being advertised, she produces a quarter-second "weep" sound, whereupon the dancer stops and shares her food. Stopping on call turns out to be important: one scientist attempted to develop a model bee to communicate with recruits, but did not know about the stop signal; when his model failed to stop, the signaling attender stung it.

Another surprise is that the dances themselves are fairly sloppy when food is nearby. No two cycles of the same dance necessarily have the same number of waggles or sound bursts, and the angle of the waggle runs normally alternates left and right of the true direction. It comes as no surprise, then, to learn that recruits attend several cycles (six is the

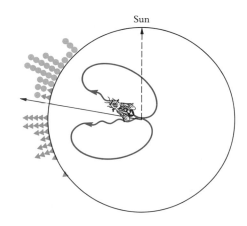

No two waggle runs are exactly the same. At distances under 2 kilometers or so, the runs alternate left and right of the true direction (dark arrow); here the food is 80° left of the sun, and the orientations of 54 runs are shown. The number of waggles also varies about an average value. Triangles indicate the direction of runs after a clockwise turn, circles the direction after a counterclockwise turn.

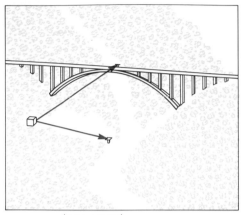

100 meters

In an effort to see if the dance language has a code for elevation, von Frisch trained bees from the side of this valley to a station on the bridge; recruits followed the ground and searched by the stream under the span.

usual number) and seem to average them together before setting a course. Once von Frisch's students trained a group of foragers about 350 meters to the northeast of his observation hive, and left it to him to deduce its location from the dances. Only after averaging dances over the course of an hour did von Frisch feel confident enough to calculate the food's location; he deduced a position that was less than 20 meters from the actual station. When he set out on foot to look, he quickly found the feeder hidden behind a bush. A typical recruit would have departed after attending dances for only five or ten seconds.

Having discovered the distance and direction correlations, von Frisch wondered if part of the dance might specify height above the ground. In the temperate zone, most flowers are near the ground, so this sort of data seems irrelevant. In the tropics where honey bees evolved, however, most of the flowers are in trees at altitudes that are significant to animals as small as bees; even in the temperate zone, honey bees sometimes encounter tall flowering trees. When he placed a hive at one end of a bridge over a deep ravine and trained foragers either to a food station out on the bridge or below it at the bottom of the valley, the recruits generally followed the land down and searched the ravine. A series of such experiments convinced von Frisch that there is no correlate for altitude in the dance.

Von Frisch also wondered how bees measure the distances and directions they report in their dances. How, for instance, do bees measure how far they have flown? One possibility is that they simply judge by the amount of effort expended, and most experiments support this hypothesis. When von Frisch glued 55-milligram lead weights on the backs of foragers (who weigh about that without a load of nectar), he observed that they exaggerated the distance to the food in their dances. Similarly, when he glued small foil flaps to the thoraxes of foragers to increase their wind resistance, they also overestimated distance. When bees are forced to *walk* to food, they begin to perform waggle dances after only two or three meters, again suggesting that they judge distance on the basis of how tired they are.

Although effort seems to be the basis of their subjective sense of distance, this does not tell us whether the bees measure effort on the trip out (when they are not burdened by a load of nectar), or effort on the way back (when the bee's weight may have doubled). They may even take the average of the two. Von Frisch found the answer to this question by training one group of bees uphill to food and another bunch of foragers to a station downhill. If they measure only one leg, there should be a significant difference. In fact, the bees flying uphill *to* the food overestimated the distance, while those flying downhill on the outward leg underestimated the journey. The same pattern appears if the training is performed into or with the wind, or if the bees are moved while feeding so that the outward and inward journeys are of different lengths. These elegant experiments made it clear that the outward trip is more important in judging distance.

The same cannot be said for the way bees judge direction. When a bee is moved to a new direction while feeding (but still within sight of the hive so that she can return directly there), her dance indicates a location halfway between the bearings of the outward and inward legs of her journey.

Even though bees seem to weigh both their outward and inward trips in determining which direction to indicate in their dance, these two portions of the foraging flight differ in other ways. For example, when we train bees along a dog-leg route to a target in an area with obvious landmarks (trees, for example), foragers tend to follow the training route out to the feeder even days later, but fly directly home. Recruits, by contrast, fly directly to the food in the direction indicated by the dances they have attended.

The degree to which a forager's loyalty to its original indirect route can persist is illustrated by a bee that we trained in 1976, who came to be known (for reasons that will be obvious) as the bicentennial bee. Three stations were placed out in a field about 180 meters from the hive, one (W) to the west, another (WSW) in the west-southwest, and one (SW) to the southwest. This forager, number 76, was trained to station W and, like the others trained to that station, was marked with her number and a spot of blue paint. When we reduced the food concentration at all three stations to slow down recruitment, the student manning station W substituted distilled water by mistake. Blue 76 soon abandoned that station and shifted to station WSW, where she was re-marked with that station's white paint. But to get to WSW, she always flew to station W and circled it once. When we needed more foragers at W, we switched the food at WSW to water in an effort to get White/Blue 76 to return to her original station; instead, she shifted to station SW, where she was, in due course, marked with the station color (red). Red/White/Blue 76 continued to reach station SW by flying first to W, circling it, then to WSW, circling again, and then flying to SW and landing. Despite her frivolous outward route, she always departed directly for the hive.

Sometimes bees fly to food by an indirect route out of necessity. When there is some high barrier in the way, such as a cliff, the forager is likely to go around rather than over. To discover what their dances indicate under these circumstances, von Frisch ran experiments near rock outcrops in rugged terrain. He also tried placing a hive next to a tall

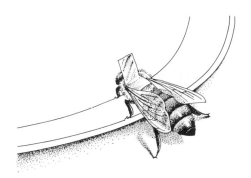

Bees carrying either lead weights or small bits of foil (to increase air resistance) overestimated the distance to the food source in their dances. This indicates that effort expended in flight is at least one basis for judging distance.

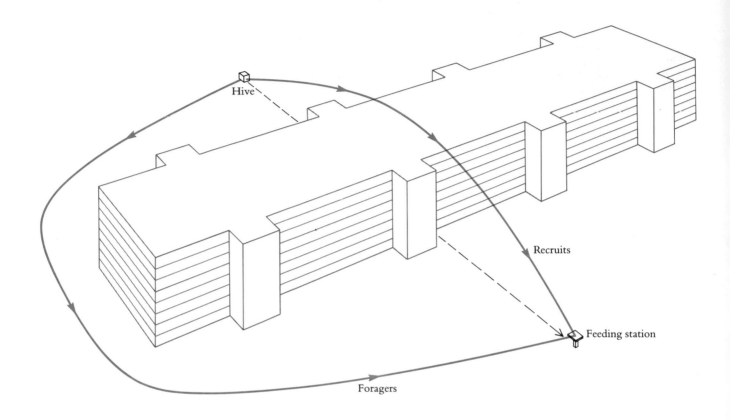

Labels on figure: Hive · Recruits · Feeding station · Foragers

Foragers need not fly directly to a food source in order to signal its direction. In this experiment von Frisch trained bees to fly around a building to a feeder; the dashed arrow indicates the location specified by their dances.

building and training the foragers around it. He wondered whether the bees, on their return, would dance in the departure direction or the true direction, or perhaps even perform a dog-leg dance. In fact, foragers indicate the true map direction, and leave it to the recruits to figure out how to get there. Faced with the building, many seem to have flown up and over.

A similar pattern is evident when foragers fly through crosswinds. Like a light plane, a bee has to turn into the wind in order to keep from being blown off course. Originally, von Frisch thought that the dances might be misdirected, since compensating for the wind makes the angle of flight with respect to the sun very different from the angle of travel (that is, the true direction of the food) with regard to the sun. In fact, the dance indicates the true direction, and it is up to the recruit to compensate for the wind. This makes sense, given that wind speed and even direction can change quickly. Whether the forager actually calculates the true direction by performing the necessary mental trigonometry, or merely averages together the inward and outward angles (the errors in which would cancel one another if the wind did not change) is not yet known.

It is more likely that foragers would compute the true travel direction on the outward flight rather than rely on averaging, since the wind may shift between the two parts of the journey. In addition, scout bees may find it essential to make this correction before returning home. Scouts are bees who have no current food source to visit and who, instead of waiting in the hive for a dance, strike out on their own to see what they can find. This is slow work, and a scout may venture far outside her familiar range around the hive, and fly a very circuitous route. Once she has found a good source of food, however, she needs to be able to fly directly home. All the many meandering legs of her route must be integrated and the effects of the changing wind factored out if she is to be able to set an accurate course.

SWARMING

The dance is used to communicate the location of nectar, pollen, water, propolis, and, during swarming, potential nest sites. Swarm dances take place on the side of the swarm cluster, where the stage consists of the bodies of other bees rather than honey comb. The process by which a new site is chosen illustrates again both the value of the dance language and the basically democratic nature of certain colony activities.

Even before swarming begins, particular foragers begin examining cavities. If bees are trained to a station next to an empty hive, they can be watched to see whether marked foragers inspect the box. The shift from ignoring the empty hive to making extended inspections is a sure clue that swarming is only a day or two off. Once the swarm has left the old hive these house-hunting visits become much more common, and the scouts that inspect the box can be observed on the swarm dancing to a location at just this distance and direction.

At the outset, scouts are likely to advertise many sites; other scouts attend these dances. A bee that has visited our empty hive box may be seen following a dance to another site, flying there and inspecting, and then returning and checking the box again. Finally, she begins dancing once more, perhaps extolling the virtues of the box or, as often as not, switching her allegiance to the new site. Having switched, she will not become fixed in her opinion: she will continue to entertain other possibilities (attending new dances and visiting those places) *and* monitor her own choice from time to time. If we pour water on the floor of a cavity that has been the subject of enthusiastic dancing, the advertisements for

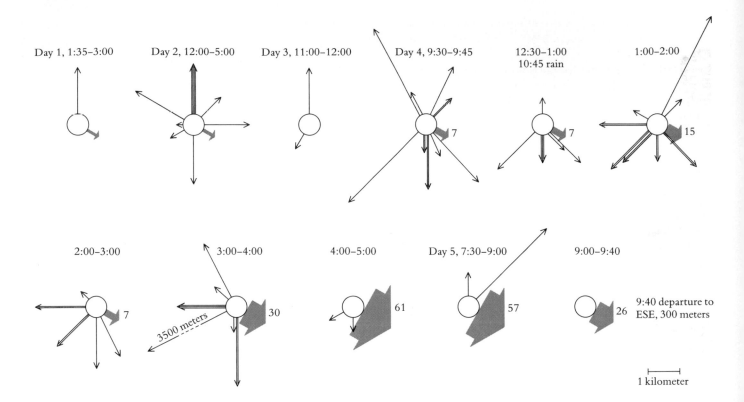

Day 1, 1:35–3:00   Day 2, 12:00–5:00   Day 3, 11:00–12:00   Day 4, 9:30–9:45   12:30–1:00
10:45 rain   1:00–2:00

7   7   15

2:00–3:00   3:00–4:00   4:00–5:00   Day 5, 7:30–9:00   9:00–9:40

7   30   61   57   26   9:40 departure to
ESE, 300 meters

3500 meters

1 kilometer

Scouts fly out from the swarm in search of new cavities and return to report their finds. They also attend other dances and check those alternatives as well. Slowly a consensus develops for one location, and the swarm departs. These charts record observed dances in a swarm that took about four days to reach a decision. North is up, the length of a line indicates the distance to the site being advertised, and its width corresponds to the number of dances observed for that site.

this site will dwindle and finally come to an end over the course of perhaps two hours.

The scouts take their time making their decisions; given that winter survival in a new cavity is a difficult prospect, it makes sense to take as much time as needed to explore the alternatives. Eventually, however, a consensus builds as more and more scouts dance for the same location; when virtually all scouts agree, the last few dissidents are ignored and the swarm departs for the cavity.

But things do not always run so smoothly. If there are no adequate cavities, the swarm may finally give up and build exposed comb on the spot. When winter comes, these colonies perish, if predators have not finished them off already. When there are two first choices, two factions develop among the scouts, each dancing for its location, and no consensus may ever be reached. Finally, the swarm may divide and the scouts of each persuasion attempt to lead as many bees as possible to their side's

When a swarm cannot find a new cavity or agree on one of several alternatives, the bees may finally give up and build their comb in the open. In the temperate zone, such a hive will certainly die in the winter, if it is not destroyed first by predators.

choice. Inevitably, however, only one of these groups will contain the queen, and the other will abandon its journey and rejoin its other half, usually while it is still en route to the cavity in question. Much remains to be discovered about which bees elect themselves as scouts, how the movement of the swarm is triggered after a consensus is achieved, and how the swarm, composed for the most part of bees that have not attended a cavity dance, is herded to the goal, which may be more than 2 kilometers away.

The Dance-Language Controversy

The idea that an insect has the second most complicated language in nature continues to astound students of behavior today as much as it did scientists when von Frisch first reported it in 1946. The dance language is certainly one of the seven wonders of animal behavior, and is probably near the top of even that exclusive list; in terms of amazement per gram of organism it must be number one. The story of the dance communication is now a prominent part of nearly every introductory biology text, and von Frisch's Nobel Prize was largely in recognition of this discovery.

Despite the institutionalization of the dance language, however, there has always been an undercurrent of doubt. One university press refused to publish von Frisch's first book on the subject as submitted because its advisers suggested that there was less to the phenomenon than met the eye. Events came to a head in 1967, when the first of a series of papers challenging the dance language appeared in America's most prestigious

Numbers allow researchers to trace the movements of individual bees.

and widely read scientific journal, *Science*. The ensuing controversy rekindled work on the dance, sharpened the thinking and behavioral techniques in the field, and provided a rare lesson in how science really works.

THE CHALLENGE

The attack on the dance language was mounted by two California scientists, Adrian Wenner and Patrick Wells, with the aid of their students. There were four basic components to the challenge: the existence of a dance proves nothing in and of itself; von Frisch's experiments were poorly designed; well-controlled experiments contradict the dance-language hypothesis; a new hypothesis based exclusively on odor accounts for honey bee recruitment.

Their points are well taken: to begin with the first, even striking correlations need not mean coevolution. Country dwellers have known for centuries that it is possible to judge temperature by counting the number of cricket chirps per minute; as temperature rises, crickets chirp faster. But cricket chirping is unlikely to have evolved to inform us of the temperature.

Consider a more pertinent example: some moths "tremble" their wings after flying, and the duration of trembling correlates with the distance flown. Could trembling behavior have evolved to communicate distance in this solitary species, or is a meaningless physiological artifact—an inevitable "winding down" after strenuous activity, analogous perhaps to panting more after jogging farther? Among stingless bees (the social, perennial bees of the New World tropics), returning foragers perform buzzing runs that excite recruits to go out and search; the duration of these runs correlates with distance to the food, but this information is not used by the recruits. How, Wenner and Wells argued, can we assume without proof that the distance correlation is used by honey bees?

The direction correlation they found to be equally suspect: ladybird beetles choose an angle to walk with respect to the sun, and so travel in straight lines; if we suddenly block out the sun and turn the surface the beetle has been traversing from its horizontal position up into a vertical orientation (like the comb of a bee hive), the beetle takes up a direction that deviates left or right of vertical by just the angle she had been walking with respect to the sun. This correlation, like the trembling of the moths, closely matches the apparent code in the dance, but also serves no obvious purpose; yet it has been observed in some dozen species of insect. Could the direction correlation of the honey bee dance also be an artifact?

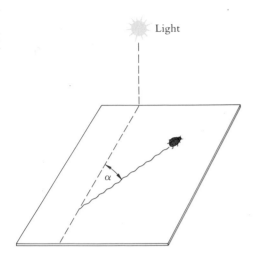

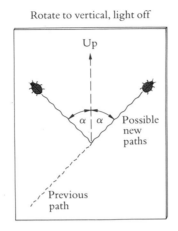

This argument evoked two basic reactions among scientists. Some, comfortable with their understanding of the dance system, refused to believe that von Frisch could be wrong. After all, the dance language was so hard to believe in the first place, was received so critically, and had been the subject of so many follow-up studies that it simply *had* to be right. This may be called the Argument from Inertia, and it applies equally well to Ptolemaeic astronomy and Aristotelian physics. The other group was clearly intrigued by the possibility of a major scientific scandal, the chance that the counterintuitive notion–that the elaborate dance correlations evolved in the absence of any functional application— might actually be correct. Academics like nothing better than a counter-intuitive argument; it proves the fallibility of common sense and the concomitant need for subtle minds to see past the obvious. Of course, common sense *is* usually a reliable guide, and the obvious *is* usually correct. The second group's line of reasoning may be called the Argument from Boredom: there is not much reason to believe it, but its conclusions are more entertaining for the spectators.

Neither camp of boosters in what grew into a well-known and widely discussed controversy did, in fact, know much about bees, behavioral experimentation, or von Frisch's experiments; each had to rely on the partisan versions offered by the California group on the one hand and von Frisch on the other. Wenner and Wells began their attack on the evidence by dragging out all the loose ends and inconsistencies about the dance, details known only to the aficionados (and readily found in any field, swept neatly under the carpet until someone figures out what they mean). They pointed out that the dance is, as we have already men-

When a ladybird beetle is allowed to walk on a horizontal surface (left), it will keep some constant angle with the sun or other light. If the light is extinguished and the surface turned up (middle), the beetle will shift to walking at the same angle with respect to gravity, though it will choose left or right of up with equal frequency. Right, ladybird beetle (Hippodamia convergens).

tioned, very sloppy for distances out to about a kilometer (the range of most foraging); if this really were a highly evolved communication system, why all this slop and noise? Next, they reminded us that very few bees recruited by dances to artificial feeding stations ever actually find them; most return to hive emptyhanded. Those that do find the food take far longer than a direct flight would require; might they not have been searching at random, and simply have stumbled across the station by chance? Experiments with species that lack a dance indicate that at short distances recruitment is almost as efficient in these colonies.

And if it were an optimized language, why has it not evolved in genera other than *Apis*—bumble bees and social wasps, for instance, all of whom could presumably benefit from rapid and accurate recruitment to food? Why, if the dance is really part of a language, are there so many distance correlations? After all, distance can be read from the number of waggles, the number of sound bursts (or the duration of either), or even from the position of the dance in the hive: foragers returning from longer distances dance farther from the hive entrance.

Having sown the seeds of doubt, Wenner and Wells turned next to von Frisch's evidence. Typical of the experiments he cited is the series of array tests that he and his students performed in the 1950s. His basic technique, which is still in use today, was to train foragers to a feeding station some distance from the hive, set out an array of similar stations offering the same food odor, and then count the number of recruits that arrive. The array can be in the form of a fan, with the training station (called the "forager station") in the middle and all the others (called "recruit stations") at the same distance from the hive but in different directions; alternatively, all the stations can be in the same direction but at different distances—the so-called "step-wise" array.

Wenner and Wells did not dispute von Frisch's report that most recruits arrive near the center of these arrays, close to or actually at the forager station. Instead, they pointed out that recruits could have found their way there without using the abstract information in the dance. Like the other thousands of hymenopteran species, honey bees might rely simply on odors to locate food. We know from von Frisch's early work that recruit bees can learn the odor of a forager's food from the scent clinging to her body; this would allow a bee searching randomly to recognize when she was near the food and home in on it.

There are other odors available as well at the food site: foragers regularly emit the Nasinov gland pheromone at feeding stations, and this scent could draw in recruits from considerable distances. Von Frisch sometimes sealed these glands with shellac, gluing the rear abdominal plates closed so the gland could not be exposed, but Wenner and Wells argued that recruits would have smelled the shellac odor itself on the dancer and used it to home in on the station in the field. Though the quantity of shellac scent exuded by a dry gland seal is small, these seals would eventually break and be repaired at the station with new applications of shellac. Indeed, von Frisch mentions that some arriving recruits landed on the shellac bottle rather than on the food.

In addition, we must not forget the hive odor that every member of a colony carries and passively exudes everywhere she goes. As Wenner and Wells point out, even just using food odors would take recruits to the center of the array near the forager station; von Frisch almost never put the forager station at the end of an array. In short, they argued, honey bees might use conventional odor cues as other bees, ants, and wasps do, and their "language" might be just a fortuitous collection of orientational artifacts with no actual role in recruitment.

For the first two papers in *Science,* Wenner and a student repeated the fan and step-wise array experiments with new controls that they felt would minimize the olfactory ambiguities von Frisch had overlooked. The experiments were first performed roughly as von Frisch's had been, and recruits arrived predominantly at the forager station and recruit stations nearby. Then the experiments were repeated with the addition of controls for odor. Though the foragers from the observation hive were trained to only one station in the array, foragers from a second "control" hive were trained to each of the recruit stations. Now there would be scent-gland odor and hive odor at each location, as well as the sight of feeding bees. As Wenner and Wells pointed out, recruits are often hesitant to land on a nonfloral target unless they see other bees already there. In von Frisch's experiments, recruits did not actually *land* at the recruit stations; they "approached" and were counted. Since the recruits at these stations could not be captured, there is no telling how often they were counted as they made perhaps several passes at one station or one at several different sites. (Recruits arriving at the forager station, on the other hand, *were* captured.) In the Wenner and Wells work, there were foragers at every station to induce recruits to land, and the recruits were always captured. The bees from the two hives could be distinguished because one colony was from a stock carrying a mutation for body color, and so looked very different.

When the experiments were done this way, the results were provocative: recruits from each hive went to the middle of the array where the odors were centered, and there was no obvious preference for the location specified by the dance.

Although the original olfaction hypothesis of Wenner and Wells included only the factors we have already mentioned, a later and more comprehensive version hinted at in 1969 and then put forward in detail in 1973 included the effect of locale odors. The idea is that foragers might

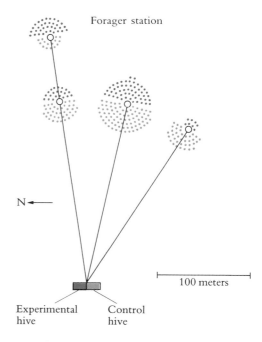

One of Wenner's colleagues repeated the "fan" experiment of von Frisch, except that he trained the foragers to the end of the array rather than to the center. In addition, he trained an equal number of bees from a second ("control") hive to the other stations in the array to provide bee odors everywhere. Recruits from both hives favored the center of the array, even though the dancing in the experimental hive should have indicated only the left-most stations.

bring back with them not only the odor of the flowers they have been visiting, but the general scents of the area they have been foraging in. If recruits build up an olfactory map of the surrounding landscape, they could "place" the locale odor brought back on the body of the forager, remembering where in the field they had smelled that particular combination of scents. This would enable recruits to begin their search in roughly the right area without any need for the distance and direction coordinates in the dance. There is some circumstantial evidence for the use of locale odors even in von Frisch's work, and Wenner and Wells had reported that recruitment is enhanced up to eightfold when the forager station is given a locale odor—the scent of trampled or freshly mown grass, leaf litter, insecticide, suntan oil, chicken manure, or even paper towels. But the role of locale odor was not investigated in any systematic way, so this aspect of the hypothesis remained speculative. Nevertheless, taken with the other odors, it could account for any example of directed recruitment without recourse to a language.

THE DEFENSE

Von Frisch, in his 70s when the challenge to the dance language came, based his defense on previous work; he did not perform any new experiments. He began his response in *Science* by dismissing the idea that odor cues left in the field could play any but a very local role in recruitment. This assertion was based on his extensive but clearly subjective experiences over the course of fifty years. For example, von Frisch said that random search aided by local odors could not explain the "surprising speed" with which recruits find the food; in his massive book on the dance language, von Frisch even states that "recruits fly rapidly and with certainty to food." Actually, no one had ever measured the speed in question, and when three studies in 1970–71, each prompted by the debate, *did* time the searches, the results were troubling: though a bee can fly a hundred meters in about twelve seconds, successful recruits usually take ten minutes or more to find a station at that distance.

The idea that odors do not travel far or linger long seems contradicted by von Frisch's own accounts in earlier publications. In one case, for example, he explained the failure of a step-wise experiment on the grounds that a vial of lavender scent had spilled in the car carrying the equipment to be set out; the odor was said to have flowed out of the car travelling along what would be the recruits' flight path, where it lingered long enough to disrupt the test, hours later.

The next part of von Frisch's reply to the challenge cited experiments that Wenner and Wells had not mentioned in their brief papers. These, he

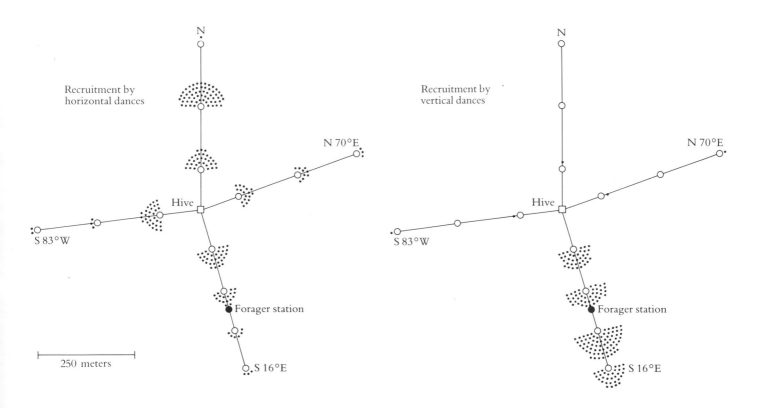

Recruitment by
horizontal dances

Recruitment by
vertical dances

In one experiment, von Frisch trained foragers to a station to the south and set out scent plates in 13 other places. When the hive was tipped over so that the dancing was disoriented (horizontal dances), recruits were observed in all locations; when the hive was righted, on the other hand, the recruits were seen almost exclusively in the direction of the food station.

felt, made the case better than the fan and step-wise array tests that had been the object of the initial attack. The best of the old experiments cited by von Frisch was probably a major inducement for Wenner and Wells to include a hypothetical locale odor in their model of recruitment. In this experiment, von Frisch had trained a group of foragers to a station about 250 meters south of the hive and set out thirteen scent plates in various directions. At the beginning of the experiment the hive was laid on its side, so that the comb lay flat, and so the dances could no longer be oriented to gravity. (Interestingly enough, bees do pretty well in hives containing horizontal combs; they raise brood and store honey on the top side of the combs and they will even perform properly oriented dances if the sun is visible; in this experiment, however, the bees danced in the dark, and so the waggle runs were disoriented.) After 90 minutes, the hive was restored to its normal position, oriented dances began, and the scent plates were again monitored.

At first glance, the results of this clever experiment appear to support the dance-language hypothesis fairly strongly: when the hive was on its side recruits went everywhere, but when the hive was vertical, the recruits arrived near the feeder. But though the distance correlation in the disoriented dances was not affected, there was no tendency on the part of the recruits to search at the correct distance. Surely if the dance communication is real, the recruits should have looked at about the right distance, regardless of direction.

Given that this experiment was performed only once, it is easy to explain it away on any of a number of *ad hoc* bases. For instance, we could argue that the foragers might have everted their scent glands more during the second half of the test. A bee's readiness to mark a food site depends on how good it is relative to other food being brought into the hive at the same time; the same food can be considered good at one time and poor at another, depending on the shifting nature of the competition. The nature of the competition *does* shift over the course of the day: flowers offer nectar at only a particular time each day; if the morning crop is first rate and afternoon blossoms scarce and of poor quality, foragers visiting von Frisch's station might have begun marking the site only during the second half of the experiment. Spatially precise recruitment based on Nasinov pheromone, therefore, would have been possible only late in the proceedings.

There are other ways of explaining this one result away (for example, a shift in wind direction at about the time the hive was reoriented), but the point is that when an experiment is not designed to control against a specific alternative hypothesis, the results are usually ambiguous. In this case, for instance, if the experiment had been repeated the next day with the times of vertical and horizontal dancing reversed, most of the possible alternatives could have been excluded.

Von Frisch concluded his rebuttal by criticizing the methods of the challengers. As already mentioned, most researchers train their foragers on low-concentration sugar solution with either no odor or a scent other than the one to be used in the experiment. Wenner and Wells use concentrated food with the experimental odor from the outset; moreover, they use concentrations of odor at least ten times as strong as those used by von Frisch. Von Frisch complained that high odor in food inhibits dancing, fills the hive with strong scents, and leaves the field full of recruits stimulated during training rather than during the experiment. Since no one monitored the dancing, we cannot know whether the foragers danced at normal rates. In a later experiment by Wenner and Wells run after the same training procedure had been carried out, however, dances were rare; this provoked von Frisch to comment that "it is a pity that [they] tried to investigate the importance of dancing with bees that never or seldom danced at all."

MORE EXPERIMENTS

It is a truism of science that for every experiment supporting one side in a controversy, there is an equal and opposite experiment bolstering the other. Each side held assumptions that the other rejected, and each designed its experiments with these axioms in mind. No wonder they argued and experimented at cross purposes. In 1969, four groups undertook experiments aimed at settling the controversy. Two of them numbered hundreds or thousands of bees individually in the hive and then watched when the bees attended dances and where they subsequently turned up in the field. Another group repeated a conventional recruitment experiment, but attempted to control for all the odors in the field. The fourth group did both.

The fourth group's experiment was performed by a group of Caltech undergraduates, including one of the authors of this book (JLG), in the desert in eastern Oregon. We chilled 4000 bees one by one until they were motionless, then numbered them by gluing convex, form-fitting, numbered plastic discs to the top of the thorax; when the bees warmed up, they flew back to the hive. Then we trained two groups of foragers in opposite directions from the hive using von Frisch's technique. As the experiment began, concentrated scented food was set out at both stations, and both groups of foragers began to dance. As many dances as possible were monitored in the observation hive, and the individual numbers of the dancer and attenders were recorded, as well as the time of the dance. In the field, monitors at the stations recorded the arrival times and numbers of all recruits and captured any newcomers. The idea was that if the dance communicated information, a bee that had attended a dance to the north station ought to fly to the north station; if she were equally likely to be captured at the south station, where the food and bee odors were the same, then the dance did not provide directional information.

The problem with this particular experimental technique is that fewer than half of the dances could be recorded since some dances occur on the invisible side of the comb, some take place simultaneously with the dance being recorded, and so on. As a result, it is possible for a recruit to be seen attending a north-station dance, depart on a fruitless search, return and attend a south-station dance without being observed by the monitor, and then turn up at the south station. She would in fact have used the most recent dance information she had obtained, but would appear to have ignored the dance she was last *observed* attending. By comparing the accuracy of recruits that arrived quickly with those that took longer (having had time to return and attend another dance), how-

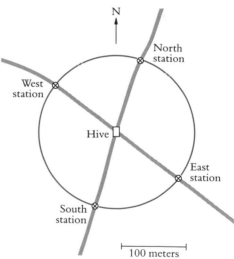

Above, gluing numbered discs onto bees' backs. Below, experimental array used in the Oregon desert experiments.

Recruits arriving soon after being observed attending a dance came predominantly to the station indicated by that dance; those taking longer than about seven minutes, on the other hand, arrived randomly. This pattern is made evident by assigning a value of +1 to each arrival at the station indicated by the dance that particular bee had observed; each arrival at the wrong station was counted as −1. The graph plots the sum of the values of each arrival. If all bees arrived at the correct station, the sum would follow the diagonal gray line; if there were no correlation, the sum would trace out a horizontal course.

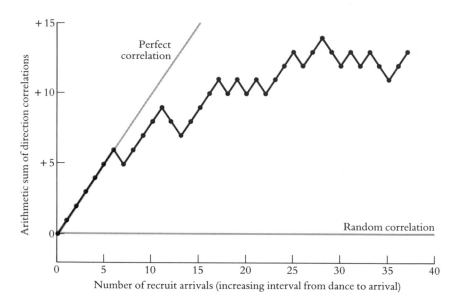

ever, we can take this factor into account. Looked at this way, 91 percent of the recruits that took less than four minutes went to the station that they had been observed seeing advertised; for those that took more than seven minutes, the correlation drops to 58 percent, near the 50 percent expected if the second dance attended indicates the same direction as the first only half the time.

In a second series of experiments, the Caltech group again trained foragers in opposite directions and placed scented food at both locations, but this time only one site had concentrated solution. As a result, most dances were for that site. To control for scent-gland odors, the Nasinov organ was sealed in both groups. Since foragers were visiting both locations, hive odor was present at each site. If bees use language, the pattern of recruitment should follow that of dancing: recruits should turn up at the station with the good food rather than the olfactorily equivalent location in the other direction. If only odor were involved, there should be no preference. Just in case there were some general bias toward one direction over another, the locations of the high- and low-quality stations were exchanged in later tests. The results of this experiment were just what von Frisch might have hoped: 93 percent of the 562 dances indicated the site with good food, and 96 percent of the 295 recruits arrived there.

What these experiments do *not* allow for is the possible effect of locale odors. The authors of the study themselves recognized this problem, and they noted that a conclusive study might be one in which the dances of the foragers were altered in such a way that recruits would proceed to a location to which the dancing foragers had never been. We had not a clue how to manage such an experiment.

The need for such a test became painfully evident in 1973, when Wells and Wenner reported an experiment that strongly implicated locale odor. In this test, which will sound very familiar except in one critical detail, they trained two groups of foragers in opposite directions, and one group was given better food than the other. The well-fed foragers did most of the dancing (65 percent—the difference in food quality was not as great as in other tests using this design) and their station obtained most of the recruits (77 percent). The difference between this experiment and the others, however, was that the hive was tipped on its side, so that the dances were disoriented—they lacked any directional information. It seemed unlikely that the recruits could have found the correct station except by odor.

There were, in fact, problems with the methods too technical to relate here—problems that could account for the results without requiring us to abandon the dance-language hypothesis—but it was clearly time for an unambiguous experiment that would allow no room for doubt.

MAKING FORAGERS LIE

One way to determine whether bees have a language is to change the dancer's relation to some pertinent environmental feature without altering the relation for attenders. In that way, we could get the foragers to lie about where they had been. If the recruits fell for the lie and went where they were told regardless of the olfactory shortcomings of that location, they must have a language; if, on the other hand, recruits turned up at or near the station that the forager was actually visiting, then the dance must provide no abstract information to the bees. The question was, how can we make a forager lie?

The experiment that finally discriminated odor from language was dreamed up during a field study on the Patagonian coast, where we were investigating vocal communication in right whales. The design took advantage of two obscure but crucial bits of information about bees. First, as we know, dances normally take place in the darkness of the hive, and "up" is taken as the direction of the sun. If, however, the comb is removed from the hive and left in the open, the dances become reoriented: a dance that had been aimed straight up in the dark will now be oriented directly toward the sun. When the sun is visible, then, the bees ignore gravity and switch to the real thing, and an extremely bright light

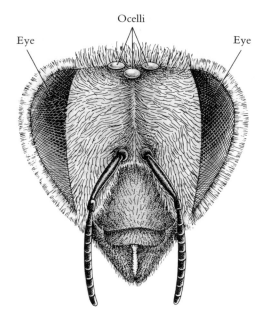

Ocelli

Eye   Eye

The ocelli of an insect are located on the top of the head between the compound eyes; they are usually almost hidden by the hairs that cover the head.

will do as well as the sun itself. As the light is moved, the dances all shift along with it.

Although the foragers shift their dances to align them with the sun, however, recruits simultaneously shift their *interpretation* of the dances, using the sun (or the bright light) instead of gravity exactly as the dancer is doing, and so no misunderstanding occurs. But a curiosity in the visual system of the bee allows us to exploit the bees' ability to shift their point of reference: in addition to the two large compound eyes, insects have three simple eyes, called ocelli, at the top of the head. These supernumerary eyes are like ommatidia in that they do not form images; evidence from experiments in which they were painted over indicates that their function is to measure general light level. Ocelli-painted bees begin foraging later in the morning and quit earlier in the evening, as though only the middle part of the day is bright enough for them; on overcast days, these bees did not come out at all, though their sisters foraged normally. When their ability to see was tested, the treated bees were about ten times less sensitive to light.

The critical step in our conclusive experiment was to paint the ocelli of the foragers trained to the feeding station. On sunny days they fly normally and dance as usual. Next, we set up a bright light as an artificial sun, visible through the glass walls of the observation hive. A sufficiently bright light will reorient all the dances—those of treated and untreated foragers alike—but as the brightness of the light is reduced there comes a point at which the ocelli-painted foragers can no longer see it, and their dances revert to their usual gravity orientation; untreated dancers continue to dance with regard to the light and, most important, untreated recruits continue to use the light in decoding the dances. At this point, then, treated foragers are using a different dialect from that of the potential recruits (gravity instead of light), and so the dances should misdirect any language-using recruits. The degree of this misdirection should exactly equal the angle between "up" and the direction from which the light shines; in fact, by moving the light, it should be possible to "aim" the recruits at any arbitrary target. On the other hand, if the bees do not use the dance to communicate, none of this will make the slightest difference.

One trouble with such experiments is that, ideally, a great many places should be monitored to see where recruits go, but each recruit station requires a person to count and catch bees. For graduate students with limited funds, this was a serious constraint. We overcame the problem by devising an automatic recruit-catching machine. It consisted of a bucket with an artificial flower that led the bees inside. The bucket contained not only food with the same odor as that being brought back by the forager,

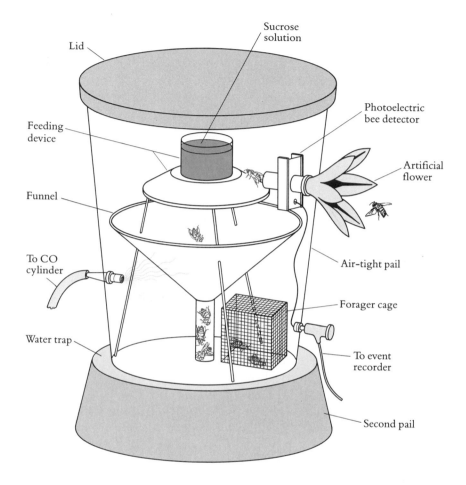

Lid

Sucrose
solution

Photoelectric
bee detector

Feeding
device

Artificial
flower

Funnel

Air-tight pail

To CO
cylinder

Forager cage

Water trap

To event
recorder

Second pail

Cross section of an automatic recruit-capturing station.

but also some anesthetized bees from the hive to exude the hive odor. As a recruit entered it passed though an infrared light beam (recall that bees cannot see red light, much less infrared), and a circuit in each bucket signalled a central device that recorded the time of arrival and the location of the bucket. The recruit then reached the food and fed. The bucket was kept filled with carbon monoxide, a gas bees cannot smell; as the recruit fed, she lost conciousness, fell off the inclined surface of the feeder, and rolled into a collecting funnel. Removed from the trap when the experiment was over, the bees regained consciousness and flew home. The bucket had to be mounted with a water trap to keep out ants, which tended to be overcome by the carbon monoxide as they crawled

Ocelli-painted foragers were trained to a feeder to the north of their hive, and an array of recruit-capturing stations was set out. Left, a light was used to aim the dances at one station in the array (heavy arrow); recruits arrived predominantly in that direction. Right, when the light was shifted, subsequent recruitment favored the new direction.

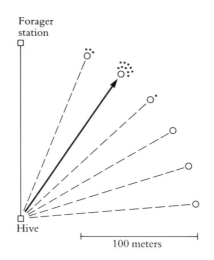

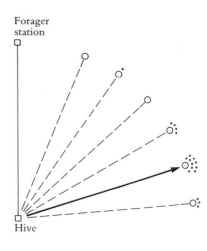

through the neck of the artificial flower. Their inert bodies would collect in the entrance and discourage new recruit bees.

With six of these devices (the limit set by the number of working channels on the chart recorder used to register arrivals), we could set up an array well away from the forager station. In the series of experiments with fan arrays, the light was kept overhead until the experiment began (so that the two "dialects" corresponded), then it was moved to aim the recruits at one end of the array, and later shifted to indicate the other end. All that remained was to see where the recruits actually went early and late in a test.

In fact, recruits fly where the dance tells them to go. In analogous experiments involving step arrays, with the forager station in a direction well away from the array to which the recruits were misdirected, they turned up at or near the correct distance. Though locale odors may be important under some circumstances, it is clear that the language really does communicate distance and direction. When the experiments were repeated using the training methods of Wenner and Wells, however, this pattern disappeared. Apparently when there is a highly fragrant food source, and when this source remains available over an extended period, dancing declines as recruits search successfully using only the odor cues.

In retrospect, Wenner and Wells were misled by their assumption that, if bees communicate by odor under one set of circumstances, then they must use odor in all cases. Yet when we look at how honey bees navigate (Chapter 7), we will see that they can indeed use several sensory systems. They can detect and navigate by the sun, or by patterns of polarized light in the sky, or by familiar landmarks. Like any crucial component in a well-engineered system, the primary system has backups in case it fails or cannot be used. The assumption that insects are, by virtue of their size or their lack of an internal skeleton, necessarily simple has frequently beguiled researchers into overly reductionistic hypotheses.

Controversies are critical in science, though, and the challenge that Wenner and Wells presented to the study of bee behavior has been of enormous benefit. They pointed out many technical flaws, logical errors, and unsupported conclusions; their challenge in fact resuscitated a field that had almost fallen asleep, provoking experiments that would never otherwise have been performed—experiments that yielded the first good measurements of recruit accuracy, search times, and other important parameters. They also stimulated thinking about honey bee evolution, ecology, navigation, and communication, posing questions that drew students into the study of bees and led to an explosion of behavioral research that continues unabated two decades later.

CHAPTER 5

The Economics of Dancing

One of the myriad sources of confusion in the dance-language controversy has been the bees' propensity to recruit by means of odors under one set of conditions, and by dancing in others. This reminds us that bees, like humans and virtually every other species of animal, must make choices—when to dance, for instance, or whether to build or destroy queen cells. Ethologists often refer to these choices as "decisions," a term that unfortunately implies that an animal consciously evaluates alternatives and makes its selection. To some of us the mere existence of behavioral variability implies decision making; yet there seems no reason to suppose that whatever logic is employed in weighing the facts is not prewired.

The formulation of conscious decisions, like all mental activities, occurs in the privacy of the mind. Determining whether bees can make logical decisions and behavioral plans—decisions and plans that are out-

In spring and early summer, many kinds of flowers bloom simultaneously, presenting foragers with a range of choices.

side the range of possibilities their innate circuitry could have evolved to deal with—is a difficult challenge, and it will be addressed in the final chapter. Our focus at present will be on the moment-by-moment, routine choices foragers must make while harvesting food. Since the same general set of problems has been faced by perhaps a hundred million generations of bees, we feel comfortable in the assumption that natural selection will have favored efficient, hard-wired circuitry over trial-and-error experimentation in solving these problems, and that there has been more than enough time for these circuits to evolve.

VARIATIONS IN THE FOOD SUPPLY

Before we look at how bees respond to the need to choose, let's look at what sorts of choices and variability they face. First, there are seasonal differences: in the spring there are enormous numbers of flowers available, but in the summer and fall the number of blooming species plummets.

In parallel with this dramatic change in numbers of blooms, there is a tenfold change in food quality: the nectar of spring flowers is very sweet; that available in late summer is very dilute. In economic terms, it is a

Concentrated nectar is readily available only in the spring, as reflected here by the threshold concentration of sugar solution necessary to interest foragers.

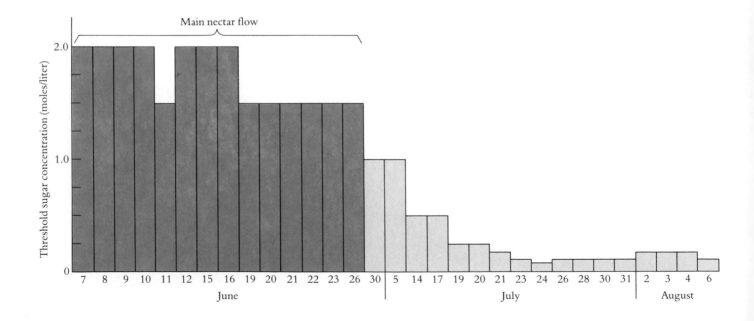

buyer's market in June, when so many species are competing for the services of pollinating insects; to attract bees, blossoms must offer more and better food. August, by contrast, is a seller's market; there is little competition between flowers, yet the number of foraging insects has risen enormously as bumble bee and yellowjacket colonies (to name only the most obvious examples) have grown exponentially. Now flowers can get away with offering low-quality food and still be certain of being pollinated.

In some sense, the plants themselves have had to choose between the high-cost spring-blooming strategy and the cut-rate late-summer alternative. Although subject to the very real risk of frost, the spring option promises a reliable supply of water, little shade from deciduous trees, cool weather, and an early start for seedlings; the late summer and fall, obviously, offer a different, generally less desirable set of conditions but without the risk factor.

Even within a season, there is considerable variability. As every gardener knows, many flowers have a distressingly short blooming season—indeed, it is even shorter in the wild, since domesticated varieties have been bred for extended blooming. The kinds of flowers available one week may be quite different from the choices available the next. Even on a given day there will be choices: some species have lots of pollen, others very little. Less obvious to us is that the quantity and quality (sugar concentration) of nectar varies from one species to another. Moreover, since most flowers provide nectar during only part of the day, the range of choices can vary between morning and afternoon.

Even within a single species, choices and variability remain. During a drought, for instance, nectar production may vary enormously between wet and dry areas, or between exposed and shaded spots. Patches of flowers can also differ in size: one spot may have plenty of forage, while another patch may be too small to provide a single load of nectar. Even if the patches are equivalent in size and productivity, one may have been canvassed by another bee so recently that the blossoms are depleted of nectar while the other may still be rich in food. In short, the world is a very heterogeneous and variable place for a forager, and choices must be made if a bee is to use its time efficiently.

There has been surprisingly little research on this variability, and yet it is easy enough to study. Fortunately, it is not necessary to sample the flowers to get a qualitative picture of how things are changing: the bees will do that for us. Virtually the only study on these questions was carried out by Thomas Seeley and his students in the forests of upstate New York. They established hives and then recorded the dancing. The bees kept them informed about where the rich patches were to be found and when they were played out. By observing the color of the pollen loads, it

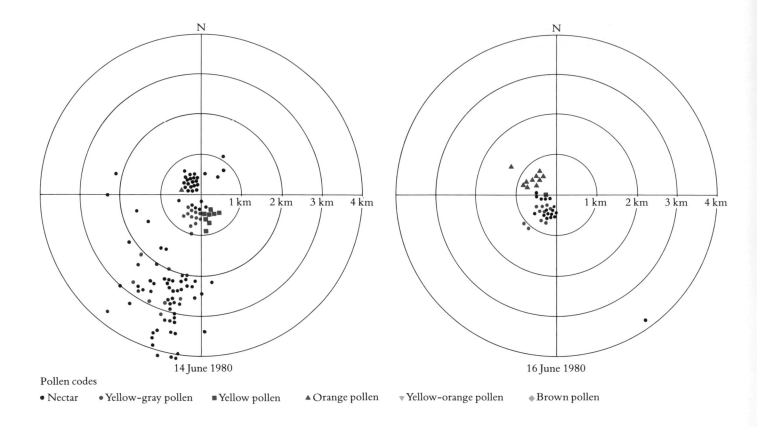

Pollen codes

● Nectar   ● Yellow-gray pollen   ■ Yellow pollen   ▲ Orange pollen   ▼ Yellow-orange pollen   ◆ Brown pollen

Patterns of pollen foraging (as indicated by forager dances) shift rapidly over even just a few days. The hive is at the center of each map. At far right, close-up photograph of pollen loads carried back by foraging bees.

was even possible in some cases to distinguish which of two different species of flowers was being harvested in the same general location.

What stands out in their results is the rapidity of change in the foraging conditions that bees face. The high-quality patches signalled by vigorous dancing come and go in a few days; the pattern on June 14, for instance, bears no resemblance to that observed on June 18, and only a slight similarity to what the bees reported on June 16. On average, the colony worked about ten patches for pollen over the course of a given day; some of these were heavily exploited while others aroused little interest. Although a typical pollen-producing patch of flowers lasts about a week, it is at its peak of productivity for only one to three days. In order for bees to track the sorts of rapid changes going on in the real world they obviously need scouts investigating the environment, on the lookout for new patches; the dance, then, provides a way of sharing this information with sisters so that the colony as a whole can focus its efforts

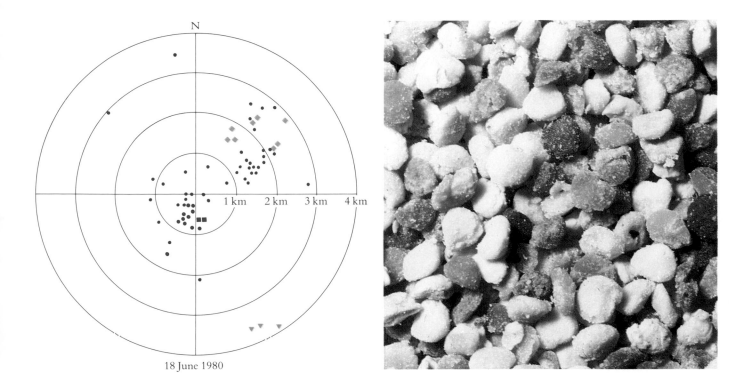

18 June 1980

on the best food currently available, and good sources will normally not slip past unnoticed.

By looking at the distance indications in the dance, we can get a picture of how extensive these scouting expeditions are. Patches turn out to be widely scattered, with half a mile or more usually intervening between one patch and its nearest neighbor. The scouts search far and wide: patches were reported up to 11 kilometers away, though 95 percent of the discoveries lay within 6 kilometers, and the majority were confined to a radius of 2.5 kilometers. Still, for an animal less than 2 centimeters, these are enormous distances.

Given that the rapid change in forage necessitates an active scouting force to monitor the floral market, how large is the hive's commitment to "research" versus "production"? The answer, predictably, is that it varies. Different researchers have found the proportion of scouts in a range from 13 percent to 23 percent of the forager force, but these different results are a consequence of when the measurements were made. If the proportion is monitored over the course of several weeks, it becomes clear that the variation is tied to the colony's needs: during a dearth of food, fully a third of the foragers are scouting, whereas when food is abundant, the scouts number fewer than one forager in twenty.

CHOICES

Having looked at the nature and range of variation in the food supply, we can appreciate how numerous are the factors a bee must weigh. Moreover, the choices confronting a scout, a forager, and a dance attender can be quite different. A scout, for example, must choose between foraging the first patch she discovers or looking further in hopes of finding a better one. She may also have to choose between searching for pollen or nectar. When she has opted for a particular patch, she then has to determine the best time to leave: as she depletes the area, accidentally revisiting blossoms she has already drained, there comes a point at which she would be better off returning to the hive. When she does get home, there is the choice of whether or not to dance. Nor do the options end here: when she reemerges to fly forth again, should she return to the newly discovered patch, thereby becoming a regular forager there, or should she look for new food sources?

A forager—that is, a bee who knows where there is food to be collected at the current time of day—has her own set of alternatives. Two are identical to questions confronting the scout: when to leave the patch and return home, and whether or not to dance. In addition, she can attend dances in the hive advertising other locations and consider switching. Honey bees may live in a socialist democracy, but their economic thinking is highly conservative: a new food source being reported in a dance must be very much better to attract a forager's interest. Bees adhere steadfastly to the advice of the old saw that "a bird in the hand is worth two in the bush." When we measured this conservative bias once, we found that foragers generally ignored dances for food three times as good, but when we upped the quality ratio to five to one, defections became common. Given the millions of years of evolution that have gone into the circuitry of choice in bees, this reluctance to switch must have solid advantages.

Dance attenders—the hive's potential recruits—are bees with no present employment. After attending a dance, they have to choose whether to fly out on the basis of these instructions, or to try other dances and compare the offerings. These bees, too, will have to choose between nectar and pollen—or, at times, water and propolis may be among the options. A recruit even has the choice of flying out to recheck a patch that played out a day or more ago just in case it might have rejuvenated itself, as can happen after a rain. Perhaps, after all, she should give up foraging and remain in the hive, fanning the thickening honey or just resting, thereby increasing her lifespan against the chance of better forage in the days or weeks to come.

At first glance, it is hard to believe that a mere bee can hope to sort all this out, and yet she does so—on the whole, quite sensibly. And while behavioral ecologists are just beginning to understand the subtleties of the "optimal-foraging strategy" of bees, these insects have been working effortlessly through the algebra of foraging since before our ancestors came down from the trees; such is the potential efficiency of innate wiring, honed and polished by countless generations of natural selection.

DECISIONS IN THE FIELD

Our use of artificial feeders, which contain far more food than an individual bee could collect if she worked at it all day, can lure us into forgetting that a bee must usually visit dozens of blossoms to gather a full load. As she forages in a patch, the bee risks visiting the same flower twice, and this risk increases as she drains yet more blossoms. Bees deal with this problem in two ways, one of which affects search pattern, the other the choice of when to leave.

Discovering the optimal search pattern—the route that maximizes the number of nectar-laden flowers encountered while minimizing the overall distance travelled—is a well-known problem in applied mathematics, where it is often referred to as the travelling-salesman problem. Human analysts begin with the advantage of knowing in advance all the locations to be visited, and high-speed computers can now be used to devise the best route. Honey bees have neither the massive computer nor the list of flower coordinates. It comes as no surprise, then, to discover that they are programmed to operate by a rule of thumb that, though by no means perfect, has the advantages of being both better than searching randomly and simple to employ.

Operationally, the rule causes the bee to depart the flower in the same direction she left the last flower if there is not much food, but to turn left or right more often if the blossom has lots of nectar. The result of this system is that when the part of the patch the forager is working is poor, she moves directly across it, perhaps stumbling into a better (less recently harvested) region. When the forager discovers a good area, on the other hand, she begins to mill around in it, choosing new departure directions almost at random. (Behavioral ecologists refer to this as a "win → stay,

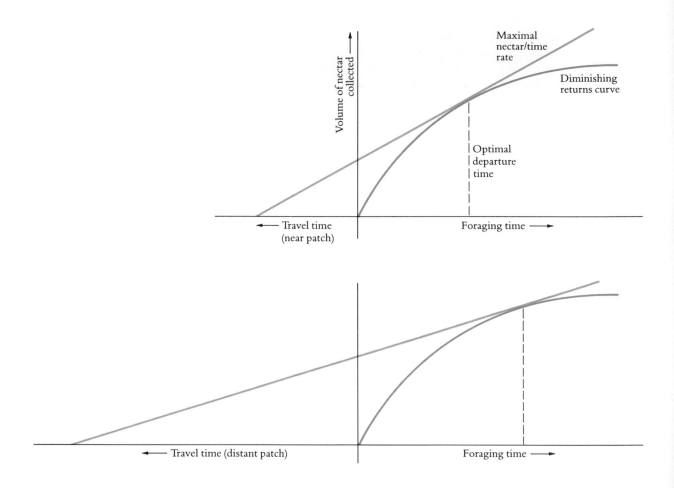

The optimal time to leave a patch depends on how quickly it is depleted (as indicated by the curving line "diminishing returns curve") and the travel time to and from the patch. The slope of the heavy line indicates the maximal overall rate of food intake. If the patch is farther from the hive, a bee will do best to linger in it longer.

lose → leave" rule.) This statement of the rule is "operational" because the variable that the bee is programmed to measure before exercising her choice is not food quality at all, but another parameter: handling time. Handling time is the amount of time the bee spends on a flower, and its only value here is that it usually correlates with the amount of food in the blossom. The threshold for lingering in an area is a handling time greater than about eight seconds per flower. As we shall see, bees frequently use this kind of strategy, determining one thing by measuring something quite different.

The flight-direction rule helps bees harvest a patch efficiently, but if the patch is small (as many are), there comes a point at which the rate of discovering new flowers becomes unacceptably low. This decline in the harvest rate is part of a more general phenomenon known as the law of diminishing returns: additional investments of time or money result in smaller net gains. The problem for the forager is to determine the optimal time to quit and return to the hive so that her net rate of nectar collection will be as high as possible; every minute wasted in a depleted patch is a minute of foraging potential lost from her brief life as a food collector.

Solving this problem, which in one form or another faces virtually every species, requires measuring two factors: the changing rate of return for time invested (that is, the amount of nectar being collected per minute) and the overhead, which in this case is the time needed to travel from the hive to the food and back. At any particular moment, the net rate of nectar collection for the trip *as a whole* is equal to the total volume collected divided by the total time, which consists of the time spent in the patch thus far *plus* the travel time necessary to get there and back.

If we graph the diminishing returns curve, we can visualize the net harvesting rate by drawing a line from a point signifying the travel time (the round trip) to the point on the curve corresponding to the given foraging time. The steeper the slope of this line, the higher the net rate of gain. Since the curve itself slopes ever less steeply with increasing foraging time, there is some point at which the straight line being drawn reaches its maximum possible slope and then begins to decline. This is the moment at which the bee ought to leave. The effect of longer travel times is to increase the optimal amount of foraging time in the patch, which is necessary to amortize the travel-time investment.

So much for theory; how do actual bees, perfectly capable of measuring these factors, behave in patches of artificial flowers offering many small nectar rewards? Easy as it is to manipulate these variables, it is surprising how little has yet been done to investigate this issue. From what has been tried, however, it seems clear that foragers *do* linger in a patch and collect more nectar when that patch is farther away. Whether the nervous system of these insects has evolved to incorporate the more elaborate refinements of optimal foraging theory remains to be seen.

THE OPTIMAL FLOWER

In deciding whether to dance, scouts and foragers evaluate both their own subjective impressions *and,* in the best democratic tradition, the opinions of others in the hive. Let us look first at the factors they evaluate themselves.

One of the more frustrating things about working with bees in the climate of central New Jersey is that it is difficult to train foragers before early July. This is a period of abundant flowering so that there is much competition, but we can increase the concentration of sugar in our training solutions to a level above what real flowers are providing. Yet still there is little interest. Any bees we do manage to train are certainly not very enthusiastic; they stubbornly refuse to dance even while their sisters vigorously advertise less concentrated nectar that takes more time to collect and lies farther from the hive. In fact, bees simply prefer real flowers, and a host of factors beyond simple sweetness go into evaluating the desirability of a food source.

Studying the variables that bees ponder is fairly easy. Two groups of foragers from the same hive are trained to two feeders, and one component of the constellation of cues is made different; the number of foragers from each group dancing in the hive is then recorded. To take the simplest possible case, a greater proportion of foragers will dance for the station with the more concentrated food. But sweetness, which we might guess ought to be the only factor, may or may not be measured directly; after all, bees use handling time rather than the actual quantity of nectar in a flower when they make their value judgements in the field.

If we think about the features that correlate with concentrated nectar, we might wonder whether bees could be measuring the actual stimulation of their sugar receptors, the thickness of the nectar (more concentrated nectar is thicker), how long it takes to suck up a full load (a more viscous solution will take longer), its weight (a fluid ounce of concentrated nectar can weigh almost twice as much as the same volume of dilute nectar), or its energy content.

It is easy to show that viscosity is important, but not as important as sweetness per se. This is done in two steps: first, we must compare the rate of dancing for a particular concentration of sugar solution with the rate for a solution with same amount of sugar but which has been artificially thickened; this in turn must be compared with the dance rate for a more concentrated sugar solution whose viscosity equals that of the artificially thickened one. Here are the results: when 70 percent of the foragers dance to the original solution, 80 percent will dance to a thickened version of it. Fully 90 percent, however, will dance to a solution that is thickened to the same viscosity by the addition of sugar, rather than neutral artificial thickening agents. Clearly, bees evaluate both sweetness and viscosity, but sweetness is about twice as important in the final valuation.

The same pattern is seen with weight: when a forager has a lead disk glued to her back while feeding, she is more likely to dance on her return to the hive; part of her judgment of the quality of a source, then, depends on the weight of the nectar load. On the other hand, the actual energy content of the food—the essential variable of practical importance—is

not measured at all: a concentrated solution of a tasteless sugar such as sorbitol, which has just as many useful calories as sucrose, holds no more interest than thickened water.

Foragers evaluate other factors beyond those that correlate with the energy value of the nectar—factors that, given their inessential quality, seem like aesthetic preferences. Bees will dance more often for a weakly scented solution than for one with no odor, but too much scent inhibits dancing. They prefer to collect food from feeders that partly enclose them—they prefer funnels to flat discs—and would rather draw the nectar from narrow slits or tubes instead of from large drops or open dishes, even when the openings are so narrow that it takes the forager quite a bit longer to imbibe a full load. These proclivities are obviously directed toward the characteristics of real flowers, and it would be interesting to know if the preferences are innate or arise through experience.

Foragers also take account of factors neither aesthetic nor directly dependent on the calorie content of the food. One element of their basic economic conservatism is particularly obvious here: a recruit will almost never dance after her first visit to an advertised patch; only when repeated trips have demonstrated that the source is reliable is she likely to dance. In a typical case, about 10 percent of the recruits danced within ten minutes of discovering a nearby source (corresponding to roughly two visits); after an hour, the figure had risen to about 40 percent and was approaching 70 percent two hours later. (This prudence disappears during times of extreme dearth; recruits will dance after the first return if the hive has a serious shortage of food.)

Bees prefer an enclosed feeder with small holes to draw the food from. They prefer a funnel to a flat open feeder.

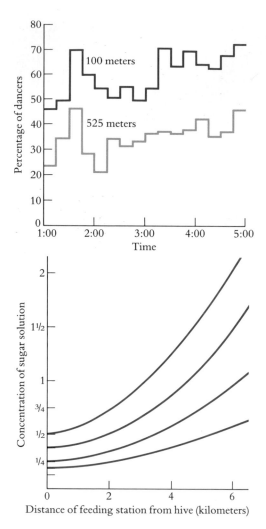

Above, at any given time of day, foragers collecting a particular concentration of sugar solution at a more distant station were less likely to dance than bees foraging the same food nearer the hive. The hour-by-hour variation in dancing reflects the changing competition from natural food sources. Below, on any given day, the concentration of sugar solution necessary to elicit dancing was higher at greater distances; each curve represents measurements made over the course of a single day. The different curves come from days with different amounts of natural forage.

Another such factor is how the food quality changes. If bees were simple robots, we might expect that the probability of dancing for a particular concentration of food at a given time ought to depend simply on its subjective quality. But if we train two groups of bees to two feeders, one with dilute food and the other with more concentrated sugar solution, and then change the poorer food to the same quality being offered at the better station, the foragers experiencing the improvement will dance more often than those accustomed to the good stuff. Bees are optimists, exaggerating positive turns in fortune but accepting a lowering of food quality without abandoning the site.

More subtle (perhaps eerie is a more appropriate term) is the reaction of foragers to changes in the weather. When a storm approaches, bees foraging at long distances stop dancing, whereas those visiting sites nearby continue to recruit. It is as if they understood that encouraging recruits to venture far from the hive when bad weather threatens is foolish, though they themselves, knowing just where the food is and so being able to get out and back quickly, are at no risk. Similarly, bees are reluctant to dance near noon. This "noontime sluggishness" is not a simple matter of not wanting to fly when it is hot, for it is evident even during cool weather. More likely it is an accommodation to the difficulty that inexperienced bees have in adjusting to the rapid movement of the sun near noon, a topic we will take up in a later chapter.

Apart from sweetness, the other obvious factor in deciding whether to dance ought to be the "cost" of obtaining the food—the travel time and the number of minutes needed to take on a full load. Bees certainly dance more often when the foraging time is low, though (surprisingly) this has not been studied in much detail. The effect of travel time, on the other hand, is very well documented. When the same food is offered to foragers at two different distances, the group visiting the nearer place is more likely to dance; when the distances are 100 and 525 meters, for instance, the foragers flying the shorter distance dance on twice as many of their returns to the hive.

A more informative way to look at this factor is to measure the threshold for dancing at different distances—that is, the minimum sweetness necessary to elicit recruitment dances as the training station is moved ever farther from the hive. On a typical day, for instance, the concentration of sugar solution that prompts foragers to dance near the hive will need to be doubled by 3 kilometers, and quadrupled by 6 kilometers. This makes perfect sense: the cost of flying (in both time and energy) is much higher when the food is several kilometers away, and must be compensated for by a corresponding increase in the number of calories brought home.

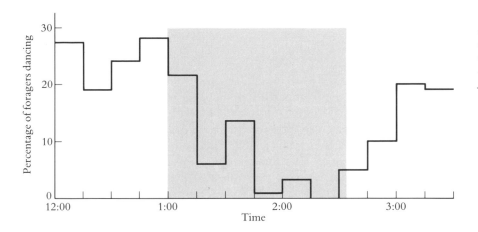

This graph illustrates the effect of competition on the readiness of foragers to dance. This group of bees collected the same food all day, but stopped dancing after another group was given better food. Dancing began again after 2:30, when the better food was withdrawn.

DECISIONS IN THE HIVE

In the measurement of dancing to food at different distances, the exact values vary both over the course of a single day and from one day to another. The reason for this variation is competition: when natural sources are scarce or of poor quality, dancing for the food at an artificial feeder increases; conversely, as the natural competition improves, dancing for a feeding station declines. Since natural nectar supplies vary from hour to hour and day to day, this sort of variability is exactly what we should expect.

To examine the time course of the foragers' reaction to a change in competition, bees were once again trained to two stations. At the start, they were offered the same food at both locations, and so the probability of a forager's dancing was the same for both groups (about 25 percent in one such experiment). At a prearranged time, then, the foragers at one station were switched to food five times as concentrated. Within about 45 minutes, the bees collecting the original food virtually stopped dancing; dances by the other group skyrocketed.

How did the bees that stopped dancing know that their food was no longer very good relative to the competition? It cannot be just that there is better food coming in, because the quantity matters as well as the quality of the competition: when the number of foragers at the high-concentration station was reduced from the original 40 to only ten, the foragers at the low-concentration station started dancing again within about half an hour. Although it is true that foragers will sometimes attend the performances of extremely vigorous dancers, and so can learn in this way about unusually good alternatives, they adjust their dance rate even if the dances of colleagues are not monitored.

In fact, foragers are informed of how good their product is relative to the competition by the dance attenders themselves. Attenders, which include both potential recruits *and* younger bees that specialize in unloading returning foragers and storing their nectar, have attended many dances, and so have a fair sample of the market. Through repeated food exchanges, they can also monitor dances vicariously that they have not even attended. When a forager advertising unusually dilute or concentrated nectar pauses to offer food samples, the attenders know immediately that the source is out of the ordinary. Apparently, they factor distance into their evaluation as well, and recruits show less interest (that is, turn away to other dances sooner and are less likely to leave the hive immediately) in dances advertising more distant locations unless the nectar is much above average.

How do dance attenders inform a dancer of their evaluation of the food? The mechanism is wonderfully simple and direct: bees returning with substandard nectar have more difficulty getting an unloader bee to take the food. After all, during times of plenty, unloaders are in short supply, and can pick and choose. They treat returning foragers like flowers, favoring those that have high-quality nectar over those with dilute food. Bees bringing in first-rate forage will be unloaded eagerly; sometimes they are emptied within 20 or 30 seconds. Those with poor forage may need to hunt for several minutes, unable to foist off more than a bit

The probability of a forager's dancing depends on how long it takes for her to unload her cargo to bees in the hive. When the unloading time is 40 seconds or less, most foragers (dark bars) dance; when more time is required to dispose of the load, dancing is omitted (white bars).

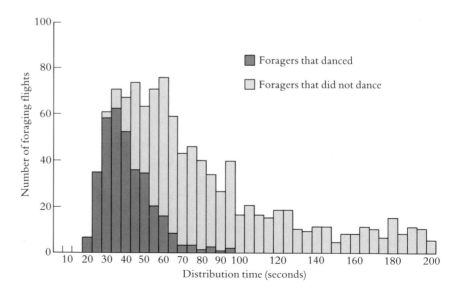

here and there to passing unloader bees. Really poor food will have to be taken by the forager to storage areas and unloaded directly into cells, the ultimate indignity.

The best study of the relationship between unloading and dancing compared water collectors with foragers returning with concentrated nectar. Initially, of course, the nectar gatherers danced on virtually every trip, the water bearers not at all. Water is needed in quantity only when the hive is overheated; when this happens, the water is spread on every available surface and fanned; as a result, the hive is cooled through evaporation, much as a breeze cools damp skin. When the experimenters heated the hive, the nectar collectors began to have more difficulty disposing of their loads, whereas the water carriers began to be mobbed by attenders. When the time for unloading water fell to less than 50 seconds in one experiment, the majority of water foragers danced—in fact, when the water was disposed of in 30 seconds or less, the probability of dancing rose above 95 percent. The ability of bees to cool a hive in this way is remarkable: a colony kept on a lava field where the air temperature was 60°C nevertheless maintained their brood comb at the optimal 36°C.

In sum, then, a forager forms her own judgment about food quality, considering the concentration, viscosity, and weight of the nectar, the distance to and feel of the flower, and the nature of the patch; in the hive she then listens to the "applause" of the unloaders, and factors this in as well. With these two sets of opinions, the bee then chooses whether or not to dance. This use of subjective criteria and audience feedback, then, results in a recruitment system that is extremely sensitive to the needs of the hive and the contingencies of the moment. As a result of this innate sense of free-market economics, a honey bee colony turns a higher and more consistent profit than any other group of social bees.

Foragers collecting water from a leaking faucet.

CHAPTER 6

Evolution of the Dance

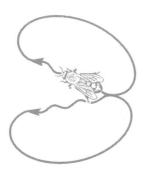

The dance language is unique among invertebrates. Its abstract conventions are capable of transmitting millions of distinct messages, and the resulting flexibility gives honey bees an enormous edge in their competition with other species for flowers. And yet the dances are sloppy, dialects vary from one race to another, and there are multiple cues for distance—all curious anomalies in what looks otherwise to be a well-honed piece of behavior. Furthermore, if the dance is such an advantage, how is it that a similar sort of communication has not evolved in other species of social insects? In fact, how could an abstract language have evolved at all?

A waggle dance by an Apis dorsata *pollen forager.*

VON FRISCH'S SCENARIO

Von Frisch formulated the first comprehensive hypothesis to account for the evolution of the dance language. He believed that the original honey bees evolved in the tropics and resembled today's dwarf bee, *Apis florea,*

A herring gull performing a threat display. The neck is extended and the wings held slightly up and out from the body, ready for action.

in many respects (though probably not size). In particular, he guessed that the first dances were performed in the open on the more or less horizontal top of the comb, and that they pointed directly at the food. In orienting their dances, these early honey bees would have used, as the dwarf bees do still, cues visible in the sky overhead.

Many communicative behaviors began as what are known as intention movements—motions necessary in the early stages of a behavior. Bending the knees, for example, is an intention movement for jumping, and we learn to recognize it as such. Among animals, individuals able to recognize an intention movement as a predictor of coming behavior might have an advantage, and selection will work to make such recognition innate. When a gull begins an attack, it lifts the wrists of the wings slightly in preparation for jabbing; other gulls instinctively recognize this gesture as a threat. Selection has also led to what is called a *ritualization* of this movement, so that it is exaggerated and unambiguous. Individuals whose threats are clearly intimidating are better off, so it is no surprise that all gulls now innately perform the threat according to what is essentially a hard-wired behavioral convention.

The intention movement from which, according to von Frisch, the dance language might have arisen is simply the run that precedes taking off. If the foragers tens of millions of years ago flew off the exposed top of the colony in the direction they were going to travel, then this gesture could, through selection, have been ritualized into a dance. In this hypothesis the waggle would still be a mystery, but the dance sound could readily be explained: since the sound is produced by the wing muscles, it could itself be the result of an intention movement for flight—warming up the flight muscles, a common preparation among insects. Von Frisch believed in addition that the ancient origin of the bees' propensity to orient their dances to celestial cues is indicated by the ability of our modern temperate-zone honey bee to do the same: when we lay a piece of comb out horizontally, the bees readily adapt to the changed situation and use the sun as their reference point.

Common morphology and behavior are the bases on which von Frisch reconstructed the honey bee's evolution. In the simplest case, a feature shared between two forms must have existed before the lines leading to the two groups diverged. Von Frisch's surmise has gained increased validity from two more modern lines of evidence, one behavioral and the other genetic. First, our students have forced the giant honey bee *Apis dorsata,* which normally hangs on huge combs that have no horizontal surfaces, to dance on horizontal comb. The foragers, like their temperate-zone counterparts, orient to celestial cues perfectly, though they have had no opportunity for millions of years to perform horizontal dances. This implies that honey bees started out dancing on horizontal surfaces. The other evidence comes from comparisons of the similar gene products (proteins, usually) of different species: by this measure, *A. florea* is by far the oldest species (perhaps ten million years old), *A. dorsata* is about half as old, whereas *A. mellifera* and *A. cerana* became separate species very recently (10,000 to 100,000 years ago). Again, this implies that *A. florea*'s horizontal dance is the original version.

To account for the distance correlation, von Frisch pointed to the same apparently functionless correlations that Wenner and Wells later used in their challenge to the dance-language hypothesis: although their colleagues seem to have no way of interpreting the information, stingless bees stimulate recruits by means of disoriented buzzing runs, the duration of which correlates well with distance. In fact, von Frisch had supposed that, at the onset, the distance information in the dance was a meaningless artifact—a behavior tied to effort expended en route—and that selection had operated on honey bees to develop circuitry capable of decoding this data.

In time, the dance would have evolved to what several experts refer to as a miniature reconstruction of the outward journey. Since for some

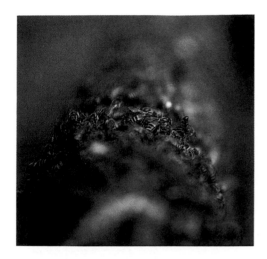

An Apis florea *worker dancing on top of the comb.*

reason bees do not fly in beelines but instead steer a few degrees to the left, then slightly to the right, and so on, the waggles might correspond to the zig-zag nature of the forager's flight path. Recruits, by following the dancer, might be "rehearsing" the outward flight they are to take.

The next step von Frisch pictured in the gradual evolution of the honey bee dance was the conversion of horizontal sky-oriented dances to vertical gravity-based performances. This is necessary for the giant honey bee *(Apis dorsata)* because it suspends its massive comb from thick limbs or overhanging rocks, and so there is no horizontal surface available. It is also essential for the cavity-living species of India *(A. cerana)* and the temperate zone species (our *A. mellifera*), since these species not only attach their comb to the top of the cavity (thereby eliminating any horizontal platform on top of the comb), but they must dance in the dark out of sight of celestial cues. Here von Frisch again invoked an orientational artifact we have already touched on: some insects convert an angle walked on a horizontal surface in relation to the sun into an angle taken up on a vertical surface in the dark. Several species do this, though most confuse left and right, and some even get up and down wrong. Through ritualization, the argument goes, selection cleaned up this behavior so that communication of direction became unambiguous.

EVOLUTION FROM A MAP?

The problem with evolutionary hypotheses is that they are often hard or even impossible to test. The events in question happened millions of years ago, and behavior leaves no fossils; we are in the position of detectives attempting to solve a crime that has no tangible clues. Often the best we can do is to explore the predictions that a scenario makes, to see if the hypothesis suggests unlikely behavior when we arrange the appropriate conditions. One reason Einstein's theory of relativity gained rapid acceptance was its implausible prediction that light should be bent by gravity. When an eclipse provided the opportunity to put this curious consequence of the theory to the test, and astronomers observed that the apparent positions of stars near the edge of the sun's disc were displaced by the right amount, the hypothesis began to gain a wide following.

How, then, does the von Frisch hypothesis fare when we look at its predictions? First of all, the idea that the dance sound is an intention movement appears to be wrong: our students have recently shown that there is no sound in the dances of the two most primitive species (the dwarf and giant honey bees). As we will see in the next section, the sound is a later addition that evolved to solve a specific problem. Of

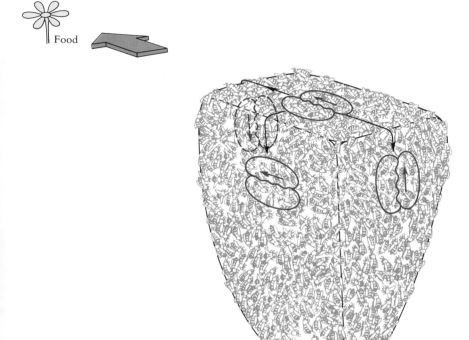

Food

Although dwarf bees normally dance on the top of their comb, they can be forced to perform on a vertical surface; in such cases, the dances are not oriented to gravity but instead point (to the extent possible) directly at the food.

course, this discovery makes the idea of the dance's beginning as an intention movement slightly shaky, though it is still possible.

Another problem is that the conversion of effort into waggles (the original distance artifact that von Frisch thought available for ritualization) does not always happen. For example, von Frisch once trained Italian honey bees (for whom a waggle corresponds to about 25 meters) up a radio tower to a height of about 50 meters. Surely the effort required to fly up is at least as great as that necessary to fly the same distance on the horizontal, and yet the foragers performed round dances. In fact, the conclusion that effort has to be measured on the way out has recently been disproven by another of our students, as we will see presently.

The idea that the orientation of the dance on a vertical surface grew almost automatically from the light-to-gravity artifact of insects is questionable too. When our students forced dwarf honey bees to give up dancing on their usual horizontal comb top and orient instead on a vertical surface, the resulting dances did not take gravity into account at all. In fact, they continued to point directly at the food as best they could.

The notion that the dance is a miniature reconstruction of the outward flight also has problems. The forager need not actually have flown out to a food source to dance for it, and the dances of the bees in the detour experiment described in an earlier chapter also contradict this picture: although the foragers had to fly about 90° right of their goal for nearly half the journey, and then 90° left of the hive-to-food direction for most of the second half of the trip, the dances in the hive indicated the true map direction rather than the two segments actually travelled.

One theme of these anomalies—these failures of the original von Frisch hypothesis to predict dance behavior—is that the bees behave as though they have a map of the foraging area and reference their dances to it. Until very recently, this was a heretical thought: only vertebrates were supposed to have the mental wherewithal for this task. In fact, prior to 1948 only *humans* were imagined to make maps. Until then, the picture of how animals got around their home areas was based on old psychological theories according to which every behavioral response was a direct consequence of a specific stimulus. According to this stimulus-response (S-R) hypothesis, rats learned mazes as a series of responses (left and right turns, for example) triggered by choice points in the maze (each a conditioned stimulus for the appropriate learned reaction). Similarly, in an animal's home range the natural landmarks (particular trees and bushes, for instance) triggered learned responses, enabling the creature to navigate along a familiar route.

This route-specific navigation hypothesis accurately describes the subjective human experience of learning to negotiate an unfamiliar area; we remember key landmarks and use them as mental map pins. But we also know that as we become increasingly familiar with a region, we can imagine the spatial relations between different locations—we can draw a plan of our house or apartment as seen from above with the ceilings removed, though we have never seen the rooms from that perspective. We can close our eyes and call to mind what things must look like in a particular place—100 meters north of where we are now, for example. Most important, humans can plan a novel route using familiar landmarks in an order different from any we have ever encountered before; we are not locked into recapitulating familiar routes, using well-worn S-R series.

There is compelling evidence that even rats form true maps of their mazes. If the walls of a familiar maze are removed and the rat released at the normal starting position, the rat runs directly to where the goal box (containing the food that served as a bribe to induce the rodent to run the maze in the first place) *ought* to have been; the animal did not need to

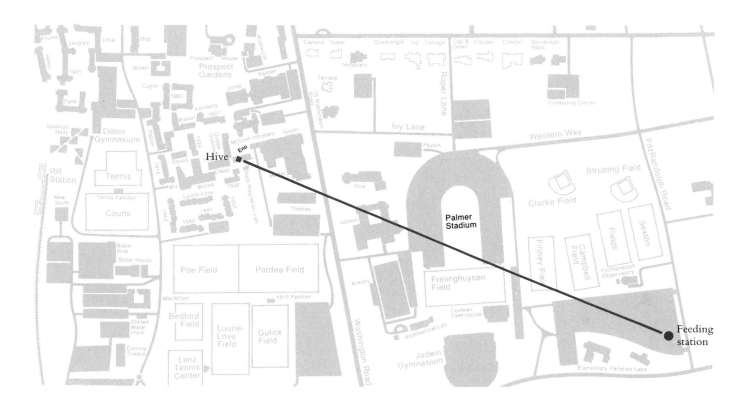

retrace its steps, making the same series of turns along the roundabout route the maze walls had imposed on it. In short, the rat knew the true map direction and distance of the food.

If bees were also found to have maps, we would need to look at the dance and its anomalies in a new light. This possibility was suggested when a student at Princeton discovered a training technique that should not have worked. He wanted to get foragers from a hive on the roof of a building down to the ground and then to a parking lot several hundred meters away, but a major road, a large stadium, several fences, and a busy pedestrian plaza (always a hazard to bee research) intervened. Frustrated, he hit upon the simple expedient of capturing bees as they flew out of the hive and carrying them in the dark to the goal. There he allowed them to feed and depart. Some flew directly back to the hive, which was out of sight; because the hive was starving, some of these foragers even danced immediately upon their return, indicating the true distance and direction of a station they had never flown to. Apparently, experienced bees left the station, looked around, recognized familiar landmarks, placed them-

Foragers were trapped as they left the hive and carried to a feeding station in a parking lot out of sight of the hive. After feeding, older foragers were able to return directly to the colony and dance, indicating the location they had been displaced to.

To see if bees have landmark maps, foragers were trained to a feeder at site A, then captured later as they left the hive and carried in the dark to site B, where they were released. Even though site A was hidden from view by trees, the displaced foragers were able to fly off directly toward it when they were released.

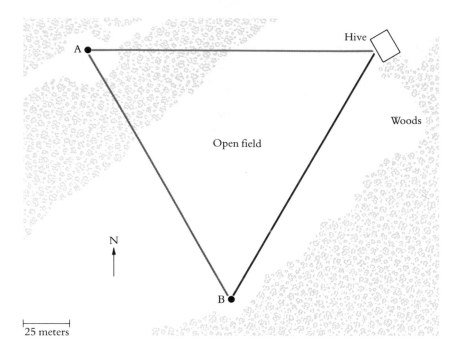

selves in relation to the hive, and set course for home. Young inexperienced bees transported in this unorthodox way circled helplessly and returned to the feeder, waiting to be carried home. Familiarity with the general area was evidently important in finding the way back home.

Suggestive as this observation was, it was not conclusive. The parking lot might have been along a familiar route to some patch of food farther away, and so recognized by the transported foragers as a route-specific stimulus. Having placed themselves on a known route, they could then have begun using the remaining S-R steps to fly home. A definitive experiment would have to be one in which the goal was not the hive, and in which bees flew a novel route to that goal.

The experiment began with training a group of individually marked foragers to a feeder in a small clearing in some woods, out of sight of the hive. The foragers were visible departing directly toward the clearing when they left the hive, and directly back toward the (unseen) hive when they had taken on a load of sugar solution at the feeder. Foragers leaving the hive for the clearing station were captured in ones or twos and transported inside an opaque container to another location well off their route. Without being fed, the foragers were released individually and tracked for as long as possible; they usually spiralled upwards to an altitude of about 5 meters and then flew off, disappearing from view a second or two later.

If the transported forager really depends on route-specific cues, the best she can do is to recognize the release point as a location along some other familiar route, and use the familiar landmarks there to set course for home; once near the hive, she could pick up the S-R trail to the clearing. If, on the other hand, the forager has a true map, she should do what we would under the same circumstances: she should use nearby landmarks to figure out where she is, determine in which direction her goal lies, and then depart directly toward it. Because of a ridge and line of trees, there was no possibility of the bees' seeing the clearing directly. In fact, foragers transported in this way flew off directly toward the clearing along what must have been a novel path.

That honey bees have a map *now* does not necessarily mean that they had one before the dance evolved; the map could have come later, as an economical way to deal with complex information. But less definitive experiments with other insects (some dating back to the 1800s) suggest that many Hymenoptera with homes to return to form true, landmark-based maps of their home range. If so, maps almost certainly predate dancing. And if bees had maps first, it is no wonder the dances indicate true map locations even when a forager or scout flies an indirect route. In this case, selection may have begun not with an intention movement but rather with a sort of map reading, resulting in a dance as a kind of "pointing," analogous to the impromptu dances dwarf bees perform when forced off the tops of their combs. Surely it was no big step for humans to begin indicating the location of herds of antelope by pointing; even converting this to a vertical surface (as in drawing a map on a cave wall) seems trivial for a creature with a true map, assuming sender and receiver can agree on how the map is being oriented (north as up for most humans, the sun's direction for bees). In fact, it is imagining the additional refinement of distance information that is more challenging. Perhaps this part really did evolve out of an orientational artifact like that seen in the stingless bees. On the other hand, it may be that we are still missing something—perhaps something already hinted at in previous experiments and buried in the data, waiting for some keen-eyed investigator to sort it out.

WHY IS THERE SOUND IN THE DANCE?

If the dance did not evolve as an intention movement, then the dance sound is unlikely to have arisen as an artifact of a flight gesture. Why then is it in the dance at all? Humans have little difficulty "reading" the

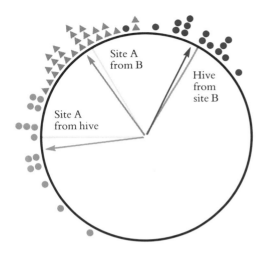

Departure bearings of the foragers displaced to site B are shown as triangles. Red dots represent the departure bearings of bees who had been captured as they arrived at the hive and released at site B; this is the distribution of directions expected if the displaced foragers had to return to the hive in order to find site A. Blue dots indicate the departure bearings of trained foragers leaving for site A from the hive; this is the distribution expected if the trained bees transported to site B had not realized that they had been moved and so set off in the usual direction adopted at the hive.

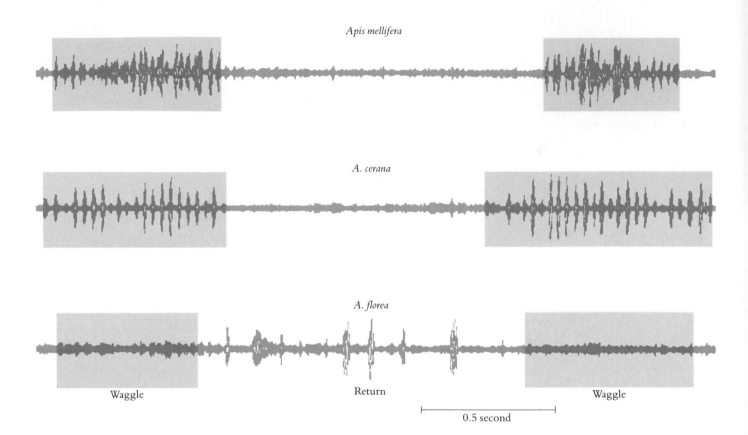

Apis mellifera

A. cerana

A. florea

Waggle   Return   Waggle

|———————————————|
0.5 second

The two cavity-nesting species of honey bee pro-
duce sound bursts during the waggle run, whereas
the open nesters do not. The dwarf bee does, how-
ever, sometimes emit a burst or two during her
semicircular return.

dance without it: von Frisch decoded the dance more than a decade before its auditory accompaniment was discovered, and concluded that
sound served simply for "emphasis."

As was hinted earlier, we have good reason to think that the dance
sound is a later evolutionary arrival. When we record the dances of the
two open-nesting tropical species, the giant and dwarf honey bees *(Apis
dorsata* and *A. florea)*, they turn out to be silent; no acoustic emphasis
seems necessary for them. It is not that these bees cannot produce sound,
though: both species use the stop signal (a quarter-second-long "weep"
that is produced exactly like the dance sound, though without its bursts).
The Indian bee *(A. cerana),* on the other hand, *does* have sound in its
dance. In short, the cavity nesters, dancing in the dark, have sound in
their dance, while the open nesters do not.

A close look at the dancer's posture reveals other species differences as
well. Whereas the Indian bees and our temperate-zone species dance with
their abdomens tucked under and wings only slightly spread, the open

A. mellifera

A. florea

The dance posture of the open nesters involves widely spread wings and a raised thorax; in addition to the usual side-to-side motion, the abdomen is also vibrated up and down during the waggle.

nesters look quite different: both dwarf and giant honey bee dancers spread their wings far apart and raise their abdomens high. Moreover, they waggle them up and down as well as side to side. Finally, the behavior of the attenders differs as well: among the cavity nesters, potential recruits hurry after the dancer, usually keeping their antennae on her body; among the open nesters, attenders tend to hang back and keep their antennae to themselves. Giant honey bee recruits, in fact, simply form a circle and let the dancer perform in front of them.

These differences all add up to one conclusion: open nesters depend more on vision, and attenders observe the raised abdomen of the dancer as she performs; in cavities, visual information is gone, and sound has evolved to replace it. This helps explain an observation that arose out of countless tens of thousands of dance recordings: occasionally, a dancer will omit the waggle sound, performing an otherwise normal dance; over the course of 6000 silent dances observed in hives of *A. mellifera,* not one bee was ever successfully recruited.

If the sound has replaced vision in the transmission of dance information, which correlates has it substituted for? Up to now, we have emphasized the distance correlation in the sound—the number of sound bursts and the duration of bursting each relate to the distance to the food. But in the dances of the open-nesting species, vision seems to be the modality used for communicating direction as well; how else can the recruits of the giant honey bee determine the direction of the dance, since they do not actually traipse along behind? Could it be that the dance sound communicates direction in *A. mellifera* as well?

It is difficult to put ourselves in the place of a dance attender, clinging to a sheet of vertical comb in the darkness of the hive, continually being bumped by unseen sisters. When, in our imaginations, we stumble upon a dance, we must try and follow its course without being able to see anything. Using our hands like antennae to grope our way along behind, we would feel the swinging body strike first one hand and then another as the dancing bee waggles, and then the movement would cease suddenly as the dancer began her semicircular return. Since there is room directly behind the dancer for only one attender, it follows that most recruits attend from the side, and so must blindly infer the dancer's orientation.

The dance sound can certainly help with this task. The antennae are receptors not only for touch, smell, and taste, but for sound as well. As ears, however, they are nothing like ours. Humans hear by monitoring the movement of a membrane (the ear drum) that encloses a sealed chamber; when the air pressure changes, as it does briefly but rhythmically when a sound passes, the ear drum is set into motion, being bent inward when the air pressure peaks, and bending outward as pressure minima pass by. Such a device is insensitive to direction, though: high pressure is high pressure, regardless of the direction from which the sound arrives. To localize many sounds we must time the arrival of a peak at the two different ears, and so determine which side received the sound first.

The antennae of bees have no pressure detectors; instead, an antenna detects the motion of air particles as they are stirred by the motion of the vibrating wings and thorax of a dancer. The antennae are like tuning forks, resonating most readily over a small range of frequencies; this range is centered on the dance tone. But as detectors of air motion, antennae are highly directional: a sound coming from the side moves an antenna maximally, but sound arriving from the direction in which the antenna is pointing does not move it at all. As a result, determining the direction from which a nearby sound is coming should be easy for an attender, and she should be able to track the dancer even in the dark.

The antennae actually have two resonances: the end portion (the flagellum) resonates to the dance sound, but the antenna as a whole vibrates

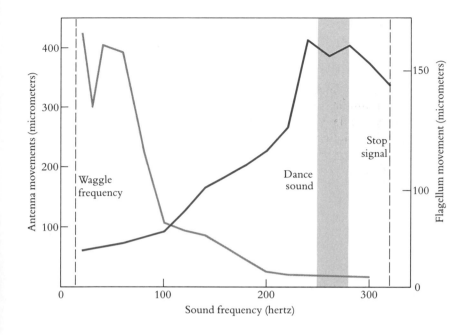

The two parts of the antenna resonate at different frequencies: the antenna as a whole (orange curve) vibrates best to sounds of 20 hertz and below, whereas the flagellum (the flexible part of the antenna, red curve) resonates at 240 to 300 hertz.

best near the waggle frequency. One of our students has trained bees to understand that, while feeding at a training station, one sound means the food will be electrified in three seconds but the other means it is safe. Bees can learn to react to either sound, taking off briefly to avoid the shock, and ignore the other. It is possible, therefore, that attenders hear and use both sounds.

The best way to investigate this question further, and completely dissect the dance in the process, would be to devise a model bee capable of producing realistic dances, sounds and all. There have been several attempts, and it is sound production that has proven to be the major stumbling block. Since the dance attenders probably need to localize the sound, it must come from the tiny model itself. One attempt was made using a hearing aid speaker, but it heated up so quickly that attenders were repelled.

WHY ARE DANCES INACCURATE?

If dances evolved to help bees recruit others, why are they so inaccurate? The scatter in the direction indication is especially striking: when the food is a hundred yards away, the divergence between one waggle run

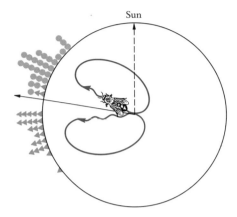

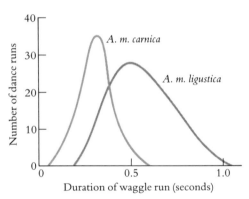

Above, different waggle runs indicate different directions to the same goal; only by averaging over many cycles can this "noise" be cancelled out. Below, different waggle runs also indicate different distances to the same goal. The dances to the same distance by two foragers of different races are compared here.

and the next is about 30°; the value is higher still when the food is closer. When we compare the dance scatter at different distances, a clear pattern emerges: as the distance increases, the scatter declines.

If, as some researchers have suggested, the bees are merely disoriented when they first begin dancing and need a few cycles to really get going properly, we would expect the first few cycles of every dance to be sloppy. But in fact, even the first few waggles of a long-distance dance are well oriented. Another possibility is that when food is close by, foragers obtain too little information en route to orient their dances. Were this the case, however, we would expect the foragers themselves to have difficulty locating the food on subsequent trips. In fact, no hypothesis based on sensory or other limitations can work: when our students measured the divergence in the dances of the other three species they found that although the scatter does decrease with distance, it is far smaller to begin with. The dances of *Apis mellifera* would probably be just as accurate as the tropical dances if there were not some advantage for them in being sloppy.

One possible reason for their lack of precision is that the bees' natural food sources are usually patches, rather than individual points. There may be no virtue in dispatching recruits to the same exact flowers a dancer has just harvested, but every reason to scatter them, within limits, about the part of the patch of a particular sort of flower the forager has just visited. In this way recruits arriving in another part of the same patch will find food, return, and dance; their recruits, in turn, will explore the area around this find, and so on until the full limits of the patch are discovered and the resource fully exploited.

If the error in the dance is actually designed to spread out the recruits, then we can make several unlikely predictions for testing. First, the size of a typical patch (the contingency of nature that the scatter would be designed to exploit) should be the same regardless of how far it happens to be from the hive. Thus we would expect the divergence in the direction indication to decline with distance (which it does) *just* fast enough to compensate for the decreasing angular size of the patch—that is, the degree of directional scatter necessary to spread recruits over a fixed area declines as the distance to that area increases, just as any object appears smaller when farther away. That the decline in angular scatter should just match the decrease in apparent size (a declining exponential proportional to the inverse of the distance) would be unlikely to occur by chance.

On the other hand, if the error is optimal, the divergence in the distance indication should *not* decline with distance. Finally, since there is no reason to suppose that patches should be systematically wider than they are long (or vice versa), the distance and direction errors should be the

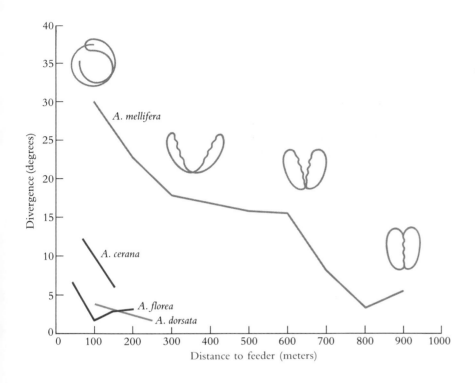

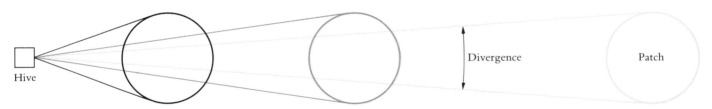

same size. Even if the optimal-error hypothesis is correct, we still need to account for why the error is smaller among the tropical species.

There are two ways to test these predictions: we can analyze the dances themselves, or we can look at where recruits go. Measuring and comparing the dances at different distances is certainly the easiest, and when we do this all three predictions are upheld out to at least a thousand meters; beyond this distance, the angular divergence reaches a minimum angle, and decreases no further with distance. Here we probably *do* run up against a sensory limitation of bees—the maximum accuracy of their gravity-measuring system, for instance.

An early test of recruit accuracy at two distances indicated that both the distance and direction error were the same size and did not change with increasing distance.

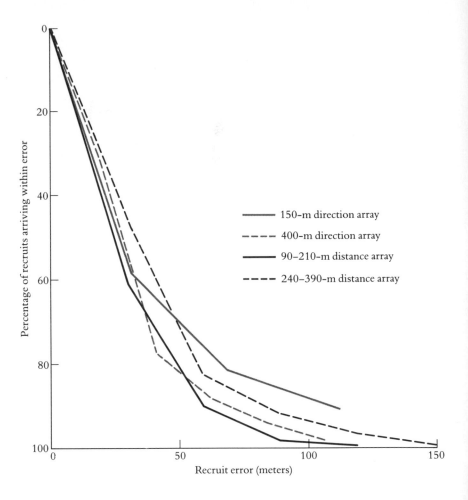

But showing that the dances predict a constant and equal scatter in distance and direction, regardless of how far away the food is, does not mean that recruits are arriving in the field in that pattern. For example, recruits might average together many cycles and so factor out the variation altogether; in fact, recruits do attend about six cycles, and von Frisch found that they arrive in the field more accurately than could be expected if they knew only what one cycle could have told them.

We made a preliminary effort toward measuring recruit scatter many years ago, using the automatic forager-capturing stations described in an earlier chapter. With only six stations and a relatively small field to work in, the data can only be considered suggestive, but the pattern is just

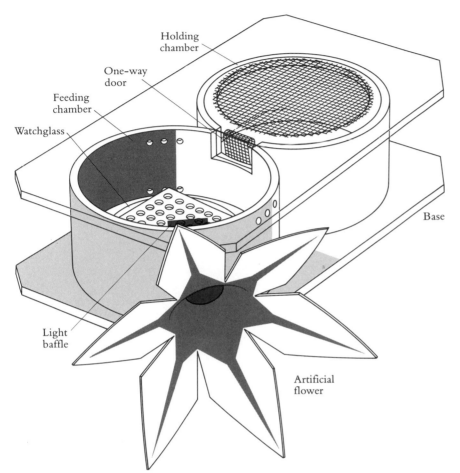

Second-generation automatic recruit-capturing station; arriving bees enter, passing through a light baffle (a flap of red cellophane—bees are blind to red). They feed, and then depart through a brightly illuminated one-way door (a flap of metal screen) into a holding chamber, where they are trapped.

what the tuned-error hypothesis predicts: distance and direction scatter are equal to each other, and do not change with a doubling of distance.

One of our students took up the challenge of measuring the scatter in detail and over a wider range of distances. He devised a new kind of recruit catcher, one that could be mass produced. As a result, he was able to field 25 stations at once and so make fine-grained measurements. He could even measure distance and direction scatter simultaneously. His results strongly support the idea of optimal scatter: distance and direction scatter are nearly the same at any given distance, and there is very little change in the size of this recruit scatter as the distance to the forager station increases.

More precise measurements with far larger arrays confirm that the distance (red curve) and direction (blue curve) scatter are about equal and change little with increasing distance.

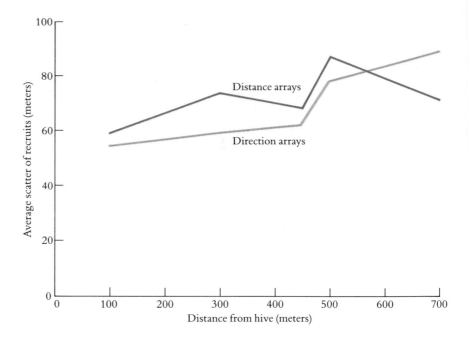

We wondered what the bees do when the goal really *is* a point source. Perhaps they do not comprehend that scatter is counterproductive in such a case, and so do nothing; or perhaps instead they reduce the divergence to compensate for the nature of the target.

As usual, the bees do something else. We compared the dances of scouts returning to the swarm to advertise a cavity (a target that is *always* a point source) with the dances to food at the same distance; there was no difference in scatter. Nevertheless, recruits seem to arrive more accurately after swarm dances. There are two possible ways they could be managing this. One is that attenders might average more dances when the target is small; the other is that the dancer might leave scent in the field, which they do for cavities and for feeding stations with abundant high-quality food.

Though the optimal-error hypothesis predicts remarkably well what recruits will do, it does not explain why the divergence in tropical species is much lower. Surprisingly, this turns out to be the easiest piece of the puzzle: in the temperate zone, forage exists mainly as extended patches of flowering annual and perennial herbs, whereas the major food source in the tropics is blossoms in trees. Hundreds of flowers open simultaneously on most tropical bee-pollinated trees, but a tree is likely to be some distance from another of the same species—that is, the trees do not grow in pure stands of the sort we have in the temperate zone. (If they did, they could rely on wind pollination, as most temperate-zone trees do. The few bee-pollinated species of the temperate forest—dogwoods, for example, and tulip poplars—*do* tend to be widely scattered.) As a result, a "patch" for a tropical bee is often a single tree, and so the optimal scatter should be much smaller, as it is.

WHY ARE THERE DIALECTS?

The four species of honey bee, and even the many races of *Apis mellifera,* all have different dialects. Have these dialects, like the dance sound and scatter, evolved as specific adaptations to the differing geographical challenges bees face, or have they arisen by chance, as we believe many human languages have diverged from a common Indo-European tongue simply because subgroups became isolated?

If dance dialects represent evolutionary optimizations that differ from one region to another, then it seems likely (as von Frisch himself pointed out decades ago) that races with short-distance dialects—dances in which each waggle corresponds to only a few meters—are adapted to foraging over a short range. Races with long-distance dialects, on the other hand, must have evolved in areas requiring larger foraging ranges, and so must often signal great distances without wasting too much time passing the message. Indeed, the north European race, *Apis mellifera carnica,* spends only one-fifth of the time required by the tropical dwarf honey bee to signal 200 meters, and only one-third of the time spent by the Egyptian race, *A. m. lamarckii.* Looking at it the other way, a Carniolan forager can indicate a food source at the limit of its range (about 12 kilometers) with a spectacular waggle run of 25 seconds, whereas *Apis florea* would need more than two minutes to pass the same information.

The obvious way to test this optimal-dialect hypothesis would be to measure the foraging ranges of the different races and species. Unfortunately, our own species has so altered the habitats in question, particularly in Europe and India, that we could not trust the results to reflect accurately the situation hundreds of thousands or millions of years ago, when the dialects evolved. A less direct way exists, however, the key to which lies in one of the hundreds of obscure experiments performed decades ago. When von Frisch's best-known student, Martin Lindauer, was studying swarming, he once offered a swarm a choice between a nest box about 30 meters distant and another some 250 meters away; to his surprise, the cluster moved to the farther cavity.

Though the logic behind this choice was not obvious then (which is probably why Lindauer did not follow up on this observation), we now

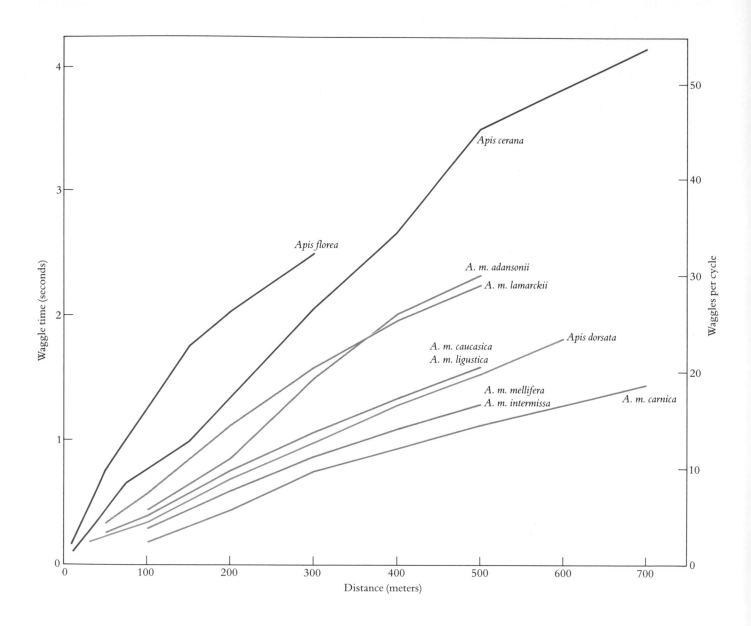

Distance dialects for all three tropical species of honey bee and several races of the temperate-zone species.

understand enough about evolution and competition to see why going farther makes sense. The swarm, as we know, consists of the old queen and her daughters; the old hive contains still more daughters, and so is very closely related. Natural selection will favor swarms that move far enough to minimize the competition between the two sister colonies; as

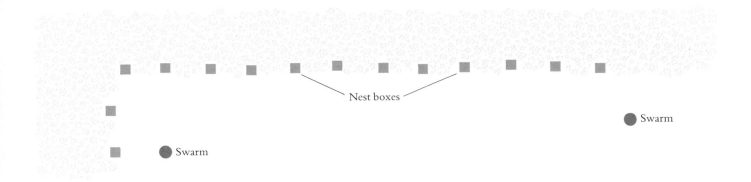

Nest boxes

Swarm

Swarm

relatives, they should not fight for the same resources. Hence, Lindauer's swarm should have flown 250 meters, or perhaps farther if a more distant box had been available.

Though swarms should disperse out of the center of the old hive's foraging range, they should not go *too* far. There are risks in moving thousands of yards: it will take longer for the scouts to survey the landscape for suitable accommodations; more honey will be used up waiting for the decision and then flying there; the chance that the queen, a weak flier at best, will get lost or worn out increases; and the farther a swarm moves, the greater the chance that it will find itself in a habitat significantly poorer than the one that supported the parent colony well enough that it was able to produce a swarm.

So, given that going too far and not going far enough have significant costs, there must be an optimal range of distances; that range should depend on the size of the foraging area the race is adapted to exploit. Of course, distance to the cavity is just one of the many factors bees must evaluate, and there will be times when a nest site very close or very far away is so much better than anything at the right distance that the calculus of swarming will dictate moving there. But if the choices are otherwise equivalent, swarms from short-dialect races should not move as far as swarms of races with longer dialects.

This prediction is fairly easy to test. We must choose an area with few natural cavities (the pine forests of Cape Cod, for example), create an artificial swarm, and set out an array of nest boxes. Placing the queen in a cage tied to a tree limb or (in our case) an artificial tree persuades the hive to swarm. When the bees are shaken out on the ground just below the queen and their hive box removed, they quickly form a cluster around the queen, and scouts take up the search. All the nest boxes must

To test for any preferred swarming distance, swarms of two different races were offered an array of identical nest boxes at different distances; this array was located on Cape Cod.

be identical—all at the same height, of the same size, facing the same direction, and so on. In an experiment carried out by the authors, hive boxes were simply nailed to trees at a forest edge, giving the swarm a choice of distances out to 1100 meters. In fact, a swarm was set up at each end of the array, one of long-dialect Carniolan bees, the other of medium-dialect Italian bees. We let them investigate the alternatives, released the queens, and watched them move in.

The results of this experiment were just what we might have expected: the long-dialect swarms chose boxes much farther away than the medium-dialect bees. Italian bees moved about 160 meters on average, whereas Carniolan bees opted for hive boxes around 700 meters away. (Since no pure strains of short-dialect bees live in North America, we could not test them; when the African bees, *A. m. adansonii,* arrive after their inexorable spread from Brazil, we should be able to repeat this experiment with one of the shortest-dialect races known.)

In the course of our observations, another fact emerged that throws some light on the evolution of dialects. We found that some Carniolan swarms showed great interest in the boxes at about 600 to 750 meters, but refused to move in. Quite by accident, we discovered that if we used larger hive boxes, there was no problem. We then altered the protocol and provided both large and small hive boxes at each distance; the swarms could occupy either one. Carniolans chose the larger boxes all seven times they were given the chance, while Italian clusters selected the smaller hives six out of seven times. Obviously there is a racial difference in optimal cavity size.

In thinking about the logic behind this difference of opinion, it occurred to us that a larger cavity would be needed if the race typically maintained a larger forager force; the African races, for instance, are famous for keeping relatively small populations and occupying very small cavities. It seems equally obvious that, if a colony is small, its

Italian honey bees (A.m. ligustica), *which have a medium-range dialect, prefer to move to a cavity 150 to 200 meters from the home hive, whereas Carniolan honey bees* (A.m. carnica), *which have a long-distance dialect, choose cavities about 700 meters distant.*

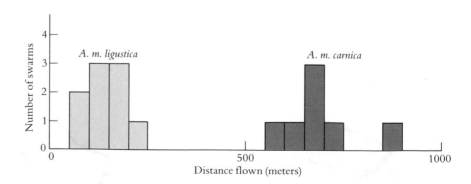

foraging range will be small; if the race forms more populous colonies, they will need to forage over a larger area. Dialects, then, may relate as much to optimum colony size as to foraging range, and certainly the Central African races have very short dialects. However, whether foraging range or colony size ought to be cause or effect remains a mystery.

But why should selection operate on colony size? What environmental factors would favor large size? As we look over the dialects, one pattern is evident: short-distance dialects predominate in hot climates, long-distance dialects in cold ones. Could it be that the ultimate driving force is temperature? This is a very plausible notion. The main threat to a colony in the temperate zones is winter; a hive must accumulate enough honey stores to survive the cold weather. The colder the climate, the more honey will be needed; not only are temperatures lower, but winters are longer. To collect more nectar, more foragers are needed, a larger cavity is necessary to accomodate them and their stores, and a longer dialect to suit the extended foraging range. In the end, then, dialects are probably a consequence of the selective pressure of climate.

Evolutionary hypotheses are often beyond testing, yet the testable ones are the only ones that satisfy. Without well-conceived, critical experimentation, many evolutionary theories are little more than sophisticated "Just-So" stories. Honey bees provide one of the best possible systems for this sort of experimentation. There are four species and more than a dozen geographical races to compare. Furthermore, seven decades of intensive behavioral work have generated an extensive body of knowledge about the honey bee's anatomy, physiology, behavior, natural history, and social system (not much is known yet about its psychology), from which evolutionary hypotheses can be formulated. Finally, so many different techniques for experimentation with bees have been developed that it is usually possible with a little thought to design a practicable experiment to test almost any idea.

CHAPTER 7

Navigation

The average forager flies more than 900 kilometers in the course of gathering pollen and nectar. Precise navigation is essential. Not only is a bee very small, so that the distance travelled in her terms is vast (roughly equivalent to 100,000 human kilometers—more than twice the distance around the earth), but her visual resolution is so coarse that only very large or close landmarks are of any use. For a honey bee, the sun's disk is invisible, and the trunk of the home tree is an indistinct blur until she is only a few meters away.

The limitations of the invertebrate visual system have been overcome by means of navigational strategies that can bring a returning forager in a featureless environment to within two meters of home from a food source a thousand meters away. Our present understanding of how honey bee navigation works with such accuracy rests largely in the willingness of foragers to dance on their return; their dances inform us of how they have used various cues for orientation—cues available during their journey to and from the food, as well as those visible while they dance.

Honey bee landing at hive entrance.

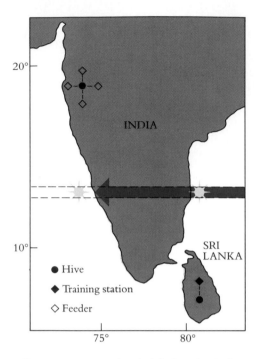

Foragers were trained to find food north of a hive in Sri Lanka; seen from this locale at this time of year, the sun moved from right to left across the northern sky. Later the hive was moved to a site in India at which the sun moved from left to right across the southern sky. Feeders were set out in several directions and the flight directions of foragers monitored. These bees searched for the food in the south, but became lost as the day progressed.

THE SUN COMPASS

The sun is the primary compass honey bees use. We know this from two kinds of experiments. In one, foragers are trained to a food source in a landmark-poor environment and then moved to a different location. The moving can be done in three ways: First, the hive can be moved overnight after all the active foragers have returned to the colony; when the hive is reopened the next morning, the bees fly out unaware of the shift. As long as the landmarks near the hive are not too different, and the shift has been at least several kilometers (so that the new location is out of the familiar foraging range of the bees), the foragers will recommence their flights as though nothing had changed. Before the hive is opened, however, we can set out stations in all directions, and then monitor where the foragers search. Using this general technique, von Frisch showed that trained foragers flew in the same direction from the new site to feeding stations as they had from the old.

The second strategy requires transporting the foragers while they are actually feeding at a training station. We then monitor which direction the bees depart in. Using this approach, one of von Frisch's students demonstrated that foragers leaving the food fly off in the direction they came from, rather than in the new direction of the hive. (The foragers soon discover their error and do find their way home.)

The third technique also requires moving the hive overnight, but for great distances—across a continent or an ocean, or to the other side of the equator. Again, stations are set out in all directions and the hive reopened, but now the sun is in a very different part of the sky: If the move is across the equator (or rather, across the latitude that the sun is shining directly down on, which is the equator on the equinoxes, but is farther north in the Northern Hemisphere summer and south in our winter), the sun's path across the sky is greatly altered. For instance, if the hive is moved from north of the sun line to south of it, the sun will go from appearing to move from left to right (east to west) in the southern part of the sky to moving right to left in the north. On the other hand, if the hive is moved a great distance in longitude only—from Europe to North America, for instance—the sun will still be in the southern sky, but the time difference will be such that the sun will be much farther east of its location the day before. When von Frisch's students undertook these heroic displacements, they were able to show that the foragers fly out and search at the same angle to the sun they had the day before, even though the sun's direction in the new place is quite different.

Yet another way to demonstrate that the sun is the bees' primary compass is to observe dances. Very soon after he discovered the dance language, von Frisch tried holding a comb with dancing foragers horizontally in the open; the dances pointed directly at the food. If the entire sky was blocked, the dances were disoriented. When he blocked a direct view of the sun but provided a mirror reflection, the dances were reoriented to the mirror image. Finally, when the horizontal comb was moved into a darkened room and a light provided (even just a flashlight), the dances were oriented to the artificial sun. All these experiments, then, indicate that the bees use the sun as their primary compass. But this discovery raises new problems: how do bees see the sun, an image too small for their eyes to resolve, and how do they account for its motion through the sky?

Even though honey bees cannot see the sun as a distinct object, they can determine its location on clear days. This hardly seems difficult; after all, the sun is where the sky is brightest. But this simple formula is subject to error when the sky is partly cloudy and the sun is behind a cloud; at such times, the light reflected from other clouds may be brighter. Even when the sun is not behind a cloud, if a bee is flying near trees the sun may be hidden from view. Because *Apis* evolved in tropical forests, this must always have been a common contingency. In any case, the bees ignore reflections from bright clouds. How do they avoid these pitfalls? Do they learn through experience how to recognize the sun, or do they innately use some cue other than relative brightness?

Von Frisch had once argued that bees might be able to see the sun through at least a thin overcast by relying on the ultraviolet light (UV) that penetrates cloud cover. (The ability of UV to get through clouds is the basis of the oft-heard warning not to sunbathe too long under overcast; smog and ordinary glass, on the other hand, are very effective UV filters.) But von Frisch hedged his bets, pointing out that UV light is scattered so much in its journey through the atmosphere (and particularly in clouds) that it should be spread out and thus hard to localize. It is because blue and UV are so easily scattered that the sky is blue: as the white light from the sun passes through the atmosphere overhead, it is the blue and UV that is scattered down to our eyes. The preferential scattering also explains why the sun is orange near dawn and sunset: the blue and UV are scattered to the side during the passage of the light obliquely through so much air, leaving mainly red and orange light.

Though it is true that, in theory, UV would be a poor clue to the sun's location, a student (Michael Brines) decided to help us actually map the brightness of the sky in the UV on clear, hazy, partly cloudy, and overcast days. Our data demonstrate that UV is the worst wavelength to use if you want to find the sun through clouds.

The potential cues the sun provides are high absolute brightness, small size (0.4° across), no polarization (most of the light from blue sky, by contrast, is highly polarized, as we shall see), and proportionally little

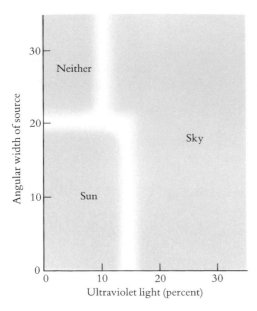

This simplified graph indicates the combinations of angular width and degree of UV light that bees will accept as indicating the sun, part of the sky, or nothing at all. To a first approximation, the degree of polarization does not matter. The sun is 0.4° across, has no polarization, and its light contains only about 10 percent UV.

ultraviolet (about 8 percent, the lowest anywhere in the sky). We established a colony in a horizontal observation hive, trained a group of foragers to a distant food source (so their dances would be long and well oriented), and offered artificial celestial cues to see how they would be interpreted. Since we knew the direction the bees should dance if they saw our bit of counterfeit sky as the sun, it was easy to figure out which cues they consider important in identifying our local star.

After offering hundreds of combinations of stimuli, we can define the minimum criteria for the sun as understood by bees. To a first approximation, the object should be less than 20° across (up to fifty times the sun's actual apparent size); it can have any amount or direction of polarization; finally, its light must be less than 15 percent ultraviolet. In other words, having navigated by the sun for days, a forager will blithely accept a 15°, 100 percent polarized, green triangle for the 0.4°, unpolarized, white circle we know as the sun. Obviously, bees do not learn to recognize the sun by personal experience; instead, they are born with a crude but diagnostic rule based primarily on its dimness in the ultraviolet.

COMPENSATING FOR THE SUN'S MOVEMENT

Identifying the sun is only the first (and easiest) challenge bees face in using this prominent landmark. The most problematic characteristic of the sun for any animal using it for orientation is that it moves: the direction of the sun changes over the course of the day from east to west, and this movement must be taken into account. Consider a forager flying out to a familiar patch of flowers: If she is flying due south to her goal at about 11:45 A.M. in late June, the sun will lie about 10° to her left. If the food is a thousand meters distant, she will arrive after a flight of about a minute. In a typical patch, she will spend as much as 30 minutes gathering a full load of nectar, and so start her return to the hive at about 12:15 P.M. If the sun had not moved while she was visiting blossoms in the patch, she could adopt a reverse orientation, steering with the sun 180° from where it had been with respect to her outward flight path. The trouble with this approach is that the sun is now 10° to the *west* of south, having moved a full 20° in the interim; if she fails to take its shifting position into account, she will miss the hive by more than 300 meters.

We know for a fact that foragers do accommodate the sun's movement more or less accurately. First of all, we can see it in their behavior, both when they depart from the hive and when they leave the food source. Some foragers spend considerable time in the hive between trips, either trying to get rid of their load or dancing, or because the hive has

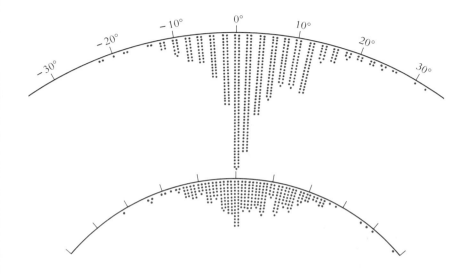

Foragers depart accurately toward the hive whether they leave immediately after feeding (top) or after being trapped in the dark for an hour (bottom).

been closed (artificially or because of a rain shower or high wind). When the forager leaves again, her departure bearing is roughly correct, even though the position of the sun has shifted. Similarly, a forager trapped in a feeder and kept with no view of the sun for up to an hour is able to depart in about the right direction, though the sun has moved west during her entrapment.

The second line of evidence comes from the dances themselves: when a forager dances for an extended period, the direction of her waggle run actually precesses a measurable amount counterclockwise to allow for the changing angle between the sun and the food. When, in a few cases, illuminating an observation hive at night has caused a forager to begin dancing for a source visited hours before, her dance direction has very approximately allowed for the sun's movement, though this landmark had long since dipped below the horizon.

The sun moves left to right in the northern temperate zone, right to left in the southern temperate zone, and either way, depending on the date, in the tropics. How do bees know which way it moves? Since honey bees evolved in the tropics, it seems unlikely that they could be born with a prejudice about sun movement—if they had been, they would have gotten lost during at least part of the year. The best bet is that bees learn the direction of the sun's movement before they begin foraging—perhaps during play flights. It also seems likely that this learning is like imprinting—that is, it may be irreversible. This is suggested

The path of the sun through the sky differs according to the time of year. The graph on this and the facing page show the course at 40° north on the summer and winter solstices. At any time of year, the rate of azimuth movement varies over the course of the day, being lowest near dawn and dusk, and highest at noon.

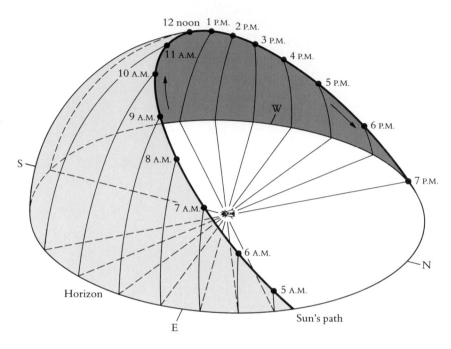

by the results of two experiments performed by Martin Lindauer. In one, he raised bees in a closed room, so that they began flying with only the unmoving lights of the room to guide them. When moved outdoors and trained to a feeding station, these foragers rapidly become lost. Apparently they had become committed to a world view in which the sun did not move, and they were unable to adjust when this situation changed.

In another of Lindauer's experiments, a hive was moved from south of the equator to north. Here again the trained foragers set off in the direction they had been trained to at the old site and quickly became lost. Apparently they compensated for the sun's movement in the wrong direction and so could not get back home after the first few flights. In fact, this may normally be a problem for new foragers as well: more than 20 percent of bees fail to return from their first foraging trip. Given that the loss rate drops to practically zero thereafter, it is possible that first-time foragers fail because they do not yet know enough about the sun's movement.

Compensating for the sun's movement, even once the direction of movement is known, is no easy matter. First, the change in the sun's direction is much slower near dawn and dusk than it is near noon. The

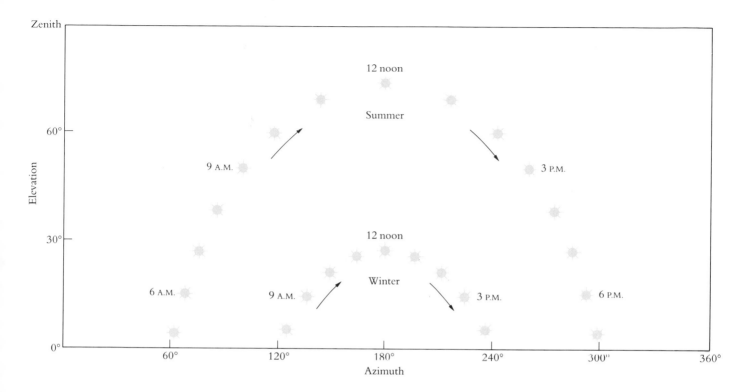

reason for this is that, early and late, the sun is moving vertically in the sky; near noon the sun is at its maximum elevation, and its movement is mainly in direction (azimuth). The most extreme example of this change in the rate of azimuth movement occurs on the equator at the equinoxes. On these days, the sun rises in the east and moves straight up; its azimuth does not change until noon, when it is directly overhead. A moment later it is in the west, and it sinks along that line until sunset. In the temperate zones, the maximum difference occurs on the summer solstice, at which time the sun's azimuth changes five to six times faster at noon (roughly 44° an hour at the latitude of New York City) than at dawn.

Not only does the sun's rate of movement vary over the course of the day, but it is different at different latitudes, as we have already implied. On any given day, for example, the sun is always higher at noon in Florida than in New England, and the difference between the maximum and minimum rates of azimuth movement is greater. Furthermore, the sun's arc through the sky is different on different days even at the same location: the sun is always higher at any given time of day as the date more closely approaches the summer solstice, and the noontime acceleration of the sun's movement (and the dawn/dusk retardation) is also

Five foragers were trained to collect food between 4:00 and 6:00 in the afternoon. One day the feeder was left empty and the times of forager visits recorded, as shown in this graph; each forager is represented by a different color. One bee checked the source twice in the early morning; the other 42 visits occurred during the training period (38 of the 42) or within 15 minutes of it.

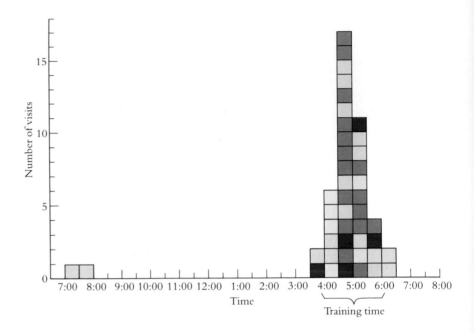

larger. In short, for humans to accommodate the sun's changing motion accurately—an ability essential to navigation until the advent of radio—we must have an accurate clock, know the date, and have a set of tables setting out the sun's movement for the day and latitude in question.

It seems unlikely that bees are born with a set of tables, though they certainly have good internal clocks. A group of foragers trained to collect food at a certain time of day, and then isolated from the normal cues that are used to reset the clock (dawn and dusk being the cues for most animals), illustrate the precision of their internal timekeepers by how accurately they turn up for their appointments on later days. This experiment can be done most conveniently in a closed room, and the bees' error in judging time in such tests has been variously estimated at five to fifteen minutes per day. For those of us that had watches before the advent of quartz-controlled mechanisms, the need to reset the hands of wrist chronometers almost daily to correct for their systematic drift, whether fast or slow, will be a familiar if distant memory. A 15-minute error would be considered unacceptable in a watch, but it is fairly good by animal standards. As we will see, there is strong evidence to indicate that bees have a unique system for adjusting their drifting inboard timepieces.

To replace the tables of sun position that our species requires, bees must have some more approximate method. One possibility is that bees use an average value for the sun's westward movement; the mean rate is 15° per hour. This system would work reasonably well over short periods (which is usually all that a bee would need) except near noon; perhaps this is why few bees forage at noon. Until a few years ago, the data taken on sun compensation were not sufficiently precise to rule out this particular intellectual short cut.

Another option for a bee would be to map the sun's movement precisely on one day, and then use it on subsequent days. This would be reasonably accurate since the course of the sun in the temperate zone does not change much from day to day, and in the height of the season (when the daily change is greatest) foragers live only about a week; the information cannot get too out of date in that time interval. To map the sun's arc on a minute-by-minute basis, however, would require a frame of reference. We would probably use a prominent landmark or magnetic north, and perhaps bees could do so as well.

Yet another strategy would be to use spherical geometry. The sun moves along its arc in the sky at 15° an hour; the arc itself is a great circle, a well-known geometrical figure; if we move the sun mentally from its last observed position along this arc at the rate of 1° for every four minutes that have elapsed, and then drop a line from that location perpendicular to the horizon, we can calculate its new azimuth with great precision. If this sounds complicated, it is, but there seems no reason that it could not be wired into an animal that requires this level of accuracy.

Finally, there is a possibility that had occurred to no one until we performed the first critical experiments a few years ago: the bees might approximate the sun's movement by extrapolation—that is, they could simply assume that the sun's azimuth has continued to change at the same rate it was moving when last measured. This technique of judging the future by the past would be more accurate than the 15°-per-hour approximation, and less complicated than the other two more accurate alternatives.

Tests for distinguishing among these hypotheses are best attempted on or near the solstice, since the predictions of the various hypotheses will differ the most at this difficult time of year. First, marked foragers are trained to find food while the hive is at one location. After several days of training, the hive is closed near midday; this is accomplished by installing a one-way door at the entrance so that foragers can return but not leave. The hive is then moved to a new location (so that the bees cannot use familiar landmarks), stations are set out offering the same food as before but now in a variety of directions, and the hive reopened. Foragers

The rate of change in the sun's azimuth direction varies, being highest at noon. By closing a hive for two hours beginning either at noon or 11:00 A.M. it is possible to discover how foragers allow for the changing azimuth by observing which feeding stations they fly to after their incarceration. The preferred direction is close to what would be expected if the bees simply extrapolated the sun's last observed rate of movement.

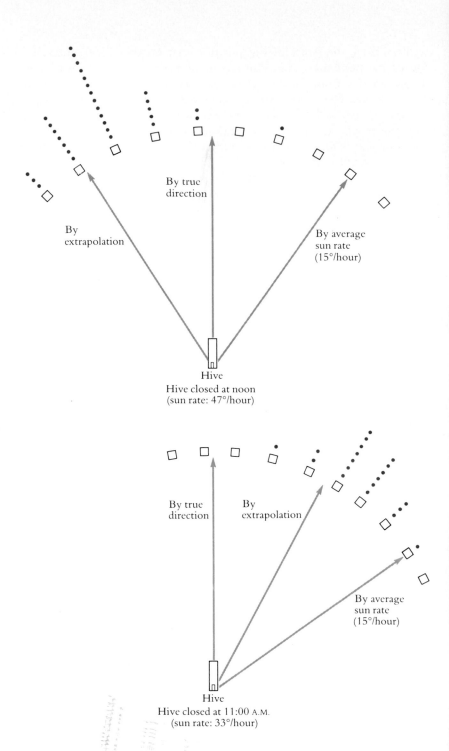

By extrapolation

By true direction

By average sun rate (15°/hour)

Hive

Hive closed at noon (sun rate: 47°/hour)

By true direction

By extrapolation

By average sun rate (15°/hour)

Hive

Hive closed at 11:00 A.M. (sun rate: 33°/hour)

reemerging after two hours of incarceration will compensate for the sun's movement by means of one system or another and arrive at the corresponding station.

For example, if we close the hive at 11:00 A.M., when the rate of azimuth change is about 27° an hour, and open it at 1:00 P.M., we can make three different predictions: bees able to remember the sun's movement from a previous day or perform spherical geometry will infer correctly that the sun has shifted by 80°, and so arrive at the station in precisely the direction of the training feeder at the former site; bees extrapolating the sun's movement at 11:00 A.M. will underestimate this value, allowing for a change of only 55°; any forager using the 15° per hour approximation will employ a correction of only 30°. In fact, the foragers made a correction of about 50°.

Similarly, if the hive is closed from noon until 2:00 P.M., the sky-map and spherical-geometry hypotheses both predict an accurate correction of about 65°, whereas a 15°-per-hour accommodation would give 30°. In this case, however, the extrapolation hypothesis predicts an *over* estimation of the sun's movement (since the rate was measured at its fastest point, and it has been slowing down over the course of the two hours that the hive is closed)—about 95°, to be precise. Again, the extrapolation hypothesis seems closest to the mark: the foragers estimate the sun's movement at about 87°. (As we will see, in the presence of prominent landmarks foragers do not need this extrapolation strategy, at least for nearby goals.)

One trend in these data is for the bees to under-extrapolate the sun's motion slightly. This could be just experimental error, but it is so consistent that it may actually suggest something about how the extrapolation system works. In order to estimate the sun's rate of azimuth movement, a bee would have to measure the sun's location at one time and then at another, and then compute the angle of movement over the time interval between the two measurements. Two problems are immediately obvious: first, how accurately can an organism with a visual resolution of 1 to 1½° actually measure the sun's direction? It is easy to see that the error will be minimized if the measurements are taken at widely separated times: an uncertainty of 1° is huge if the two fixes are taken five minutes apart, during which time the sun will have moved only 1° on average, and 4° at most. If the measurements are taken an hour apart, though, a 1° uncertainty would be trivial in the face of the typically large movement in summertime, ranging from 15° per hour to 45° per hour between 8:00 A.M. and 4:00 P.M. This brings us to the second problem: the rate determination is really accurate only for the time halfway between the first and second measurements—30 minutes in the past if the interval is an hour. In other words, any estimate is out of date before it

The "last-observed rate of movement" is, in effect, about 20 minutes old, the result of averaging over the previous 40 minutes, as these experiments by Martin Lindauer indicate. When the feeding station was moved continuously to keep a constant angle with the sun, the bees' dances were aimed 10° to 20° to the left—that is, in the direction the station used to be. When the station was moved only every 30 minutes, the dances started 10° to 30° to the left, but then began to catch up. When bees were reared in a closed room with no view of the sun, and then trained outdoors to a moving feeder, there was no inaccuracy at all; apparently these bees had grown up with the understanding that the sun does not move.

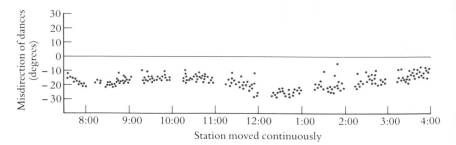

Station moved continuously

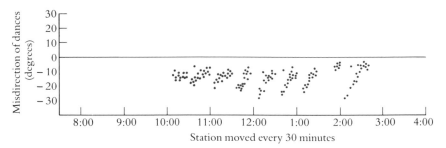

Station moved every 30 minutes

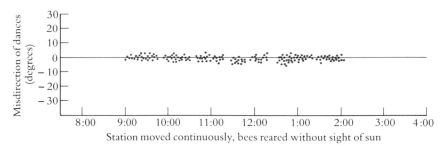

Station moved continuously, bees reared without sight of sun

is even calculated, and the longer the interval, the worse the problem. There must be some optimum measurement interval that minimizes this problem while also minimizing the error that arises when fixes are taken close together.

From the data in our sun-compensation experiment, we can calculate a rough value for this error: the extrapolation rate the bees seem to be using matches the sun's movement about 20 minutes before the hive is closed. This would be the value expected if the measurements are taken at 40-minute intervals. At first sight, this seems a much larger interval than anyone would have guessed, but, as often happens, there are some old forgotten experiments performed by von Frisch and his students that, in retrospect, bear on this question. Martin Lindauer once tried training bees with a feeder that moved from east to west with the sun. In one case, he moved the station every minute or two; in the other case, he

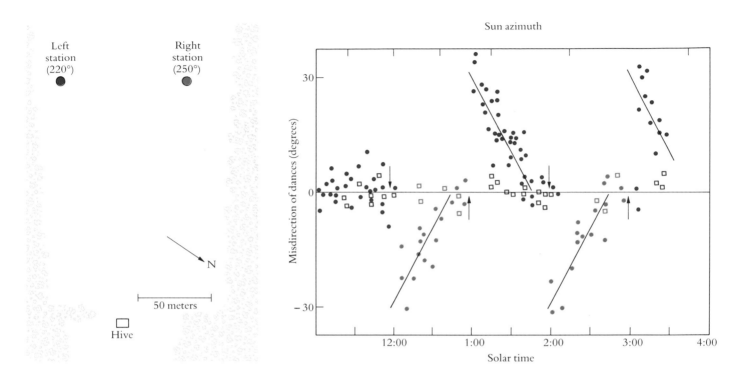

When we repeated Lindauer's experiments, we moved the feeding station every hour 30° to the right or left, alternately. Dots represent dances of trained foragers, and squares the dances of the bees that they recruited. The dances became accurate after about 45 minutes.

shifted it only every half hour. The curious thing was that the foragers' dances did *not* indicate where the station was (relative to the sun) when they were last there, but rather its angle 15 to 30 minutes in the past. When the station was moved at half-hour intervals, the dance angles would almost catch up with the true direction before the feeder was once again relocated.

This is just what we would expect if the bees' estimate of sun direction is about 20 minutes out of date, but as Lindauer's experiments were not carried out with this question in mind, they are not conclusive. When we repeated them in an effort to get a precise measurement, the results were just the same: the dance angles started out indicating the location 22 minutes in the past, caught up, and were then correct. When the station was moved, the foragers began by indicating the old location, then shifted slowly but systematically into the correct alignment. The period of adjustment is roughly 44 minutes. Systems analogous to this one are probably common when animals must make estimates on the basis of inaccurate or noisy data. By averaging over time, allowing the random errors to cancel each other out, they would achieve a true value. Indeed, this is just what recruits do when they attend the sloppy dances in the hive and compute a mean value on the basis of about six cycles of data.

The giant honey bee of the tropics, *Apis dorsata*, will forage on moonlit nights, something our temperate zone species will not do. (There are some reports of the Central African bee, *A. mellifera adansonii*, foraging after dusk.) With the moon as the only beacon in the sky, the source of what little light there is for seeing landmarks, do the bees reference their dances to the moon, or to the unseen sun? One of our students, Fred Dyer, measured the dance directions both before and after sunset, and concluded that the bees ignore the moon, apparently extrapolating the sun's azimuth below the horizon.

POLARIZED LIGHT

Though the sun is the primary navigational compass of honey bees, there are times when it is unavailable—under overcast, for instance, or when it is behind a cloud or tree. Foragers do not fall to the ground helpless under these circumstances; they have a backup system to take the sun's place.

The primary backup was discovered by von Frisch in just the way he discovered that the sun was the main compass: he observed dancing in the open on a horizontal comb. We have already mentioned that when the sun is blocked and a mirror image of it is provided, the dances are oriented to the reflection. More remarkably, though, when the sun is simply blocked, there is virtually no effect: the bees continue dancing in more or less the same direction. Clearly there must be some cue in the blue sky overhead not obvious to us.

Von Frisch dug deeper into this mystery by using a horizontal observation hive in a tent with only a small opening. Through this gap von Frisch inserted a piece of stove pipe so that he could show the dancers any part of the sky that he chose. He found that as long as the bees had a view of at least 10° of blue sky not too close to the sun, they could orient pretty well; a thin haze would cause problems, and overcast destroyed the orientation altogether. Next, von Frisch tried interposing various color filters between the sky and the dancers, and found that only those that passed ultraviolet light still allowed the bees to dance correctly; thus the cue had to be in the UV.

Von Frisch guessed at this point that the secret compass might be the patterns of polarized light created by the scattering of sunlight in the atmosphere overhead. But this speculation could not be tested because he had no UV-transparent polarizers. During a lecture trip to the United States, however, von Frisch met Edwin Land of the Polaroid Corporation, and he returned to Austria with one of Land's newly developed polaroid filters. Sure enough, when von Frisch interposed a polaroid

Von Frisch used a short piece of stove pipe to show dancers in a horizontal hive a restricted patch of sky.

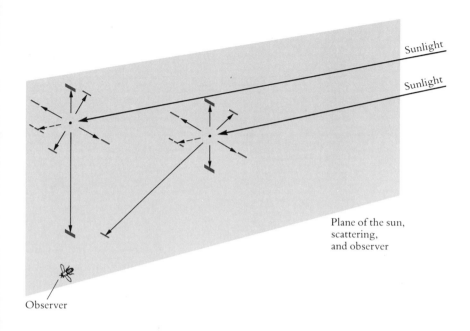

Sunlight

Sunlight

Plane of the sun,
scattering,
and observer

Observer

Polarization is created by the scattering of light by air molecules. The angle of polarization is always perpendicular to the plane of the incoming and scattered light, and the degree of polarization is related to the angle of scatter, being largest at 90°.

between a dancer and the piece of blue sky visible to it, she reoriented her dance; when he rotated the filter, the angle of the dance changed as well.

Polarization refers to the direction in which light waves vibrate as they travel through space. This direction is always perpendicular to the direction of travel. Thus, a light wave may have vertical polarization (in which case it is pictured as vibrating up and down as it travels), horizontal polarization, or it can be polarized in any other direction in between. All light waves are polarized, but sunlight (and the light from most bulbs) is a mixture of waves in all orientations, and so there is no net polarization. The invisible symmetry of the polarization pattern in the sky was first explained by Lord Rayleigh in the late 1800s. Light coming from the sun is unpolarized; when it scatters off air molecules, a net polarization results which is perpendicular to the plane containing the sun, the scattering molecule, and the observer. So, each molecule in the sky sets up its own pattern of scattering around it, but the only part of interest to us is the light scattered down to a bee near the ground.

From the bee's point of view, the light scattered to it from any point in the sky will (in the simplest case) be polarized perpendicular to the line linking that point and the sun. As a result, the pattern of polarized light in the sky will encircle the sun, surrounding it like a set of concentric fences. In addition to affecting the direction of polarization, scattering

The theoretical result of scattering in the sky is a symmetric pattern of polarized light surrounding the sun. At any point in the sky the polarization is perpendicular to the great circle connecting the point and the sun (allowing for the distortion induced by representing the celestial hemisphere on a flat surface), and the intensity of the polarization is greatest 90° away from the sun.

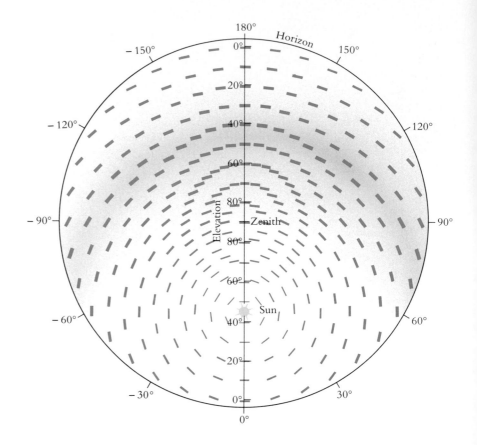

creates differences in intensity: light scattered perpendicularly to the line of sunlight will be almost completely polarized, but that scattered by greater and lesser angles will be diluted by a certain amount of unpolarized light; the greater the difference from the optimum of 90°, the less intense the polarization. For the bee, this means that the strongest polarization will lie in a circle 90° from the sun (a circle that, of necessity, lies partly hidden below the horizon); the weakest will be in the sun's direction and in the sky opposite the sun (also below the horizon).

In theory, then, a honey bee could look at a piece of the sky, determine the angle and degree of polarization, draw a great circle perpendicularly through the plane of polarization, and use the degree of polarization to determine how far away on that circle the sun must lie. By spherical geometry, then, the bee could find that point, drop a line perpendicularly to the horizon, and thus determine the sun's azimuth. This complex calculation is unlikely to be the way bees solve this problem, but it illustrates that all the necessary information is there. In fact, there is even more to be extracted: the brightness and color of the sky also vary with the distance from the sun, a consequence of the greater scattering of UV and blue light.

Is this information really up there? This line of reasoning is based on Lord Rayleigh's theoretical calculations, but Rayleigh ignored the inconvenient possibility that some of the light reaching the earth from a particular direction might have gotten there by being scattered *twice*; the effect of the second scatter is not just to weaken the pattern, but even to distort it, particularly near the horizon. In addition, Rayleigh presupposed an ideal atmosphere, unpolluted by dust, water vapor, hydrocarbons (produced by trees as well as by cars), and so on, all capable of complicating matters beyond the easy reach of theory. It seems clear that an essential step in understanding how bees use patterns of polarized light is actually to measure them in the UV.

With Michael Brines, a student who enjoyed the technological aspects of the project, we undertook this project a decade ago. In addition to the conceptual difficulty of measuring something invisible to the human eye, we soon discovered the many technical difficulties that had dissuaded others. In the end, we did succeed in mapping the sky in the UV (and in the blue and green wavelengths corresponding to the other two pigments in the bee eye) on clear, partly cloudy, hazy, and overcast days with the sun both near the horizon and high. The results convinced us that the patterns of degree of polarization, brightness, and color were too variable—too dependent on humidity, clouds, slight haze, and so on—to be of any use for navigation; only the pattern of polarization *angles* was fairly reliable, and not even that near the sun and horizon.

The next step was to learn whether bees are wired to ignore everything but polarization angles, and if so, how they use the angles to infer the location of the sun. Like von Frisch, who had looked into these questions in a preliminary way, we used a horizontal hive in a dark room, offering the dancers artificial light cues to see how they would orient to them. Like von Frisch before us, we found that brightness, color, and degree of polarization are ignored. But what about gradients? After all, bees require a minimum of 10° of sky to orient themselves; and a patch that size has obvious gradients: the degree of polarization changes systematically across the patch, as does the brightness and the color. Perhaps the reason bees cannot use a smaller piece of sky is that a smaller section has less obvious gradients. It is conceivable that even though the absolute values of color, brightness, and degree of polarization are unreliable cues because of various atmospheric effects, their gradients might be stable enough to be used by the bees to judge direction. In fact, they are not; not only are gradients unreliable in the real sky, but dancing bees

The actual patterns of polarization in the sky were measured with a device that could be aimed by computer and scanned half the sky in only a few minutes.

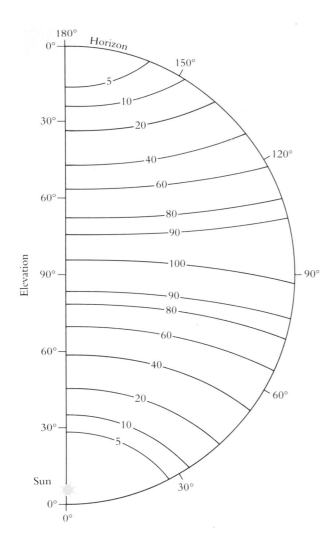

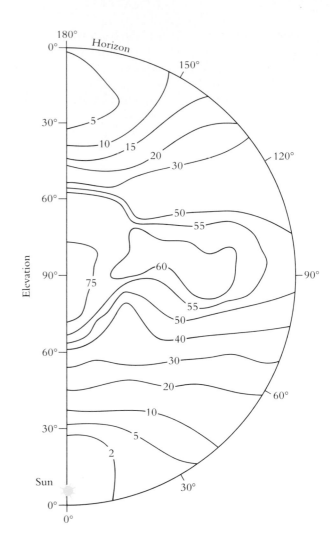

The actual patterns frequently do not match the theoretical one, particularly in degree of polarization and sky color. Compared here near dusk are the expected (left) and observed (right) patterns in degree of polarization (given as percentages).

do not use them even when available. The reason bees seem to need a 10° patch is not to extract gradients, but just to have enough light; if the brightness of the artificial patch is increased to well above that of the real sky, the minimum area needed drops down eventually to just 1° wide.

If bees do not use brightness, color, or degree of polarization to orient themselves, a major difficulty immediately arises. The problem is most obvious if we look at the spherical geometry of locating the sun. What a bee seeing a patch of sky might know is that the sun lies on a great circle passing perpendicularly through the angle of polarization in that patch; without more information, the bee cannot know how far away the sun is along that arc. Now if the bee sees *two* patches, there need be no difficulty: the two circles defined by the polarization angles of the two patches intersect in only one place above the horizon (there is a second crossing below), which is where the sun must be. But if the bee sees only one patch—and all the tests described here so far use only one—then there should be a whole range of possible azimuths at which the sun could be. Yet bees are clearly able to orient by a single patch of sky.

Things are not necessarily bleak. If the bee knows the sun's elevation at the moment, then the great circle running perpendicularly through the polarization in the patch of sky will intersect the sun's elevation in only two places. How does the bee decide between these two alternatives? Does she beg the question and dance both directions, choose one at random, or mysteriously infer which is correct? We trained bees to a feeder, allowed them to dance to an artificial sun in a horizontal hive to calibrate directions, and then substituted an artificial sky patch at a predetermined elevation and with a particular angle of polarization. The dancer, seeing this highly polarized light rich in UV, adopted a new dance angle corresponding to one of the two alternatives. All the dancers selected the same alternative, and their choice was always to interpret the patch to be the one lying farther from the sun.

This farther-from-the-sun rule can be thought of as an arbitrary convention: dancers orient their dances as though this were the only possibility, and recruits decode the dance in the same way; the language works because both sender and receiver use the same convention. In fact, the rule is better than its alternative—pretending that the patch is the one closer to the sun—because often the degree of polarization in the closer alternative is too low and the pattern thus too faint for the bees to use during flight. Although it may seem quite artificial to use a horizontal hive and sky patterns, this is probably just the situation faced by the earliest honey bees, living in the open and dancing on the tops of their comb; the branches overhead and the clouds in the sky must have presented the dancers with a very partial view of the celestial vault. The sun would often have been obscured, so that the bees would frequently have been thrown back upon deciphering solar azimuth from one or a few isolated patches of sky.

The farther-from-the-sun rule ought to break down for vertical polarization patterns: in these special spots in the sky, two patterns at each elevation lie symmetrically left and right of the sun; they correspond to alternative sun positions equally far away. When dancers are faced with this choice, they consistently opt for one of the alternatives—the one

Bees seeing only one patch of sky eliminate the ambiguity between the two possible locations of the sun by means of rules. If bees are shown either of the two patterns circled at 20° elevation (representing two patches of sky with the same polarization angle in the large circle at right), they always dance as though the pattern is the alternative farther away, as shown in the diagram at lower left. (The dots represent the direction of individual dances; the arrow indicates the dance direction expected if the bees simply interpreted the artificial pattern as the sun; the short lines are the two directions expected if the bees use the pattern to infer the sun's location; only the direction more distant from the sun is elected). The circled patterns at 60° elevation in the large circle represent the special case of vertical polarization in which the two alternatives lie equidistant from the sun. The dancers opt for only one alternative (center diagram below). When shown a patch of sky at the zenith, bees dance in both of the possible directions (lower right).

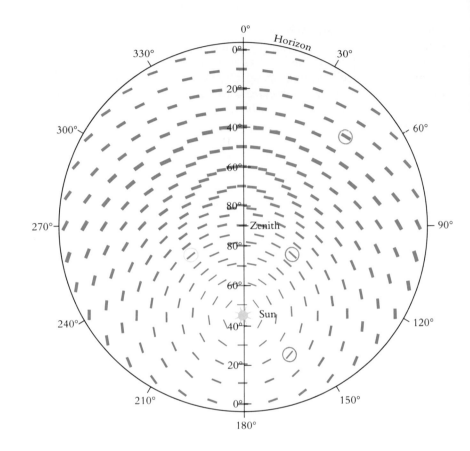

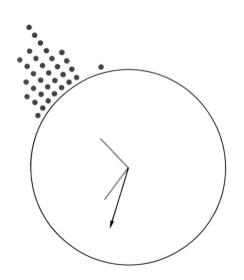

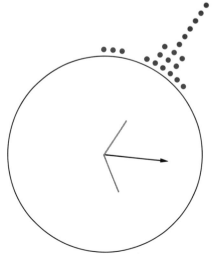

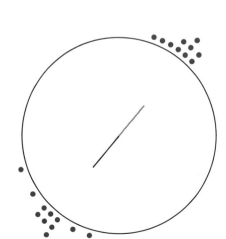

lying to the right of the sun. This right-hand rule really *is* arbitrary, since either alternative is equally suitable, as long as dancer and attender agree on which to use.

Finally, there is one point in the sky for which neither rule is of use: the zenith, the point directly overhead. The angle of polarization along the sun's azimuth and in the direction 180° opposite is always horizontal—it has to be, since the meridian is a great circle that intersects the sun and runs vertically through the sky, and the angle of polarization is always perpendicular to great circles passing through the sun. A patch at the zenith is equidistant from the two alternative sun locations, and left and right have no meaning because the pattern is directly overhead. For patches of this sort, the dances in fact do point two directions; individual dancers orient both ways in the course of a single series of cycles.

Bees can infer the location of the sun from polarization angle alone, using rules to choose between alternatives when there is ambiguity. But how do they calculate the alternatives in the first place? One possibility is that they perform spherical geometry; this would be very accurate, but if bees do not adopt this approach to compensate for the sun's movement, it seems unlikely that they use it to infer the sun's location from polarization patterns.

A second possibility is that the bees use memory (as they do, we shall see, in compensating for the sun's movement when prominent landmarks are available); the bee might simply remember the sun's position in the sky pattern from her last trip, or even from the same time on a previous day. The same horizontal-hive experiments performed with artificial patches of sky or sun on overcast days suggest this strategy. When the sky is obscured by clouds, there is no polarized light pattern, and the orientation of dancers in our horizontal hive is more scattered. If the bees use spherical geometry to interpret the artificial patterns, they ought to be able to run that calculation as well on a cloudy day as a sunny one. If the bees had some doubt about the real sun's azimuth, the scatter could reflect that uncertainty; but when offered an artificial sun, the dancers are well oriented. It seems possible that the dances are scattered because they rely on fading memory rather than on recent experience, though these observations do not prove this.

Finally, there is the possibility that bees use an approximation, as they do in extrapolating the sun's azimuth. In fact, a group of Swiss researchers have developed a detailed model for how such an intellectual short cut might work. They propose that the bees ignore the sun's elevation *and* the elevation of the polarization pattern, and instead use the following rule (slightly simplified for clarity): the angle from a patch of sky to the sun's azimuth is equal to the polarization angle of the patch, where vertical polarization is defined as 90° and horizontal as 180°, with the proviso

The innate pattern imagined by the fixed-angle hypothesis is here compared with the pattern in the sky predicted from Rayleigh scattering. The discrepancy between these two patterns is greatest for vertical polarization patterns.

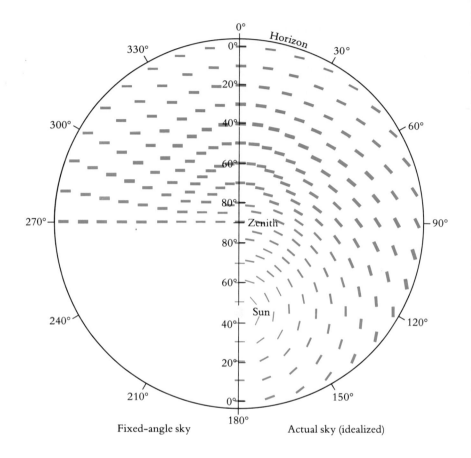

that all angles will be interpreted to lie between 90° and 180°. (The rider is necessary because any polarization angle has two interpretations; an angle 120° clockwise from horizontal, for example, is also 60° counterclockwise from the horizontal.) To the bee, in other words, all patches having the same polarization angle lie in the same direction.

This rule-based hypothesis is wonderfully simple, but very inaccurate when the sun is at a high elevation or the polarization angle is close to 90°. This need not be a disadvantage in communication—it is just a convention, and if dancer and attender both use it, no confusion will result. The problem is that if either attempts to use it in the field to orient to a patch of sky, she may well get lost. Perhaps the system of dance orientation is different from the system used when flying, though this seems

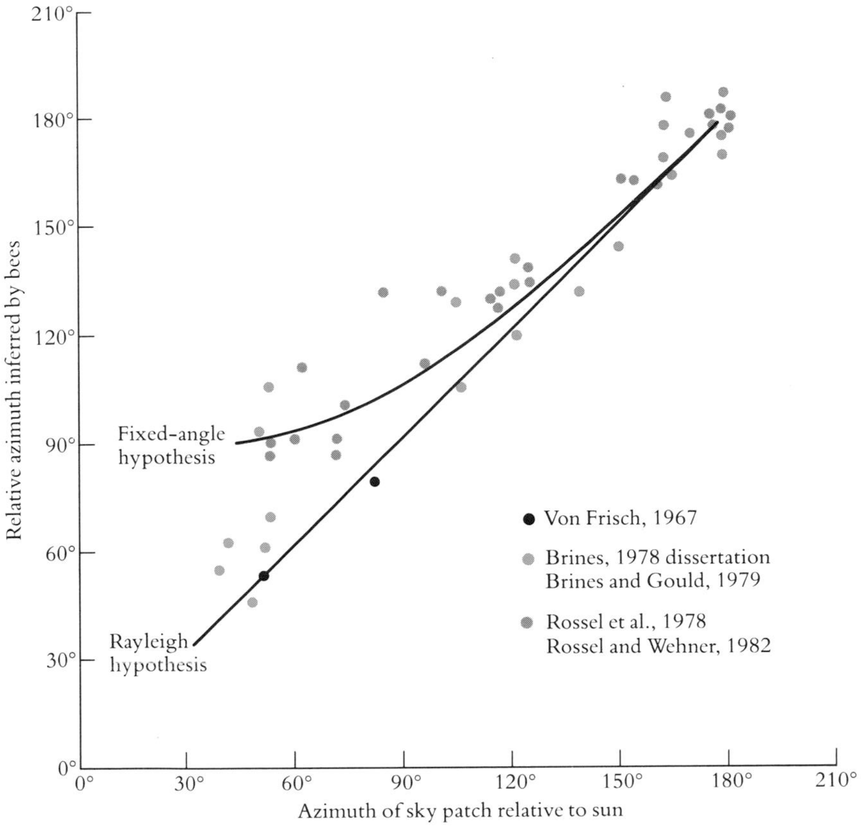
210°
180°
150°
120°
90°
60°
30°
0°
Relative azimuth inferred by bees
Fixed-angle hypothesis
Rayleigh hypothesis
Von Frisch, 1967
Brines, 1978 dissertation
Brines and Gould, 1979
Rossel et al., 1978
Rossel and Wehner, 1982
0°
30°
60°
90°
120°
150°
180°
210°
Azimuth of sky patch relative to sun

Data collected by different groups support different hypotheses for how the sky patterns are decoded. It is not yet clear why these data are contradictory.

unlikely. Oddly enough, the Swiss group's data firmly support their hypothesis, right down to the enormous errors it entails, whereas scanty data collected by von Frisch and much more extensive observations by our group do not. For example, our bees do not necessarily dance as if the sun were 90° from the patch of sky whose polarization is vertical; instead, their dances closely approximate the true position of the patch in the sky. This difference has yet to be resolved. It could be the result of a slight difference of experimental technique, or perhaps the two different races under study have separate systems. In any case, the resolution of such controversies is a stimulating challenge; the truth behind them is, as often as not, different from and more interesting than any of the imagined alternatives.

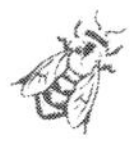

LANDMARKS

The polarized-light backup system is useful when the sun is obscured and patches of blue sky are still visible, but what do foragers do under overcast? Von Frisch never solved this problem, arguing variously that foraging and recruitment are low when the sky is cloudy, or that the sun is visible to bees in the UV. As we have already seen, direct measurements of the sky indicate that there is definitely no UV in the sun, and yet, at least in North America, foragers continue to fly to feeders and recruits to arrive at them even under overcast. Perhaps other celestial cues are available, or maybe the foragers are using landmarks for navigation but their dances are disoriented, so that the recruits must find their way by odor. We can rule out much of this line of speculation by one simple experiment: We take an observation hive into the open and turn it on its side with a full view of the overcast sky; the dancing is disoriented, indicating that there are no celestial cues. Next we return it to its normal vertical position; now the dances are oriented. The bees must know where the sun is even though they cannot see it; otherwise, how could they indicate the angle between the sun (gravity) and the food?

Familiar landmarks might be involved. As soon as von Frisch began to train bees over long distances, he began to notice an effect of landmarks. If he trained along a dog-leg route, for instance, with the turn near a prominent tree, foragers would continue to fly to the food by way of the tree; a dog leg in an open field, on the other hand, is ignored, as the foragers adopt the most direct route. Similarly, if he paused during training near a major landmark, it was difficult to get the bees to move farther when the training was recommenced; the bees had become "stuck."

Von Frisch and his group performed definitive tests of the influence of landmarks on trained foragers by training bees in one location and then shifting them overnight to another. Once, for instance, the hive was established next to a lake with an east-west shoreline, and the foragers trained about 180 meters to the west; the hive was then moved during the night to a north-south shoreline, and stations set out to the north, south, and west. The west station was in the actual training direction, while the south station occupied the same location relative to landmarks. When the foragers began collecting the next morning, 14 of 16 flew along the shore to the south station. Clearly, a prominent landmark can take over from the sun in guiding flights to familiar locations.

How prominent the landmarks must be remains to be determined. Roads and forest edges are very good when the training is along them. Even a line of trees in the distance can work if they are close enough: a stand about 60 meters away, with an angular height of 15° as seen from the

Training array

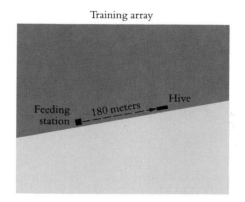

N

Testing array

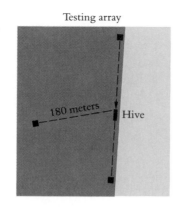

Experienced foragers can use prominent landmarks in navigating, and will even ignore the sun. In this experiment the bees were trained to find food along the shore of a lake; during the night, the hive was moved to a place where the shore ran in a different direction, and stations set out as shown. Most foragers kept the water on their left and flew along the shore.

hive, was pretty effective (13 of 21 foragers were fooled after the move), but the same stand at 210 meters (with an angular size of only 4°) forced the foragers to go back to using the sun. An isolated tree or clump at 100 meters was ignored.

The bees' system, then, uses prominent, nearby, unambiguous landmarks in preference to the sun once the route is familiar, and doubtless this is why the foragers from some colonies can continue foraging under overcast. But how can they continue to orient their dances? One possibility is that foragers not only know the direction of the food with respect to these useful landmarks, but they remember as well the sun's course through the sky relative to these beacons. With Dyer, we tested this idea by training bees along a tree line in one location and then moving the hive overnight to another tree line running in a different direction. Instead of just monitoring the flight directions of the foragers, however, we recorded the dancing.

When the hive was reopened on a clear day, most of the foragers were fooled, and followed the tree line to what we will call the landmark feeder; a few went instead in the true direction, apparently relying on the sun for guidance, to what we will call the compass feeder. The subsequent dances in the hive accurately reflected where the foragers had flown—that is, the compass-station bees indicated the same direction danced before the move, but the landmark-station bees indicated the new direction of their feeder. So, though they ignore the sun for navigation while being misled by landmarks, foragers still take account of the sun's position and use it to orient their dances.

When the move was performed and the hive reopened on a cloudy day, however, the pattern was different. First, *all* of the foragers turned

Although experienced bees may ignore the sun in setting course, they still use it to orient their dancing. In this experiment, most foragers used the forest edge for navigating in the new site, but (on sunny days) their subsequent dances were accurately oriented. When the move was made on a cloudy day, though, the dances indicated the direction they had flown at that time on the previous day.

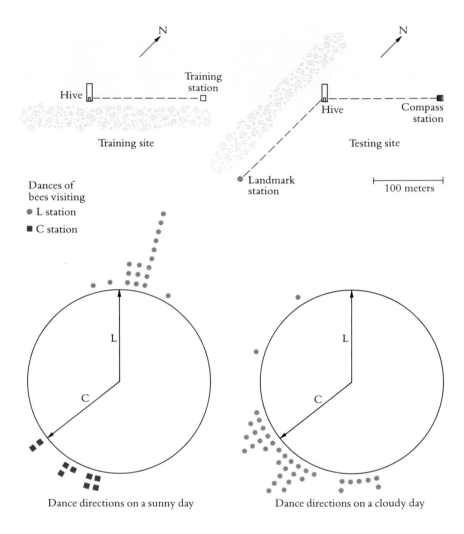

Dance directions on a sunny day   Dance directions on a cloudy day

up at the landmark station; this is not too surprising since they could not have used the sun even if they had wanted to. More interesting, the dances indicated the direction the training station had been at the previous site; the foragers remembered yesterday's sun azimuth relative to the tree line and used it to orient today's dances; recruits were able to decode these instructions and find the food. If the sky started to clear, there would be a period of confusion as bees began to switch over to the actual solar angle; if the sky then clouded up again, many would switch back to recycling the previous day's dance directions, while others appeared to have been recalibrated successfully and would stick with the new direction.

This experiment shows that when there are prominent, unambiguous landmarks near the hive, experienced bees commit to memory the sun's position relative to the landmarks for the entire day, and then use this memory to orient both flights and dances under overcast. Experienced recruits are also able to decode the dances by using their memory of the sun's movements, and steer to the advertised goals. In the tropics, this ability takes on an added dimension: Dyer has demonstrated that the dwarf honey bee, which lives on exposed comb outdoors, correctly orients horizontal dances under complete overcast, something our temperate species cannot do. The secret of this ability is that the bees become familiar with the landmarks visible from the dance floor, and use them in just the way our bees use nearby landmarks on their foraging flights. As the results of the map experiment that was described in the previous chapter also showed, honey bees have a sophisticated ability to use the features of their environment to orient their flights almost regardless of conditions. Indeed, despite their poor visual resolution, they seem much better qualified to navigate than almost any other species, humans included.

MAGNETIC FIELDS

We have seen that bees have three navigational systems, all redundant, each necessary to fill in when the information for the others is unavailable. Have we reached the end? What happens under overcast in an environment without unambiguous landmarks—a forest, for instance, where every tree must look like every other to a creature as shortsighted as a bee? After all, bees live in trees and they evolved in tropical forests; the paucity of distinctive landmarks in such places may have been an important selective factor in their evolution. In fact, no one has ever tested forager orientation under these circumstances, though it would be easy enough to do so—on overcast days in the desert, for example.

If bees did turn out to have yet another backup, it would probably be magnetic. The system of last resort for homing pigeons under overcast and out of sight of familiar landmarks, for instance, is the earth's magnetic field. And, indeed, there is plenty of evidence that bees also sense the earth's field, though not that they use it as a compass while foraging.

The most clear-cut evidence is the orientation of comb in a new hive. After the swarm moves into an empty cavity, it must very quickly build several sheets of parallel comb to hold brood and food. The bees must

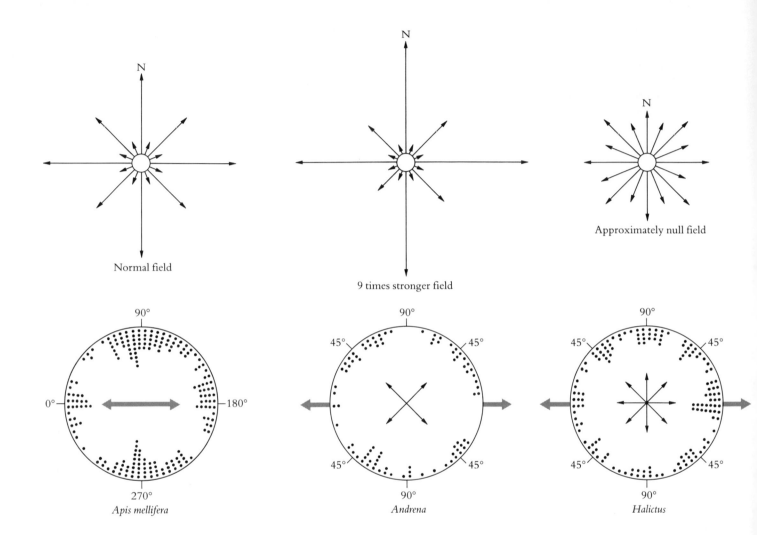

Normal field

9 times stronger field

Approximately null field

Apis mellifera

Andrena

Halictus

*Above, when forced to dance on a horizontal sur-
face with no visual cues, bees begin to orient
themselves to the earth's magnetic field. The
length of these arrows represents the number of
dances observed in each direction. Cancelling the
field eliminates the directionality, whereas
strengthening the field exaggerates it. Below, the
willingness to orient to meaningless cues is widespread among insects; these diagrams represent the
body orientation of bees simply standing in an
arena bathed in polarized light. The direction of
polarization is indicated by the orange arrows.*

agree on the direction in which to build, and apparently they have a
convention: the comb should run in the same direction as that in the old
hive. This direction is determined magnetically: if the field is rotated so
that magnetic north as felt in the new hive actually points east, the comb
will be aligned 90° from the direction used in the old hive. If a powerful
magnet is placed on the hive, producing a field that radiates in all directions, the bees build strange cylindrical comb never seen in nature.

Most of the other magnetic effects observed seem real but senseless.
For instance, bees forced to dance in a horizontal hive with no visual cues
will, after a week or two, begin dancing to the eight points of the com-

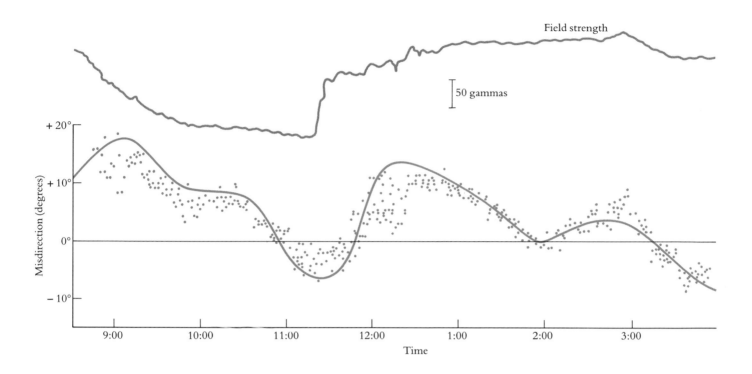

Field strength

50 gammas

The residual error in the dance is affected by the direction and change in the earth's field. The solid line through the dots (representing dance misdirections to a feeder over the course of the day) is the predicted direction based on a formula incorporating direction and the rate of change of the field.

pass; strengthening the magnetic field increases this tendency, whereas cancelling the field causes it to vanish. This orientation is of no use: the dance of a single forager will point in eight different directions over the course of many cycles, none of which necessarily corresponds to the direction actually flown in foraging. This "nonsense" orientation is actually fairly common among insects; bees and other invertebrates, for example, are likely to stand in one of four or eight orientations to polarized light.

Another pointless but interesting effect is seen in the normal dance on vertical comb. From the outset, von Frisch noted small but systematic errors in dance direction. All the foragers visiting a particular location would get the angle wrong by about the same amount; the size of the error would change in the course of the day, but the pattern of the errors was similar from one day to another. He tentatively concluded that there must be some built-in error in the gravity-measuring system of bees, but later, Lindauer discovered that the error vanished if the magnetic field felt in the hive was cancelled. Moreover, he discovered that the exact magnitude of these errors depended on how the strength of the earth's field varied.

A Helmholtz coil used to cancel the field in a hive.

We normally think of the earth's magnetic field as static: north is north. In fact, however, there are small variations. The earth's field arises from two sources. By far the largest is produced by the movement of the earth's molten interior; a smaller component is a consequence of atmospheric ions—charged particles—being swept around the earth by the jet streams. The movement of ions creates a magnetic field, and so this small atmospheric component contributes to the net field. The interior field is relatively constant (at least in terms of decades), but the atmospheric component changes as the jet streams move north and south in the daily cycle of warming and cooling. The result is a daily pattern of change in the field of strength. This change is small, averaging only a fraction of a percent of the total field, but bees apparently can sense it, at least as reflected by their dance errors. (Homing pigeons also appear to be affected by magnetic alterations of this magnitude; this sensitivity may be the basis for their ability to determine their location on the surface of the earth—a magnetic-map sense.)

A possible use for this extreme sensitivity is resetting internal clocks to correct for drift. For an animal that lives in a dark cavity, the usual cues—sunrise and sunset—may not be depended on. An ability to use the daily pattern of field variation would be quite useful. Lindauer finds that even subtle magnetic disturbances disrupt the time sense of bees, at least when they are isolated from the natural daily cycle of light and dark. How this sensitivity manages to interfere with the dance is another question.

We first became interested in magnetic sensitivity when Mike Brines discovered, quite independently, the magnetic orientation of horizontal dances performed in the dark. What might the sensor be? There are three possibilities: a permanent magnet (like a compass needle) that might rotate into alignment with the earth's field; an induction sensor (like a coil of wire, in which an electric current is induced when the coil moves through a magnetic field) and paramagnetism, a phenomenon by which a magnetic field induces a temporary field in another material. With two geologists (Joseph Kirschvink and Kenneth Deffeyes), the search began with various tests to see whether bees have any permanent magnetism.

Geologists have extremely sensitive devices for measuring magnetic fields. These superconducting magnetometers are used to determine the direction of the earth's field when a rock was formed; small magnetic particles incorporated in the rock are predominantly aligned with the field as it existed then, and these measurements can help reconstruct the changes in the field itself as well as the movement of the rocks or the continents they have been a part of since. To our surprise, honey bees can be quite magnetic, and that magnetism arises from magnetite, or lodestone, as it is more commonly known. The magnetic crystals (there can

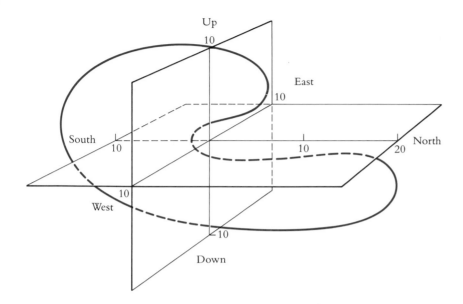

The normal daily pattern of change in the direction of the earth's magnetic field at Princeton during the winter. Units are gammas.

be millions of them) are formed during the pupal stage when the bee is no longer eating, and are concentrated in the front of the abdomen.

Subsequently, in collaboration with Charles Walcott, we discovered the same crystals in homing pigeons, and magnetite has since been identified in a variety of navigating creatures, including dolphins, tuna, salmon, and monarch butterflies. Later, we found that there were even more paramagnetic crystals of magnetite—crystals that have a steady magnetic orientation only in the presence of an external field such as the earth's. Behavioral tests indicate that these indirect detectors are the more likely candidates for sensing the earth's field strength. Theoretical calculations indicate that there are more than enough paramagnetic crystals to account for the reported sensitivity of honey bees, but the tests that will prove their role in honey bee navigation remain to be performed. The question of whether a magnetic compass is used during flight remains open as well.

CHAPTER *8*

Flower Learning

Many occasions in the life of a worker bee require learning. Guard bees, for instance, must learn and remember their colony's odor in order to identify strangers; unloader bees must remember the way from the dance floor to the storage areas and back. Most of the examples of learning that we have touched on so far, though, have concerned navigation. Foragers must learn which direction the sun moves and, if possible, commit to memory its path through the sky relative to prominent landmarks. Bees must remember the sun's current location in order to orient dances and foraging flights; they must learn the distances to various food sources as well, again both for dancing and for subsequent trips. Recruit bees must learn location and odor from the dancer. They must remember land-marks and form them into a mental map. The list goes on and on.

The first hint that honey bees could learn, however, had nothing to do with navigation. Aristotle noticed that each foraging bee is faithful to a

Forager in a learning experiment.

particular species of flower at a particular time, foraging solely on it and ignoring others. This sort of constancy requires learning enough about a flower to recognize it, and to distinguish its species from others. From this simple observation has come one of the most complete pictures we have of how learning and memory are organized to aid in guiding complex innate behavior.

COLOR

Von Frisch began his career by employing the methods of the great Russian physiologist Ivan Pavlov to investigate the sensory worlds of animals. In the course of his studies of digestion, Pavlov discovered that dogs began salivating for food *before* it actually appeared in the dish in front of them. The dogs had come to recognize certain noises that were associated with getting food, or certain sights, such as the appearance of the technician responsible for feeding, that *predicted* the arrival of food. Anyone who has a dog knows how good they are at recognizing the signs of an impending walk, such as the rattle of the leash. Even a pet guinea pig knows the sound of the vegetable peeler and an apple being sliced. This form of learning is now known as classical conditioning (or Pavlovian conditioning), to distinguish it from other kinds of learning discovered since. Von Frisch realized the value of classical conditioning for ethologists (zoologists specializing in animal behavior): if he could train an animal to respond to a cue that predicted food, this would prove that the creature could sense that signal.

The unpromising species von Frisch began with was the lowly goldfish, which he suspected could hear. He would play a note on his flute before each feeding and, in time, the goldfish would rise to the surface when the note was played, apparently expecting food. The logic as Pavlov described it was that, initially, an unconditioned stimulus—that is, an innately recognized cue, known as a "sign stimulus" to ethologists—would trigger an unconditioned response—an innate, automatic reaction that ethologists call a "motor program":

$$US \rightarrow UR.$$

By providing a novel conditioning stimulus just before the US, Pavlov could bring an animal to recognize this CS as predicting the US, and so to perform the response to it:

$$CS + US \rightarrow UR; \quad CS \rightarrow UR.$$

For the goldfish, food on the surface was the US, rising to eat it the UR, and the note on the flute the CS.

Unfortunately for von Frisch (but luckily for the study of bees), this discovery was ridiculed by the leading authorities on the sensory abilities of fish, who remained secure in the certainty that fish do not hear. In the face of this stonewalling by the zoological establishment, von Frisch turned his attention to honey bees, a species with fewer experts, and therefore with less dogma. To test for color vision in bees, a sense previously denied to insects, he performed essentially the same experiment he had tried with the fish. He trained a group of foragers to sugar solution in a watch glass that rested on a card of a particular color. After several visits by the bees, he removed the feeding dish and its card while the foragers were back at the hive and set out instead an array of cards with empty watch glasses. In some experiments, the cards were of many different colors; in others, he used an array of many shades of gray but with one card of the training color. He then observed where the returning foragers landed. The logic of a gray array was that if bees have black-and-white vision, they would confuse one of the shades of gray with the training card.

Except when he trained on a red card, von Frisch's bees landed preferentially on the card with the training color; red, however, was confused with dark gray, indicating that bees cannot see red as a color. On the other hand, von Frisch discovered during control experiments that his foragers *could* distinguish two cards that were the same standard shade of gray but that had been supplied by different manufacturers. He thought at first that there must be some difference in the odor of the cards, and that the bees were learning to recognize the olfactory stimuli, but this turned out not to be the case. Finally, he found the cue: one of the cards reflected more ultraviolet light, which is seen as a separate color by bees. This was a startling discovery; the prevailing viewpoint at the time (around 1910) was that our species, being the most highly evolved (by our standards, at least), was the best at everything; "lower" animals were, to a greater or lesser degree, sensory and intellectual cripples.

Although von Frisch's interest was limited to exploring the sensory abilities of bees, later researchers have studied color learning for its own sake, seeking to understand how bees acquire and use information about flower color. One student investigated *when* bees learn color. By allowing approaching foragers to see one color before landing, another while feeding, and yet another while circling during departure, she could offer a choice among the three hues when the bees returned, and see what was remembered. In fact, a forager remembers the color seen on its arrival at a food source. More precise measurements indicate that the last three

Bees remember the color seen in the last three seconds before landing. Colors visible at other times have little effect, as indicated by the bees' inability to choose the training color over a single alternative.

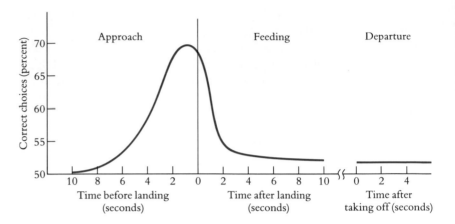

seconds before a bee lands are the crucial moments in the formation of color memory. That bees should remember the color seen *before* tasting the food is just what Pavlov would have expected: to be learned, a CS generally precedes a US.

Bees do not learn the color of a food source immediately. To determine the time course of the learning, we must train a bee to a colorless food source, and then add the color beginning with a certain visit. Learning is then tested by offering the forager a choice between two colors on a later trip, the color she has been trained on and an alternative. (The alternatives must be carefully calculated to be as inherently attractive to naive bees as the experimental ones. Attractiveness is determined by offering various alternatives to new recruits, who have no idea of the flower color. Then the relative intensities are adjusted until the bees choose them equally often.) By testing foragers after one, two, three, or some greater number of visits and recording the frequency with which they land on the correct color, we can trace the acquisition of color memory. Testing is always done with new feeders containing no food; we must be sure that bees are not cuing in on odors that they have left behind while feeding.

The general result of such tests is that, after feeding once on a training color (or, rather, seeing it as she arrived), a bee will choose it twice as often as the alternative. After three visits, she is able to make the right choice four times out of five; by eight visits she is up to better than nine out of ten, a level of accuracy no further amount of training can improve upon.

Although bees can learn any color that lies within their range of color vision, they learn some faster than others. This odd bias in learning is

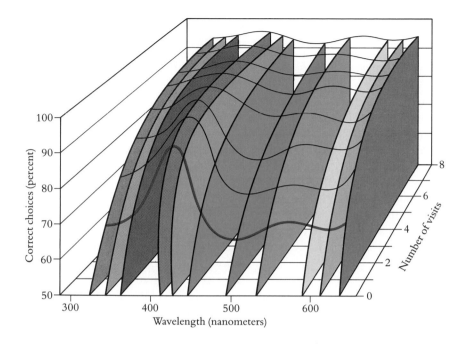

Wavelength (nanometers)

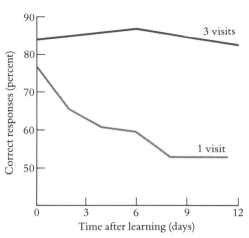

Time after learning (days)

Left, the color-learning curves for 11 wavelengths are combined here to emphasize how quickly violet is learned compared to green; the heavy red curve indicates the frequency of correct choice after one visit. Above, when a forager has visited a flower at least three times, she will remember its odor, color, shape, and location indefinitely without further visits—for the rest of her life unless she learns about a new flower available at the same time of day. If, on the other hand, she has visited the flower only once, her memory decays over about eight days, until she cannot reliably choose the correct flower over an alternative.

such that violet targets are committed to memory at the nine-out-of-ten level after only one visit; after three trips, accuracy saturates at 95%. Blue-green, on the other hand, is learned more slowly than any other color. These biases do not reflect anything as simple as the different sensitivities of the color receptors: neither violet nor blue-green corresponds to the three peaks of bee vision—UV, blue, and green.

The time course of memory acquisition is half the story; the other is forgetting. It makes no sense for a bee to remember the color of a flower unless it is a reliable source of food; once the species has stopped blooming, it probably pays to forget what was once a good kind of flower to harvest. As it happens, a bee that has visited a flower only once begins to forget about it two days later, and loses all trace by eight days; a forager that has fed three times, on the other hand, never forgets about the blossom unless it finds something new to visit at that time of day. The record for memory retention is held by a bee trained in autumn to a feeder; she stopped foraging when the cold weather came, and when she was tested the following spring, 183 days later, she still remembered the location and color of the training station.

Vertebrate memory is characteristically sensitive to disturbance in the first few minutes after something is learned or experienced; a blow to the head frequently wipes out the victim's memory of the events leading up

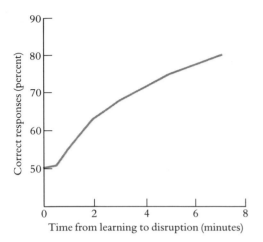

The sensitivity of a bee's memory to disruption is greatest just after learning (at which point she selects randomly between two patterns after being chilled or shocked), but rises steadily until, after seven minutes, trauma has no effect.

to an accident or assault. The usual interpretation of this widely studied phenomenon, known as retrograde amnesia, is that during the first few minutes, memory is in a sensitive form (known as short-term memory), most of which is forgotten automatically; we look up a phone number, remember it long enough to dial, and then forget it. The things we actually commit to long-term memory are processed before storage; after this consolidation period, memory is much less sensitive to shock.

Bees seem to have the same memory stages. When a bee is chilled or given electric shock within a minute of learning, the experience vanishes from her memory and she chooses later at random. If the disruptive treatment is delayed until about eight minutes after learning, the memory has been consolidated and is immune to shock or cold; the strength of the memory (as measured by the accuracy of the bee's choices) is intermediate for shorter delays. This time course for consolidation into long-term memory is similar to those found in rats, pigeons, and humans.

Although trauma is the usual way to block memory consolidation, other experiences do almost as well. We all know how easy it is to forget what we are thinking about when interrupted (particularly by children), and bees interrupt themselves when they revisit a feeder. If food is close to the hive and the forager does not pause to dance, she can return after only two to four minutes; revisiting during consolidation actually slows learning, even though she is being distracted with the same information.

The general pattern for color learning, then, is for the bee to note the color of the flower as she approaches and lands. She begins to consolidate that impression if she finds food there, and adds to the strength of the memory with subsequent visits up to a maximum of 95 percent certainty. If the bee undergoes no trauma at the critical moment and is not taught another color at the same time on a later day, the memory is permanent. The value of this system, obviously, is to enable the bee to recognize reliable sources of food as she wanders through a patch looking for additional blossoms to harvest.

ODOR

Von Frisch's original studies of odor learning were motivated by his desire to understand how recruitment works. He saw recruits approaching not only the feeder advertised by dancing in the hive, but the scent bottle that had been used to give odor to the food. He guessed that the recruits learned the odor when their antennae touched the body of the dancer; the scent of the food had been adsorbed onto the waxy hairs of the forager's body. Indeed, the odor need not have been in the food at all.

Once von Frisch trained foragers to collect droplets of sugar solution on cyclamen flowers, and placed a bouquet of cyclamen and another of phlox near by; 127 recruits found the choice pair, all of whom landed on the vase of cyclamen blossoms; all ignored the phlox, even though they found no food on the cyclamen bouquet. Nor need the foragers even touch the odor-producing surface directly; leaving the scent to evaporate from a piece of filter paper under the feeder, separated from direct contact with the forager by a piece of metal screen, worked at least as well as having the foragers actually walk on an odor-saturated surface. Odorless feeders and flowers, by contrast, are rarely found by recruits unless marked by foragers with scent-gland odor; indeed, odorless feeders elicit more Nasinov-gland exposure than those with highly scented solutions.

The olfactory "resolution" of bees was measured indirectly by von Frisch early in the century. He trained foragers to a particular tiny patch of flowers in a botanical garden; the flowers were baited with concentrated sugar solution. Even though some 700 species were in bloom, recruits were found only on the one kind of flower being advertised. Since each species has its own aroma, it seems likely that bees can learn to recognize the scent of a particular kind of flower with great accuracy.

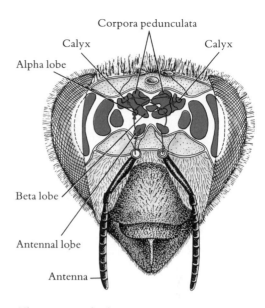

The anatomy of information processing during olfactory learning is traced here. The active site moves from the antennal lobe to the alpha lobe to the calyx.

Just as there are some colors bees learn faster than others, there are odors bees seem more willing to memorize. The scent learned most rapidly is geraniol, which is a pheromone, a component of the Nasinov-gland secretion. In general, though, any floral odor or bouquet of odors is learned quickly, whereas nonfloral scents take more time. So far as is known, though, *any* odor can be learned as a food cue, including the alarm pheromone and scents normally repulsive to bees (including the aroma of Lysol and the decay-like odor of butyric acid).

Thanks to the work of Randolf Menzel, a former student of Lindauer, we even know something of the anatomy of odor learning. Menzel developed a technique for training restrained bees: present an odor to one antenna, and a moment later touch the antenna with a drop of sugar water; the bee reflexively extends her proboscis to search for the food, and is fed. Very quickly, the odor alone elicits the proboscis extension. (This is simple classical conditioning: sugar water is the US, extension the UR, and the odor is the CS.) Menzel removed a piece of the bee's "skull" to expose the brain, and then tried chilling different bits of the brain with a cold needle shortly after training. He found that the sensitive site—the location where the active process of consolidation was taking place—actually moved as the interval after training increased. At first, only chilling of the olfactory lobe attached to the antenna used in training would disrupt the memory (as judged by whether the bee responded to the odor when it was presented later). This lobe receives the input from the antenna, processes it, and then passes it along to the brain. That this

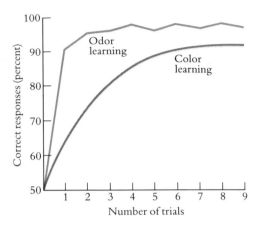

A typical odor is learned much faster than an average color.

activity goes on for almost two minutes before moving on was a surprise.

The next sensitive site is the alpha lobe of the mushroom body in the bee's brain, but only the one on the same side as the trained antenna. The mushroom body is a structure that is generally largest in the insects with the most complex behavior, and it has long been suspected to be important in learning. Chilling the alpha lobe in the first two minutes has no effect on later memory, nor does chilling after about four minutes; only during the two minutes in between does the memory processing appear to be taking place here.

The next way station is the calyx of the mushroom body, and at this point the memory is found on both sides of the brain; this means that now either antenna can sense the training odor and elicit a positive response. After six minutes, there is no place in the brain (at least, not near the surface) that chilling can block later memory; very likely, consolidation is now over, and the memory has been transferred into long-term storage.

Although bees learn both colors and odors as CSs, they do not learn them at the same rate. Odors are typically learned to a level of 90 percent correct choices after a single visit (geraniol to 95 percent, the alarm pheromone to 85 percent); the accuracy of choice increases to above 95 percent after four trips. An ability to use two cues to identify the species of flower being foraged is obviously an advantage, enabling the bee to be more accurate in her choices. Psychologists studying classical conditioning tended to use only one cue at a time, and so were somewhat surprised to find that different CSs are learned at different rates. Moreover, when psychologists did use two signals in conjunction (a procedure called compound conditioning), they assumed that the two cues would be equally salient to the animal. Honey bees demonstrate that this need not be the case: when the cues are separated, so that the returning forager can choose between the right color with the wrong odor and the correct odor with an unfamiliar color, the bee invariably selects the alternative with the training scent. These discoveries and others helped convince many psychologists that there can be powerful innate biases in learning. This phenomenon becomes even more obvious in other aspects of flower learning.

SHAPE

We can distinguish flowers not only by odor and color, but by their distinctive shapes; can bees do the same? The early work on this question suggested that shape learning was crude at best: bees could learn to dis-

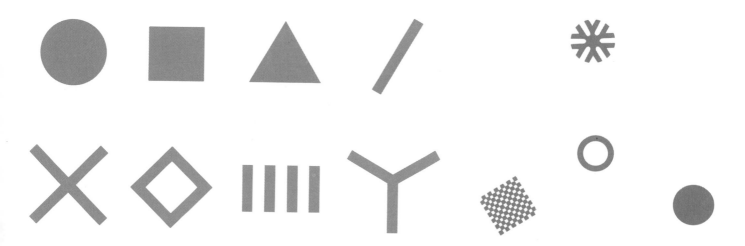

tinguish complex from simple figures, but could not be taught to distinguish two complicated shapes or two simple silhouettes from each other. The generally accepted conclusion for the next thirty or forty years was that bees could not remember shape pictorially as we do, but instead categorized objects as "busy" or "simple." The idea was that the bees sensed complexity in terms of the ratio of outline to area, so that a cross, which has a large perimeter but little area, was counted as complex, whereas a square of the same area, having a relatively short perimeter, was judged to be simple. Even when later researchers showed that the ability of bees to discriminate shapes was actually better than this, the results were interpreted to mean that bees stored not the shape but the actual value of this outline-to-area ratio (a quantity now usually referred to as "spatial frequency"—the number of edges per unit area).

Along with this crude nonpictorial memory, early workers discovered a strong spontaneous preference on the part of recruits to land on "busy" shapes. Offered a choice between a circle and a petal-like pattern, bees choose the artificial petals; confronted with the petals and the even more disrupted pattern of a checkerboard, recruits opt for the latter. This is a highly adaptive prejudice for recruits: leaving the hive, they know only the approximate location and the odor of the food; if they are not to waste time approaching every grass blade and stone to check for a floral scent, they must have some innate guidance. Bees understand that flowers are usually colorful, contrast well with their backgrounds, and have a high spatial frequency and a central UV-dark spot.

By the mid-1970s, it had become obvious that bees could learn to distinguish even similar shapes, and the innate preference for complexity was obvious in such tests. When foragers are taught to find food on a

Left, early experiments on shape learning suggested that, although bees could learn to distinguish any figure in the top row from any in the bottom, no two figures in the same row could be distinguished. Above, recruits are attracted to visually "busy" patterns—the checkerboard is preferred over the flower shape, the flower over the others.

Bees learn more complex shapes faster than simple ones.

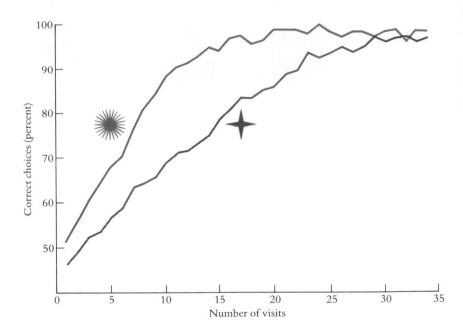

23-pointed figure, their choices reach 90 percent accuracy in 12 visits; when the training shape is a simple four-pointed star, by contrast, 22 trips are necessary. In either case, however, the eventual accuracy is almost the same, saturating at about 97 percent. The idea that bees remember only spatial frequency was modified to accommodate the discovery that bees can also take into account other factors including the angles of the lines in the figure, the proportion of different colors, and so on. But the basic idea remained dominant that bees store information in terms of a list of values—parameters—rather than as a picture.

The hypothetical parameter-based memory of bees (and, by extension, of insects in general) was enshrined as a major difference between vertebrates and invertebrates. Its imagined advantage was neural economy: less space in the small brain of an insect would be taken up by a short list of parameter values than by a picture. Consider how small an area is required in a newspaper for a classified ad listing the essential features of a car—its mileage, make, year, color, model, and so on; few car dealers and virtually no private sellers feel it is worth the space (which is to say, the money) to include a picture in their ads. Just as a brief description of a car would enable us to locate it even in a crowded parking lot with reasonable certainty, so, too, a short list of essential features could enable a bee to recognize the species she is specializing on among the limited range of flowers in the area.

Another line of evidence against pictorial memory is that bees fail to *generalize* shapes. Most vertebrates, when rewarded for responding to a pattern with a certain overall shape, will treat another pattern with the same general contour as similar—we tend to notice both the trees *and* the forest that comprises them. When bees are presented with the same kind of training and then tested on novel patterns, they refuse to make this leap: trained on a triangle composed of three smaller triangles, they showed no preference between a triangle composed of ten small triangles and a square composed of 25 smaller squares; they failed to generalize the outline. This is easily explained in terms of parameters: the spatial frequency of the training figure was much smaller than that of either of the test stimuli; neither matched well, and so the bees rejected both.

Though all these data seem reasonably convincing, and the hypothesis of a parameter-based memory is attractively counterintuitive, the experiments do not actually exclude pictorial memory. We first realized this when we were asked to write a review paper on honey bee learning, and so took the time to read the "Methods" section of the crucial papers—a part of scientific articles so obviously irrelevant to all but aficionados that it is usually printed in small, close type. Several questionable techniques and assumptions seemed to underlie the studies. For example, many of the experiments presented shapes on horizontal surfaces, which allowed the bees to circle and see the pattern from various angles rather than from a single orientation selected by the experimenter; since bees cannot twist their heads, a vertically presented pattern can be seen from only one perspective.

Another potential problem is that, in many cases, the bees were rewarded on one pattern in the absence of an alternative unrewarded pattern. Early psychologists discovered that rats behave as though they know almost nothing about the shape of a training pattern unless they also learn to avoid an alternative. (Learning that a cue predicts the *absence* of a reward is known as "conditioned inhibition"; our lab has discovered it to be very important in the process by which gull chicks come to recognize their parents, and we suspect that its role in natural learning has been seriously underestimated.) When a task is simply too easy during training, a rat learns only the slightest clue—the part of the shape in the lower right-hand corner, for instance. If bees also adopt this kind of intellectual short cut, memorizing only what are called "part figures" when the task is simple, they might well appear to be attending only to parameters.

On reflection, the failure of bees to generalize does not rule out pictorial memory either. The pervasive human impression that conscious visual experience faithfully represents whatever our eyes have seen is simply mistaken. From the moment a photon falls on a rod or cone in the retina,

Bees trained on the three-triangle triangle at the lower right and then asked to choose between a multi-square square and a multi-triangle triangle with more elements had no preference.

our nervous system begins a cascade of systematic distortions, exaggerating some features (edges, for instance) while suppressing others. Moreover, we know that the visual systems of different species focus on different cues—cats and toads, for example, are especially sensitive to movement and may not even notice static objects. Because of the way their visual system is wired, bees may well pay excessive attention to the interior details of an object, rather than to its overall shape.

Finally, most studies seemed to assume that if bees had pictorial memory, they would learn whatever they could see. Remembering all the visual details in a scene is known as "eidetic memory," and it is exceedingly rare; as far as we know, it has never been documented except in humans, and even then only in a handful of exceptional cases. It is easy to test oneself for eidetic memory: look at this page for a moment, close your eyes, and begin reading from memory starting with, say, the seventh line from the top. Or look at your bookshelf; if you are close enough, you can probably read any given title; now close your eyes and conjure up the spine of the third volume from the right on the second shelf. For nearly all of us, visual memory is of surprisingly low resolution; perhaps we can remember more different scenes as a result. In any case, requiring bees to have eidetic resolution in order to qualify for pictorial memory is simply not reasonable.

TESTING THE PARAMETER HYPOTHESIS

Distinguishing pictorial storage from a parameter-based system is not easy; almost any two patterns differ at least slightly in some parameter. Take a circular target divided horizontally into an upper and lower semicircle; imagine that one of our alternative patterns has a blue top half and yellow lower half, whereas the other is yellow on top and blue below. These two patterns have the same spatial frequency, color area, and line angles (a long horizontal line plus the circle as seen against the background), but they differ in the "polarity" of the color boundaries: one has a blue-above/yellow-below horizontal line, while the other has the reverse; the circle-background boundaries also differ. A bee storing these parameters could tell these two patterns apart without recourse to a pictorial memory.

The essential difference between parameters and pictures is that only a pictorial system necessarily records the spatial relationships between *noncontiguous* elements—that is, if a pattern consisted of two widely separated blue petals, with one above the other in one alternative while the other version had them side by side, no simple parameter would encode this difference. The test, then, is to offer patterns differing only in the spatial *arrangement* of the elements.

The actual experiment is a bit more complicated, and the details illustrate some of the problems and pitfalls in studying the learning of a species that is ready to use inadvertent cues to solve the problems experimenters pose. For example, though we offer both a training pattern with sugar solution and an alternative without food, it is important to put water in the latter pattern's feeder (a small plastic cylinder in the center of each artificial flower with several tiny holes through which the bees can feed); otherwise, the bees will learn to recognize which feeder has fluid in it, ignoring the pattern on the "flower." The patterns must also be switched back and forth so neither is consistently on the left or right; otherwise the bees learn to go to, say, the right-hand feeder regardless of pattern. During the course of training, some foragers become lazy, landing first at the pattern nearest the hive for a taste, and then moving to the other if there is only water at the first; this careless attitude must be eliminated by punishing the bee with a jet of air, a treatment that restores careful scanning of both alternatives before landing. It is also important to test only one bee at a time; otherwise, they wait for other hovering foragers to land, relying more on the behavior of their sisters than on their own memory. Finally, all testing has to be performed on fresh targets with empty feeders so that the bees do not use their own odors, left behind during training, as cues.

The actual device we used in these initial experiments was a rotating box with a pair of feeders on each of four sides. The patterns were painted on funnels or discs and plugged into the feeders. Two sides were

Each face of this device, used to train and test for shape/pattern learning, offers a choice of two artificial flowers. During training, the inner box is rotated between visits so that the rewarded pattern is not consistently on the right or left.

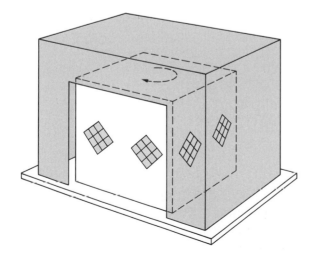

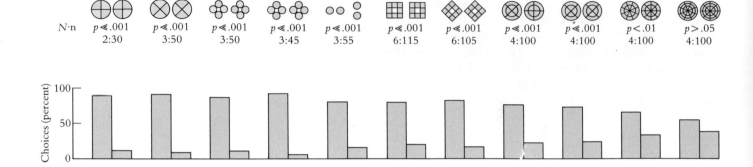

Bees were trained to the pattern shown here on the left in each pair. They were able to learn to distinguish any two patterns until the number of elements was increased to 24.

used for training, one with the reinforced pattern on the left (and the water-filled alternative on the right), the other with this arrangement reversed. After each visit of a forager during training, the box was rotated to present the other training side. During testing, one of the other two sides was rotated into view; one testing side had the reinforced pattern on the right, the other on the left, but all feeders were empty. A trained forager indicated her choice by simply landing on one of the alternatives. Finding no food, she would take off again, and one of the training sides could be rotated back for her to land on. To our total surprise, the bees had no trouble distinguishing patterns whose parameters were identical. Apparently bees do have pictorial memory after all.

RESOLUTION OF FLOWER MEMORY

Given that bees can store a pictorial representation of the flower being harvested, what is the resolution of the picture? We measured it by increasing the number of elements in the patterns until the foragers could no longer distinguish reliably between the reinforced and unreinforced "flowers." As the decision became more difficult, the bees adopted a characteristic behavior: they would approach the funnel and hover at its entrance, then move to the alternative and hover there; the bees would move from one to the other, studying each, and then land on one. Because the bees always hovered at the same point, it was possible to calculate just how large the elements in the pattern appeared to them while choosing. At the threshold of statistical significance (about 60 percent correct when 100 separate choices were analyzed) the individual elements of the pattern appeared to a hovering forager to be roughly 8° across; thus, the effective resolution of the bee's mental picture must be about 8°.

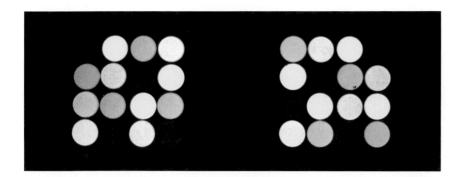

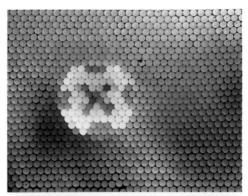

Above left, patterns used in tests to see if bees remember every element of a pattern. Above right, bees probably compensate for the low resolution of their flower memory (top) by simply flying closer to the target (bottom).

This is pretty grainy for a picture (roughly the width of the index, middle, and ring fingers together held at arm's length), and a far cry from the 1 to 1.5° (thumb-width) resolution of honey bee vision; no wonder earlier investigators were tricked into thinking bees could only remember in terms of parameters.

We worried that perhaps our bees were not actually using the entire pattern for matching; like lazy rats, they could be relying on only a piece of the pattern for making their choice—the upper center of the flower, for instance. We looked into this possibility by giving the bees a more difficult artificial flower: it consisted of 16 "petals" arranged in four rows of four petals each; the petals came in four different colors (four petals of each color per pattern) arranged randomly. As before, we trained by rewarding bees on one pattern while the alternative offered only water, but when we tested, the alternative pattern was new: it differed from the training pattern only in the color of certain petals.

As a result, if the bee remembered just one bit of the training pattern, then there was a good chance that the alternative offered during testing might be the same in that area, differing only in color elsewhere. Apparently bees do remember and use the entire pattern, since they were just as accurate at this task as they had been in the earlier tests. This experiment also showed that foragers can remember at least four colors; earlier researchers had thought that two might be the limit.

Given that bees remember the entire pattern, why is it that the flower picture they store is so crude? On the one hand, the less detailed the picture, the more separate photos a bee could store: an eidetic photo would require 28 to 64 times as much space as the low-quality picture they do remember. (The range of values reflects the variation in the resolution of honey bee vision, which is more detailed in the upper part of the eye.) On the other hand, the better the stored picture, the farther away a bee can identify the flower, and so the fewer false approaches she would be lured into making. There should be an optimum resolution, and our guess is that the ability of a forager to fly as close to a flower as she wishes allows her to use a very grainy picture for matching.

These experimental results opened the possibility that the alternative offered in training might serve no purpose. What if bees are simply more honest than rats, and so do not need a similar, unrewarded alternative to maintain their attention to detail? There are two ways to ask this question: First, we can repeat the experiment without the alternative to see if they learn just as well. A second method is to run the experiment normally, but then test with a *novel* pattern and the unrewarded alternative experienced during training; in this case, the forager should actually *avoid* the familiar pattern because she has learned (through conditioned inhibition) that this "flower" is always filled with water, whereas she knows nothing ill of the new one. In fact, both approaches demonstrate that bees learn from their mistakes, remembering the bad or indifferent as well as the good.

TIMING AND HIERARCHY

When do bees learn about shape—as they arrive at a flower or during departure? An experiment performed six decades ago suggested that the approach phase is more important, but that work used the same inadequate techniques that had led to the parameter theory. The trick here is simply to train with one shape visible before landing and another after. To switch the patterns quickly without disturbing the bee, we projected the flower patterns from slides onto a ground-glass screen mounted on a box. The images were projected from within the box so that the bee would not be confused by her own shadow. One slide had a three-petal pattern on the right and a four-petal one on the left; the other reversed the arrangement. One pattern was chosen for reinforcement. The left-right positions of the patterns seen on approach were alternated as usual, and the left-right position of the rewarded alternatives as well, by using two ground-glass sides of a rotating box. In either case, one pattern was always seen on arrival, the other on departure.

The results are clear cut: the approach pattern is the only one remembered. Again, this is just what we would expect from classical conditioning, but this CS is acquired more slowly than either color or odor.

Not only is shape learned more slowly, but it occupies a lower position on the hierarchy of cues used by foragers to decide whether the flower is of the same species already visited. Only when both the color *and* odor are correct does the shape become crucial. This is not to say that

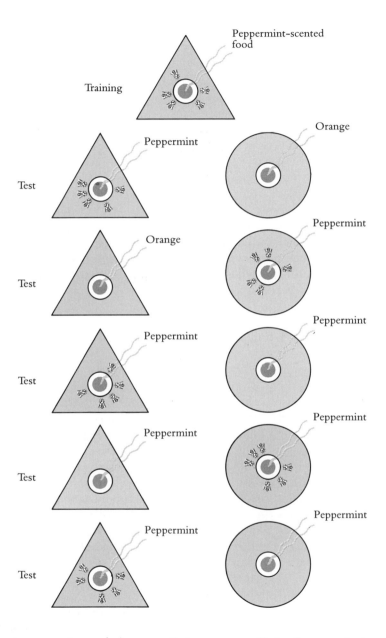

Training

Peppermint-scented
food

Test — Peppermint

Orange

Test — Orange

Peppermint

Test — Peppermint

Peppermint

Test — Peppermint

Peppermint

Test — Peppermint

Peppermint

The hierarchy used in selecting between flowers is illustrated in this series of tests. The bees are trained to a blue, triangular, peppermint-scented feeder, and in subsequent tests the correct cues are separated between two alternative targets.

bees ignore color and shape until they can smell the flower; obviously, the visual cues will usually be encountered first and used to guide the approach. By the time the bee can sense the flower's odor, then, she has all three cues at her disposal; it is at this point that the hierarchy is invoked.

Above, shape and color vary within a species. These domesticated daffodils show how far this variation can go. Below, some flowers are bilaterally symmetric—that is, they look like their mirror images.

In some sense, this innate prejudice matches the variability of flowers in the natural world. Odor is a very reliable species cue; lilacs always smell like lilacs. Color is subject to more variation: lilacs can be purple, violet, pink, or even white; moreover, the apparent color of a cluster of flowers depends on their age, the background (a well-known "context" illusion common to both humans and bees), and the ambient lighting—the color quality of light is different at dawn from that at midday, on cloudy days and sunny ones, and in the green shade of a tree as opposed to out in the open. Shape recognition requires the highest latitude: not only is there natural variation in shape (compare two lilac clusters), but the apparent shape of even one blossom depends on whether you are looking at it from above, the side, or head on. Shape also changes with different stages of petal opening, not to mention wind and herbivore damage. Bees, fortunately, do not need to work out these relative reliabilities through trial and error; they know about them in advance and are led by what we could call a "matching program" to weight their comparisons in a particular (and very sensible) order.

MATCHING FROM MEMORY

There are also matching rules governing the operation of shape memory itself. It is well known from experiments on vertebrates (humans included) that there is a nearly universal tendency to "confuse" left and right—that is, to recognize a shape or an object's mirror image automatically as the thing itself. Children, for instance, have great difficulty initially distinguishing a lowercase d from a lowercase b, but no tendency to confuse either with a p. We must learn to suppress this innate "ambiguity" in order to read: for many of us, left-right mistakes persist in other contexts well into adulthood. Some authors have argued that this automatic reversal is the inevitable consequence of a bilateral nervous system, though why this should be so has never been adequately explained. It can also be understood in terms of selection: is mirror-image ambiguity a net advantage or disadvantage to animals in general? Given that food is usually either bilaterally symmetrical—that is, the object looks just like its mirror-image reversal—or looks like its mirror image when facing the other way (as a deer facing left versus the same creature facing right), an ability to generalize from one perspective to its reverse ought to be a useful learning shortcut for any species not dependent on a written language.

Flowers are almost always bilaterally symmetrical, and so both the bilateral-nervous-system argument or the adaptionist hypothesis would predict that bees should confuse left and right. On the other hand, the

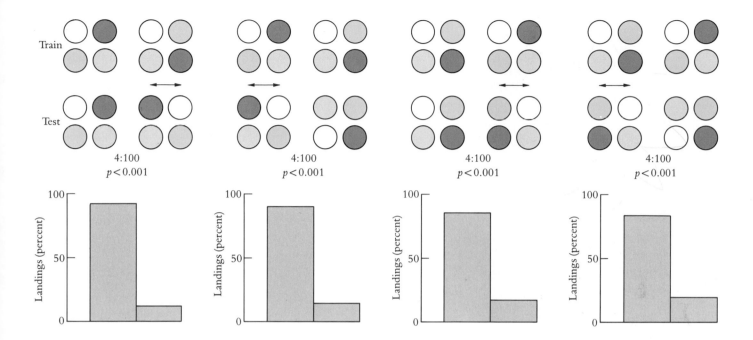

In each of these pairs of patterns, the rewarded training pattern was the one on the left. Bees can distinguish a training pattern from its mirror image, but will accept the reversed pattern ($\leftrightarrow$) if the correct one is not available.

pictorial-memory results notwithstanding, insects are supposed to be so different from vertebrates—different in kind rather than degree—that the nervous-system generalization might not apply (the visual fibers in vertebrates cross to the side of the brain opposite from the part of the world being looked at, but in insects they do not). When tested, as usual, neither of these hypotheses proved correct.

In the experiment, foragers were trained to find food on a four-petal, four-color pattern, with an alternative offering only water; the bees quickly learned this discrimination. The test then offered the original pattern and its mirror image, neither with food. If bees have a left-right ambiguity, they should be unable to discriminate the two patterns. In fact, they were just as good at choosing the correct "flower" as when they were tested against the original, randomly selected alternative used in training.

Does this mean that bees are totally different from vertebrates? We tried the test in another way: this time, instead of offering the correct pattern against its reversal, we offered the reversal versus a novel pattern. In this version of the experiment, the bees went overwhelmingly for the mirror image. Apparently, bees store flower pictures as they see them, and prefer a perfect match, but when the learned pattern is not available

Flowers with radial symmetry.

they automatically recognize a left-right reversal as close enough, and opt for it.

This result is at odds with the notion that left-right ambiguities are automatic consequences of brain organization. It calls into question the techniques used in many experiments on vertebrates in which an animal is trained to respond to a pattern—for human infants, to the point of boredom. The subject is then offered the mirror image, and if it continues to respond (or becomes increasingly bored) the animal is judged unable to tell the reversal from the real thing. By this test, however, bees would appear to have a total left-right ambiguity; only when they are offered a *choice* does the true nature of their matching/recognition system become obvious.

Flowers, one of the few classes of objects that bees must recognize, are also often radially symmetrical—that is, a rotation of some number of degrees up to 180° leaves the pattern unchanged. A cross with equal arm lengths can be rotated 90° or 180° and still look the same; a tulip can be rotated 120° with no change; zinnias and marigolds can be rotated through a series of small steps with no obvious alternation in appearance. Other flowers cannot, especially the the blossoms of the lupine family and similar flowers—sweet peas, for instance, and snap dragons and clover. Can bees accept a rotated pattern as the one they have learned, or must flowers keep a constant orientation in order to be recognized by their pollinators?

Some animals do, in fact, have what appear to be rotational ambiguities. When pigeons are trained on an outline always presented in a consistent orientation and then asked whether a new figure has the same shape, their ability to recognize similarity is not affected by rotation: the response time required to respond positively to a 60°, 90°, or 120° rotation is the same, and identical to the time needed to react to an unrotated copy. For humans, on the other hand, reaction time rises in direct proportion to the degree of rotation—a 30°rotation requires longer than an unrotated figure, and 120° takes even longer to identify. We must actually turn an outline in our minds to see if it matches; the nervous system of pigeons does this instantly and automatically.

To see in what ways bees have been endowed by their evolution, we can train them to one pattern—a four-petal, four-color artificial flower again—and then offer both a 90° rotation and a novel pattern. In testing, the bees clearly tell us that they know nothing about either. In some way, then, bees are more like people than pigeons. The adaptive value of a rotational ambiguity for pigeons is clear: these seed eaters view food from above that is lying on the ground, and a seed, by its nature, is an object whose orientation is irrelevant. For early humans, who survived by hunting antelope and small game, on the other hand, an ability to recognize one of these creatures upside down would be of little use. Indeed, given how hard a motionless antelope is to see in the first place, a propensity to spot certain distinctive features against the backgrounds they have evolved to match (an ability that makes our species an excellent hunter) would lead to a lifetime of false alarms if our brains had evolved to accept prey-like patterns automatically in any orientation.

A rotational ambiguity like that of the pigeons would be of little use to bees when flowers are oriented vertically, as the majority are. But where *horizontal* flowers are concerned, it would be an advantage for a bee to be able to recognize a blossom when approaching from a new angle, particularly if the flower lacked radial symmetry. Just to be safe, then, we decided to test for rotational ambiguity with horizontal targets. Since bees regularly circle feeders and so get to see the pattern from any and all perspectives, we constructed a translucent box that allowed foragers to see the pattern from only one quadrant; their access to a view from the other 270° around the target was blocked by thin netting. After training, they were offered a choice between fresh copies of the previously rewarded pattern and its water-filled alternative, both rotated 180° to provide a novel perspective. The bees now had no trouble recognizing the correct pattern. Apparently the bees' matching circuitry operates according to context, searching for rotational matches only when appropriate. As far as we know, this kind of sophistication in the neural machinery for recognizing a familiar object is unknown outside honey bees.

There are other questions that one could ask the foragers. For example, humans have an ability known as size constancy: we can recognize familiar objects at many distances. Our matching circuitry does not require an object to occupy the same amount of space on the retina during both learning and recognition. It is not known whether bees are similarly equipped, or whether they can identify a flower as familiar only when, in approaching it, they hit the precise distance from which their original "photo" was taken.

Many animals also have object constancy—an ability to recognize a familiar object when it has been rotated obliquely into a unique orientation, presenting a side the animal has never seen before and can therefore only "hypothesize." Can bees perform this trick as well, or must they circle until they find the familiar point of view? Only aggressive experimentation will tell whether their minuscule brains are capable of feats that still resist the best attempts of defense researchers, who are working with (thus far) little success to devise a circuit that can recognize a tank in a field or a fighter on a runway from any distance and perspective, and target them for destruction.

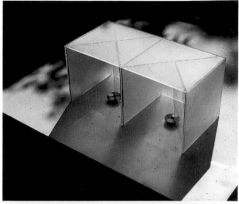

Above, device for testing whether bees can recognize a horizontal pattern from a novel perspective; the netting keeps the forager from viewing the training target from the back. Below, the shape of flowers varies according to the perspective of the bee.

LANDMARKS

In addition to a flower's odor, color, and shape, it has a location. As we have seen, bees have two perspectives on location: a site has a certain distance and direction, which is the data transmitted in the dance, and it has a certain relationship to nearby landmarks, information that becomes increasingly important to experienced foragers. Early on, von Frisch realized that bees see and react to familiar landmarks long before they can make out the feeder itself; these markers can be used to guide a bee in the last stages of its journey until it gets close to the target, much as a pilot emerging from an extended period above the clouds uses landmarks such as roads, towns, and lakes to home in on an airport.

The first experiments on how bees use landmarks near a food source yielded very curious results. When a forager was trained to find an inconspicuous feeder (perhaps a tiny hole drilled in a flat board and filled with sugar solution) that had been surrounded with landmarks, she would search accurately after several visits, and she would look in the same place relative to the markers even if the whole array had been moved away from the food hole. This was not too surprising: Niko Tinbergen had shown the same ability on the part of a species of digger wasp that captures and kills honey bees and must find the entrance to her underground burrow after a successful hunt. The odd thing is what the bees do when they return to a landmark array that has been altered.

If a bee matched her memory of the surrounding landmarks as they appeared from the food source—a pictorial panorama—with what she saw on her return, we would expect that removing some of the markers altogether would have little effect; after all, she could still match the remaining ones. But when all the landmarks on one side were removed, foragers inevitably searched closer to the remaining ones. If they were matching to a stored photo, this would seem likely to produce a very poor congruence.

On the basis of these data, Alun Anderson, who had performed the first experiments about 1970, proposed a memory system in many ways analogous to the simple parameter-based scheme for flower memory. He suggested that, rather than remembering pictorially, bees might simply recall whether particular sectors of the horizon as seen from the food source had landmarks. Such a system would register not the shape, number, or color of landmarks, but merely a yes-or-no record of horizon-sector "occupancy." As a result, removing the landmarks on one side of a food source *would* require a forager to move closer to the remainder in order to fill up the same number of sectors. The experiments did not establish the number or size of the sectors a bee might divide its world into (though four appeared to be the minimum), nor did it rule out the

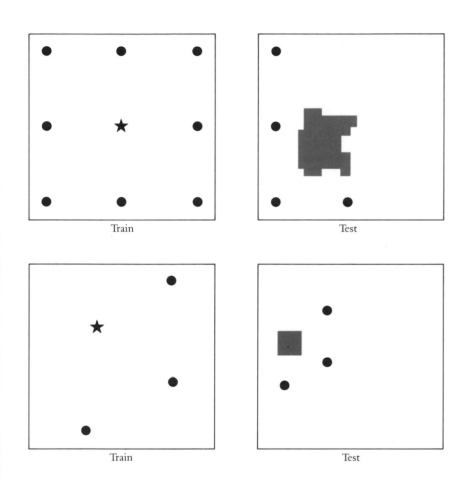

Train

Test

Train

Test

In one set of experiments (top), bees were trained to find food (star) in the center of a landmark array (painted wooden cylinders standing upright on a board); when some of the markers were removed, they searched closer to those that were left. (The colored area shows where they landed.) In another set of tests (bottom), the size of the array was altered; the foragers looked in the spot from which the landmarks could be seen to lie in the same direction as during training.

possibility that the data for each sector might include color or spatial frequency.

About a decade later, another group reported experiments that strongly suggested to them not only that bees have a photographic memory of landmarks, but that it is actually eidetic. They trained the bees to a food source that had three markers off to one side, and then altered the size or spacing of the landmarks (or both). Their bees searched in the same relative location, as though triangulating on the landmarks; hence, when the spacing was increased, the foragers searched for the inconspicuous food source farther away, at about the distance from which the markers would appear to have the same *angular separation* they had when the bees had seen them during training. Again, there was no test for an ability to remember shape or color, nor was there any measure of the

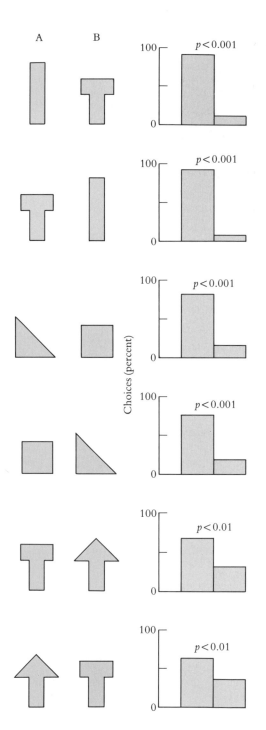

resolution—a piece of data that would be essential to support the re-markable claim of eidetic memory. In fact, it seems entirely possible to account for these data on the basis of sector occupancy, as long as we require a minimum of eight sectors: when the spacing of landmarks is increased, a sector-attuned bee will have to move farther away to get the proper sectors filled.

We decided to actually measure the resolution of landmark memory, to see if there was any truth to the crude but plausible sector hypothesis. Our training device consisted of a piece of white plexiglas with 225 tiny holes drilled in a 15-by-15 array. Unscented food was placed in one, and the foragers had to find it by using various artificial "landmarks." The location of the food-filled hole, therefore, always bore the same relation to the landmarks, though it could be anywhere on the plexiglas sheet.

After each visit, the food had to be moved (and the landmarks along with it) or else the bee would learn to search in the same general area of the board and ignore the training stimuli. After several visits, we would set out two alternative landmark arrays and allow the bees to choose; if a forager selected the right one, she obviously had remembered that cue. So, for example, when we used upright blue cylinders during training and then offered both blue and yellow markers during testing, the unerr-ing choice of the blue array told us that bees remember the color of the landmarks. (Well, not quite: bees might have a spontaneous preference for blue. To be sure, we had to repeat the experiment with yellow land-marks during training and then offer a choice between blue and yellow sets during testing. All the learning experiments described in this chapter have been run in reciprocal pairs in case of such a bias.)

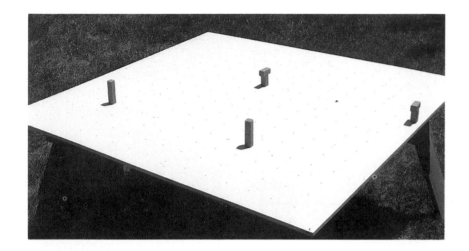

In tests of landmark memory, foragers were trained to find food by using certain landmarks, regardless of where they happened to be on the training board (photograph on facing page). They were then presented with a choice between two arrays (photograph at left). Results of landmark-learning tests (margin of facing page) indicate that bees remember the color and shape of markers. In this shape test, the bees were trained using the markers in column A and then tested with a choice between those and the markers in column B. The third column shows the percentage of correct and incorrect decisions.

Next we tried shape, using alternatives of equal size (as seen from the food hole). When the markers were large, the bees did very well, clearly remembering shape (even when all the possible parameters were equalized), but when the differences became subtle, errors began to creep in. By systematically varying size, we were able to measure the resolution of landmark memory: to be noticed, a feature must be at least 3.5° wide. This is much cruder than the bees' real-time vision (1° to 1.5°), which means that the memory is not really eidetic. More interesting, the resolution is much better than that of flower memory (about 8°), which means (as researchers have always assumed, though with no proof) that flowers and landmarks are remembered separately, rather than as part of a combined, all-purpose panorama.

If bees have a medium-resolution pictorial memory of landmarks, how did they manage to convince anyone that they relied on sectors? The results themselves are correct: when we repeated the original experiment, our bees, too, searched closer to the remaining landmarks. But what if the foragers were getting landmarks confused with one another, mistaking one of the remaining markers for one that had been removed? Perhaps they were matching selectively rather than looking for the best overall fit to the entire pattern. We tested for this by repeating the experiment with two different landmark colors—blue and yellow—alternated with each other in the array. Now when one side of the array of landmarks was removed, the bee's moving closer to the rest would result in a color mismatch. And, in fact, when any possible ambiguity is eliminated through the use of color, returning bees search accurately even with a partial array.

When the landmarks surrounding a food source are all quite similar (top row), bees trying to use a partial set get confused, using some of the remaining ones as though they were ones now missing. (Numerals indicate number of landings at each spot.) When the experiment is repeated using landmarks of two different colors (bottom row), so that this sort of mix-up is not possible, the bees orient correctly.

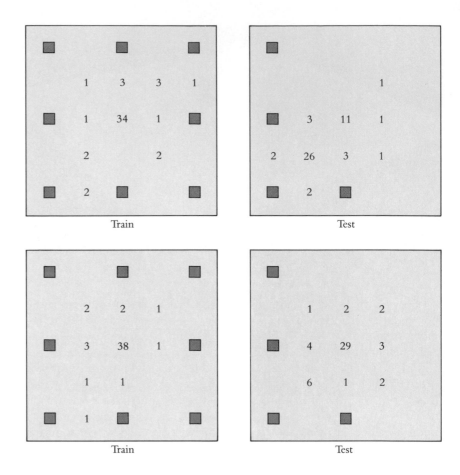

The confusion of the bees in the original experiment tells us something about how these insects are programmed to perform landmark-based triangulation: just as human navigators choose the most widely separated landmarks to take bearings from (in order to reduce the influence of measurement errors), so too bees focus on well-spaced markers, ignoring missing intermediate landmarks—indeed, not even noticing their absence.

That bees' pictures of flowers and landmarks are of different resolutions is not really surprising. A bee can always fly as close as she likes to a flower to see if it is the right one, but she does not enjoy this luxury when using landmarks: the essential details must be stored for use at the food site, since flying closer to a landmark for a better look takes her away from her goal. Everything she is going to use must be used at the

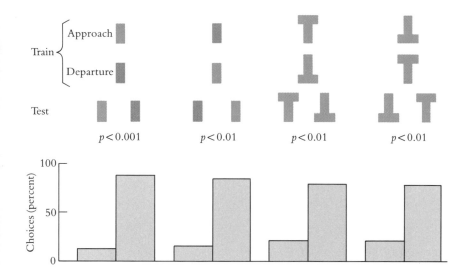

Bees learn the shape and color of landmarks when they leave the food.

correct site, and every bit of resolution is potentially helpful. That the actual resolution of landmark memory is two to three times worse than real-time vision (and so requires four to nine times less space to store) indicates that there really is a limitation to the amount of visual data that a bee can accommodate in its brain.

Another question that suggests itself is *when* in the cycle of approach, feeding, and departure bees learn landmarks. This can be studied by simply changing the color or shape of the markers while the bee is feeding, and then offering both alternatives when she returns. The answer is that it is during the circling flight *after* feeding that landmarks are committed to memory. This reinforces our impression that shapes and landmarks are learned separately: not only do they have different resolutions, they are photographed at different times. In theory, classical conditioning does not permit animals to learn CSs after the fact, but wherever this seems the best way to do it, animals are programmed that way. These departures from the usual pattern help to remind us that natural selection invented learning, not vice versa; the usual CS-then-US pattern is not a law imposed on nature, but rather the result of evolution of the optimal temporal relationship for the task at hand. Usually, the CS *must* precede the US if it is to be predictive for future encounters, but when it is there *after* the US as well as before it, it cannot matter when the learning gates are opened. It may be that the foraging honey bee simply cannot take two pictures at once, and must wait until she departs to snap the second shot.

CHAPTER 9

Programmed Learning

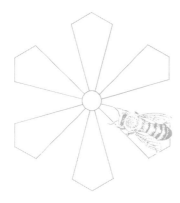

In looking at what bees remember about flowers, a subtle but consistent theme is how prearranged much of the learning seems to be. There are sensory biases wired into the system, such as the ones that ordain that bees will learn violet faster than green, multi-petal targets sooner than circles, and so on. Preexisting neural arrangements store low-resolution flower shapes and medium-resolution landmarks. The bee is also wired to time its course of learning in advantageous ways, so that it learns color and shape before landing and landmarks afterwards. Its object-matching systems are sensibly arranged to accept mirror images in a pinch, rotations only when a blossom is oriented horizontally. This innate "preparation" for learning runs counter to traditional psychological notions, which stress the flexibility of the learning process. In fact, honey bees often seem to learn in the manner of a computer program, pausing for input at prearranged steps in the program. What is the evidence that bee

A gull chick pecks at the red spot on an adult gull's beak.

learning is guided innately to solve predictable problems? Is this strategy of instinctively orchestrated learning unique to insects, or is it a hidden theme underlying the behavior of animals in general?

TIME

Bees have a time sense, which they use to compensate for the movement of the sun in their dancing and navigation. They also use their mental clocks to keep track of when flowers of a particular species are open and secreting nectar. A bee taught that food is available from a feeder during a particular hour of the day will return to the feeder about the same time the next day. If we continue the training for a week and then leave the feeder empty, the bee may check the source once or twice at other times of day when she has nothing better to do, but will make repeated, fruitless visits beginning perhaps 15 minutes before the regular feeding time and ending about 15 minutes after it is normally over.

In psychology, this propensity to remember something best 24 hours after it has been learned is called the *Kamin effect;* honey bees and certain other nectar foragers carry this tendency to an extreme. For instance, if we train bees to a blue, triangular, peppermint-scented feeder from 9:00 to 10:00 A.M., and then to a yellow, circular, lemon-scented feeder

After training to two different patterns at two times of day, foragers offered both simultaneously will nevertheless continue to favor the one they fed from at that time during training.

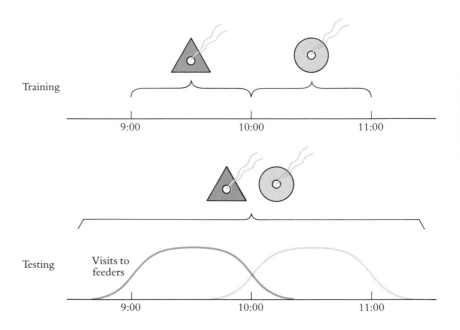

in the same location from 10:00 to 11:00 (repeating the training every day for four or five days), foragers become committed to this pattern. On the next day we can set out *both* feeders side by side, each filled with sugar solution, and watch the bees as they visit. Foragers will begin arriving about 8:45 and land exclusively on the blue triangle; the yellow circle—the more recently visited feeder of the two—will be ignored. At about 9:45, however, foragers will begin to switch to the yellow circle, and by 10:15 the blue feeder, still well stocked with sugar water, will have been abandoned. More amazing still, by about 11:15 virtually all the foragers will give up foraging at the site, even though both feeders continue to offer food.

It is as if the memory of foragers were organized like an appointment book, with "blue peppermint triangle at site X" written on all the lines between 9:00 and 10:00 A.M., and "yellow lemon circle at site X" entered on the blanks from 10:00 to 11:00; by 11:15, the foragers have moved on to other appointments. This idea is consistent with the curious observation that a forager cannot be taught that two kinds of flowers provide food at the same time of day. If we alternate the color of a feeder between visits, the bee does not learn that food may be found on either yellow circles or blue triangles from 9:00 to 10:00 A.M., but rather acquires no preference whatsoever for color or shape, and is just as willing to land on novel shapes and hues as the ones that she has been feeding from. It is as if the entry spaces in her mental appointment book had room for only one set of characteristics, and somehow the contradictory information precluded any storage.

The nature of this interference when the training patterns are alternated becomes clear in another experiment. If we train a forager for several days to the blue, triangular, peppermint-scented source, then she can unerringly select the odor, color, or shape whenever we offer a choice of individual cues. But if we then change just one component—the odor, say, which we might switch to anise, leaving the rest of the feeder the same—the bee no longer recognizes the color or the shape and must relearn all the cues. Apparently, one change is interpreted as a wholly new flower, and the entire entry is erased. When we alternated flowers, then, each new pattern erased all memory of the previous one. It is not that *additional* information triggers erasure: adding odor after training foragers to an unscented blue triangle does not disturb the color and shape memory. Empty spaces on the appointment book's entry lines may be filled in, but erasing any part of the entry to substitute one piece of data for another expunges the entire line.

Nor is this time-linked memory system restricted to classical conditioning, which is a matter of learning to recognize something on the basis of a new cue—a nectar-rich flower by its odor, color, shape, and location, for instance. The other major form of learning discussed by most psychologists is *operant conditioning*. This second kind of learning involves the creation of a *novel behavior* to solve a problem—that is, learning to *do* as opposed to learning to *recognize*. When a rat is taught by an experimenter to press a lever to obtain food, the behavior (the operant) is novel (as opposed to innate, like the Unconditioned Response of classical conditioning) and is discovered by the rat through trial and error—that is, it learns from its successes and mistakes as it solves the problem of how to get food or avoid danger. Similarly, when a chickadee learns how to open a sunflower seed efficiently it is benefitting from its own errors, discovering what works and what does not, eventually solving the problem so well that it can hull a sunflower seed in seconds.

This sort of trial-and-error learning is a major part of a honey bee's life: every flower has its own morphology, requiring a particular approach pattern and a special set of leg and proboscis movements to get to and at the nectar. From their experiences with a series of blossoms, foragers become more and more efficient at harvesting a species. Indeed, this may be one reason they specialize; as the famous economist Adam Smith pointed out in the eighteenth century, it is more efficient to perform one task over and over than to switch back and forth. We wondered if the memory of how to harvest a blossom would be stored in a time-linked manner as well, available to the bee only at particular times of day, or if the harvesting technique might instead be indexed by flower shape or odor, and therefore be at a forager's disposal whenever it might be needed.

We attacked this question by building a device that could teach a bee how to land on and feed from flowers. Our plastic blossom consisted of six long petals radiating from a plastic feeder. The task for the forager was to learn *which* petal to land on (and with it the behavior necessary to alight on the proper one). Normally, bees will land on the bottom petal of a vertical flower (and fully 56 percent of naive recruits chose this one to settle on), so to get rid of any innate bias we insisted that foragers use the lower right petal in one experiment, and the lower left one in another. To land on either of these floral runways, a bee must make a noticeable turn and swing its body out into alignment with the petal.

We convinced them that they really wanted to land on the petal we had selected by punishing them (frightening them, actually) for mistakes. Behind each petal was a solenoid connected to a control panel a short distance away; when a bee alighted on an incorrect petal, an observer pushed the button corresponding to that petal, current flowed to the solenoid, the rod of the solenoid extended instantly, and the bee was knocked violently off that part of the "flower." Foragers quickly learned

A device for studying operant learning by bees. Above, a solenoid behind each petal flips off bees that land in the wrong way. Below, a bee landing, at an angle, on the correct petal.

which petal was safe, and how to land on it gracefully and precisely, walk to the center, and feed.

In one experiment we used a yellow "blossom" with flat-ended petals and a blue alternative whose petals had pointed ends. Bees were trained to land on the lower right petal of the blue flower from 9:30 to 11:00 A.M., and then the lower left petal of the yellow flower from 11:00 to 12:30. When tested without punishment on a later day, the foragers selected the correct petal of the correct flower more than 80 percent of the time (versus 9 percent for new recruits). This tells us that they can learn to land on particular petals of particular flowers, but not whether color, shape, or time is the storage key.

To find out which way bees "index" flower-handling techniques, we repeated the experiment but used only the blue flowers; before 11:00 A.M., foragers had to land on the lower left petal, while afterwards it had to be the lower right. Now when tested on a later day, bees could not use differences in color or shape to decide how to land; instead, when they began to arrive at or just before 9:30, they could opt for their most recent experience on a flower of this color or shape, which had been the lower right from 11:00 to 12:30 the previous day, or they could rely on

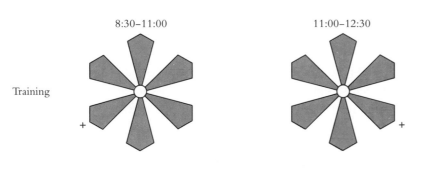
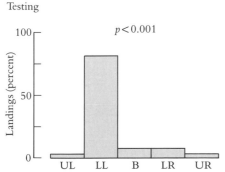
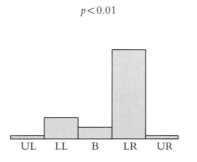

Bees will land on a target in the same way they landed at that time on the previous day. (A + indicates the petal to which the bees had been trained.)

their memory of what landing technique was appropriate at that time of day—the lower left petal. The bees overwhelmingly chose the time-linked option, indicating that operant learning is also stored according to time of day.

ALPHA CONDITIONING

Compared to the level of detail at which we know what bees learn and how they store different cues, we have little information about how individual cues are processed before being entered into the appointment book. How, for instance, is information from the color-sensitive cells in the eyes combined before being transmitted to the storage matrix? How is the data from the many more different types of olfactory receptors integrated to produce something useful to be remembered? The nature of cue storage is the Holy Grail of modern neuroethology, and perhaps bees have something to tell us that could help unravel this mystery of mysteries. What little we do know points toward a strategy not unlike that used for scoring standardized tests.

It is very difficult to investigate what is actually going on inside the neurons in a bee's brain: to record from neurons, experimenters must immobilize the bee and insert delicate electrodes into its brain. The learning task must be simple and not require flight, so odor learning is commonly used. Even so, the cells are very small, and the brain moves slightly every time the bee extends its proboscis to tell you it has learned; this movement in time dislodges the electrodes, so any experiment must be quick. Despite all these problems, one of Randolf Menzel's students has recorded from a few neurons in the antennal lobe before and after learning, and has discovered a most interesting phenomenon: the only cells that show learning—that is, fire rapidly after training when the learned odor is presented—are neurons that have a slight response to that odor *before* training, and also react well to sugar on the antenna.

This suggests something about how at least odor memory is organized in bees: neurons in the antennal lobe learn only when they are already wired in to the US *and* CS before training. In retrospect this makes sense; how can a cell learn if it does not already receive input from the two cues to be associated? In psychology, learning when there is a slight innate response to the CS is called *alpha conditioning;* learning serves to amplify a preexisting propensity. Indeed, Pavlov was almost certainly studying alpha conditioning, since dogs salivate a little in response to almost any novel stimulus. In bees, the overt response (proboscis extension) to the CS (the novel odor) is absent, but the neural response is in place; we call this sort of innate preparation for learning *covert* alpha conditioning. The obvious conclusion is that odor learning in bees may be organized like a gigantic multiple-choice examination, with all the potential answers already identified; experience, then, serves to select the correct alternative.

Could there be a cell for every odor? Neurobiologists refer to the idea of a cell for every possible stimulus that might be encountered as the grandmother-cell hypothesis: if true, there must be a cell present from before birth that specifically recognizes your grandmother. This seems unlikely as a mechanism for visual memory, since far more cells would be required to cover all the alternatives than even a human brain possesses. But for olfactory memory, with the number of odors individually distinguishable by even well-trained humans measured in the low thousands, the hypothesis is more plausible: a one-cell-per-odor system would require less than half of a percent of the bee's brain.

Another possible strategy for odor learning—one more likely to be applicable to the difficult problems posed by shape memory—is that all the cells involved in olfactory learning might "listen" to all classes of odor receptors. (If this alternative is correct for odor learning, then the alpha-conditioning cell mentioned earlier would already have learned the training odor before the experiment began.) Most neurons consist of dendrites that receive signals from other cells, an area where these electrical inputs (some stimulatory, some inhibitory) are combined, an axon along which the neuron sends its own signal if the net stimulation from other cells passes its threshold, and synapses through which the cell passes that signal to the dendrites of the next cells in the circuit. A neuron may have dozens of dendrites, receive input from hundreds of cells, and, after "evaluating" the incoming data, transmit its "conclusions" to scores of target neurons.

Information in the nervous system is collected on the dendrites of an interneuron, integrated there, and then passed down the axon of the cell to its synapses, where the information is transferred to the dendrites of other cells.

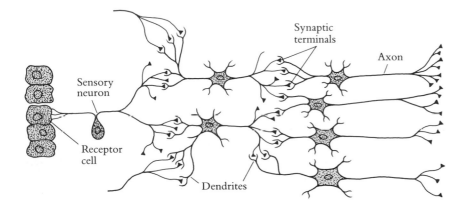

The likely circuitry of classical conditioning, from Aplysia *to honey bees to mammals, includes sensory filtering to select just the USs appropriate to the behavior in question. These are passed to a releasing circuit where, if the level of stimulation is high enough, the behavior (UR) is triggered. The possible CSs are also wired in weakly to the releasing network; these connections are strengthened when the USs arrive at about the same time as the CSs. The nature and number of the CS connections control the speed and specificity of the learning.*

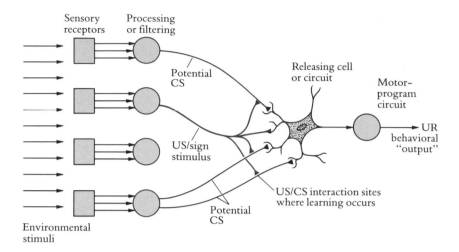

From studies of learning in the sea slug *Aplysia* by Eric Kandel and his colleagues, it is reasonable to conjecture that conditioning results in changes in sensitivity at the synapse/dendrite junction. Work on crickets has revealed cells that integrate the output of dozens of sensory receptors, with an organized connection pattern of certain receptors to particular dendrites. With this very plausible pair of assumptions, we can imagine olfactory-lobe cells that monitor *all* two dozen or so classes of odor receptors, one class per dendrite. To learn, then, an olfactory-lobe cell would have to record the stimulation pattern associated with food—that is, which inputs were active and to what degree, and which were silent; as a result of learning, there would be changes in the sensitivity of different dendrites—changes that would faithfully match this pattern. The cell, then, would become a "filter," a kind of template for the receptor pattern characteristic of the learned odor. According to this model, instead of each cell acting as one box on the answer sheet to be "filled in" if correct, every neuron would correspond to an entire page, and each dendrite would serve as one of the possible nonexclusive multiple-choice alternatives.

This learned-template system would require only one cell for each time of day that could be entered in the floral appointment book—perhaps as few as 50 to 250 cells would be required in all to cover the entire day, depending on the intervals between entry lines in the mental diary. There could even be a compromise strategy: several cells could be able to learn at any given time of day, each with its own subset of favored odor receptors. Any of these approaches can reconcile the behavioral and neurophysiological data, and account for the small size of the olfactory lobe as well as the speed and accuracy of the learning. Most important, they illustrate that there is enough known about bees to generate a fairly limited set of testable hypotheses, and so give some tangible form and substance to the otherwise airy and unconstrained speculation prevalent about the nature of memory.

Turning to shape learning, for which we can reject in advance the hypothesis of one cell per possible learnable stimulus, we again have very little neurophysiological data to go on. Combined with the behavioral results, however, it is enough to indicate the general outlines of what must be going on. The visual system of animals systematically emphasizes and suppresses the patterns of light that fall on the retina. In vertebrates, where this series of transformations is easiest to study, the output of the photoreceptors is first organized into dots: rods are wired to higher-level nerve cells that respond best to white dots surrounded by black, and another class that prefer black dots surrounded by white; neither kind reacts to a solid white, black, or grey background. Cones are wired into their own sets of higher-level neurons, encoding various color combinations such as green spots surrounded by blue.

These spot detectors are found in the retina, and some cells even respond best to spots moving in particular directions at particular speeds. In the retinas of lower vertebrates and the brains of birds and mammals, the next level of detectors integrates the input of many spot detectors, encoding line angle and even particular directions of line movement. At a higher level still, cells that integrate over many second-level detectors are sensitive to concave or convex shapes, or have characteristics too complicated to be categorized. And there are any number of yet higher levels. Our visual system, it seems, devotes most of its effort to sorting out various abstract features. While our subjective impression as humans is of an accurate point-by-point representation of the world (with, we might admit, some enhancement of edges and spots), the data being circulated in the brain is in quite a different form. Indeed, many people blind because of damage to the part of the brain responsible for conscious visual experience (rather than because of damage to the eyes themselves) are unable to see anything, but if pushed to guess can describe the shapes of objects in front of them accurately. Clearly a great deal goes on subconsciously in the abstract language of visual feature detectors, and it may be here, rather than in the part of the visual world our brain shares with us, that learning and matching from memory take place.

In the far smaller visual system of bees there are spot, line, and movement detectors to be sure, but also the kind of highly complex cells seen in vertebrates. One especially interesting cell was found to encode a vertical green line 80° to the right of the bee's body axis extending from 30° below the vertical to 50° above, with a bright blue spot 10° in diameter

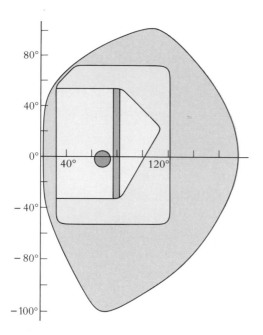

A complex feature detector in the honey bee visual system.

located on the horizon 70° to the bee's right, both seen against a pattern of blue-green backgrounds. As the bee recorded from was a forager, we have no way of knowing whether this was a grandmother cell, innately tuned to this unlikely combination of stimuli, or a memory cell, that encoded a scene of some importance from the experience of this particular bee; the latter seems more likely. And given the rather low resolution of the measurements, we cannot be sure whether this memory was of a flower or of nearby landmarks. The important point, though, is that a single cell can record a simple panorama, just as a single cell in the olfactory lobe can encode an odor. And just as the subjective experience of a scent is the result of a pattern of activity of an ensemble of only moderately specific receptors, perhaps too the visual memory recorded by the complex cell in this bee is a collage of separate inputs from line and spot detectors.

Is visual memory, then, the result of differential activation of synapse/dendrite junctions, each specific for one of many possible combinations of color, simple shape, and location in the visual field? Such a system, in which each cell encodes an entire answer sheet of a multiple-choice questionnaire, requires all the potential components to be wired in advance (which probably explains why bees do not remember motion or polarization, though they can see and react to both) but requires very few cells to store a picture. Each cell with a memory stored in its dendrites could then act as a filter to identify the degree of match with the current visual input. In flower memory, perhaps these cells are time-linked, available for matching only at their specific time of day; in landmark memory, perhaps a match activates a location on the bee's mental map.

If at least some of the bee's visual memory works this way, then there are clear behavioral predictions that can be made, and definite tests that can be performed. Bees are well understood and easy to work with, giving us the dual advantage of knowing enough to make plausible hypotheses about memory, and then to test them, an opportunity offered by virtually no other species. For example, if landmark pictures are stored this way, there should be no size constancy possible; if there is no size constancy, it should be possible to fool foragers with simple tricks, to lure them, by choosing the stimuli properly, into making false matches. All these intriguing questions wait to be answered.

PREDICTABILITY AND VARIABILITY

Regardless of how cue-specific information is processed before storage, the inescapable conclusion is that bees are born with an innate filing system for flower information, indexed exclusively according to time of

Harvesting pollen and nectar.

day. Information from a preselected set of alternatives is entered on the appropriate space on the line, since empty blanks can be filled in later. Bees do not need to learn for themselves that this is the optimal arrangement by experimenting with alternative filing systems over the two or three weeks of their lives as foragers; the recording system is in place when they are born.

The mental appointment book also tells the bees, in an indirect way, what to learn and, more important, what to ignore. The world is full of stimuli that could be memorized as a forager hovers near a flower—the shape of the plant's leaves, the pattern of clouds in the sky overhead, the direction the blossom happens to face, the ambient temperature and humidity, and so on. If bees filled their minds with such rubbish there would be little room for the critical information about the species being foraged, and subsequent searches would be wasted on irrelevant matches or rejections.

Psychologists have discovered that higher vertebrates will learn not to use certain cues because they have no predictive value; this is how the real CS is picked up by a rat in a training box while irrelevant visual, auditory, and olfactory cues inadvertently provided by the apparatus and the outside environment are ignored. For the stimuli that bees attend to at all—the color, odor, and shape of the flower—the same system for extracting useful correlations is at work, but the point here is that any

number of other perceptible cues are categorically ignored, even if they
are relevant. For example, though bees are exquisitely sensitive to polarized light and movement, they simply cannot learn that any particular
polarization or movement is associated with food, even if this is the only
cue with predictive value. This selective blindness reflects the absence of
any useful correlation of this sort in real-world flowers.

Through natural selection, bees have become sensitive to one set of
potential cues in the context of flower learning and blind to another; in
other contexts, different sets of biases are in operation. These preconceptions about what to learn arise not, as we might guess, from any lack of
attention or refusal to perceive a cue; instead, they are the consequence of
there being no place to *store* the information in the appropriate array of
memory cells. The time-indexed array for storing flower information,
for example, simply has no blanks for movement, polarization, or humidity; the information is taken in, but it cannot be stored. Other arrays
may accommodate a different set of cues—in fact, there is evidence that
bees, though they learn what their hive looks like (usually the tree it is in
and the cavity entrance), cannot store its color even if it is brightly
painted.

The prearranged flower-learning program of bees is adapted to deal
with what we might call the predictably unpredictable. Bees are generalists, foraging from a wide range of flowers; specialist species, by contrast, concentrate on a single species or a small group. As generalists,
bees must learn what the flowers they are harvesting look like; there is
not enough room in their brains for an innate field guide to the world's
flowers. But though the exact shape, color, and odor of the species that is
most attractive at the moment cannot be predicted in advance, the characteristics that are useful to learn, *and* the hierarchy with which they
should be employed during matching, *can* be predicted: odor, color, and
shape. By selecting for wiring that guides bees through the learning
process, information storage, and then retrieval and matching, evolution
has produced bees that forage more efficiently than competitors lacking
these custom-designed genetic cheat sheets.

THE INSTINCT TO LEARN

Given that learning is instinctively guided in bees, how special is their
system? Are their needs so simple and their lives so predictable (and their
minds so small) that they can (or must) rely on innate guidance, or is this
the way animals generally learn? The advantages of learning faster and
more reliably when the situation has a degree of predictability ought to
be an advantage for any species, large or small; but we are so accustomed

to having learning and instinct presented as mutually exclusive opposites, the former a particular human forte, the latter a crutch for the lower orders of life, that it is difficult to take seriously the possibility of innately guided learning in higher vertebrates such as birds and mammals. After all, we decide what we will learn, not our genes. Or do we?

When we look carefully at birds while keeping in mind the lessons from the honey bee, the role of innately guided learning becomes pretty obvious. Consider one of the standbys of ethological investigation, the gull chick. This creature hatches into a world full of sights and sounds, most of which are irrelevant and potentially distracting. For a newly hatched chick there is one overriding priority: getting fed. This requires identifying an adult gull and begging from it. Both steps are innate: The sign stimuli—the ethological term for USs—that release begging in herring gull chicks comprise a narrow vertical bar marked with red that is moving horizontally; these three cues are diagnostic of an adult herring gull beak, which has a red spot near the tip and is held vertically while being waved slowly back and forth in front of the chicks. The young respond by pecking at the red spot, and their pecks are an innate motor program (or UR, in psychological parlance) that causes the parent to regurgitate food.

The cues necessary to evoke begging are very schematic. Chicks will peck just as often (even a bit more often) at a flat cardboard cutout painted to look like a herring gull head. In fact, a model laughing gull head (black face, red beak) is just as stimulating, and a disembodied bill

Gull chicks recognize a parent gull by its beak and red spot; this recognition is so schematic that a rod with several red spots is preferred to the normal pattern.

of either species is equally good. The best response of all, though, is reserved for a wooden dowel with several red spots; moved in a horizontal arc. This so-called supernormal stimulus embodies the optimal combination of sign stimuli: red spots in a vertical arrangement, moving horizontally. Though necessarily schematic, the use of sign stimuli to trigger and direct behavior ensures that the young do not waste time and energy pecking experimentally at nearby grass, stones, their own feet, parents' wings, or clouds in the sky.

This system of innate signs and countersigns works well enough for the first two or three days, but the chicks soon become mobile and begin to explore. Gulls nest in tightly packed colonies, and neighboring gulls will eat any other pair's chicks should they wander within range. As a result, it is important for the young to learn to recognize their parents as individuals as soon as they are old enough to leave the nest. They must seek them out for food and protection, while avoiding other birds. By five days, chicks reared in the wild lose their interest in models, having learned to recognize their parents, whereas birds hatched and raised in the lab come to prefer models that "feed" them. But we know from our own experiments that not any model will do: a chick fed by a model that lacks the releasers for pecking learns nothing about its parents. The sign stimuli for begging are also the releasers for learning the CS—the individual appearance and voice of each parent.

This time-linked system for focusing the learning of chicks parallels that of bees: innately recognized cues direct and trigger memorization, and the creature knows instinctively when to learn and what to do with this information later. The preordained unfolding of parent-learning in gulls works because the situation is predictably unpredictable: the chick will certainly have parents to learn about, the parents will certainly have long, narrow bills with red markings and will wave them back and forth, but there is no way to predict in advance exactly what a particular parent will look and sound like. As a result of this innate guidance, learning is faster and more reliable than it would be if the young were left to reason it all out for themselves, and selection has doubtless favored individuals with ever greater degrees of the appropriate genetic learning prejudices.

It might be objected that the young of a species are an exception; perhaps adults, wiser and with more time available for working out cause and effect, are able to learn what they like. Instinctive learning might be evident only when time is short, an emergency measure perhaps, an exception to the usual pattern of flexible learning. But there is no reason to believe that learning programs like the one chicks have for parent recognition are unusual in adult birds. The average gull will see its eggs several times a day as it rolls them in the nest (a maneuver necessary if the embryos are not to become stuck to the inside of the shell) and

Even adult birds regularly fall for supernormal stimuli. Compelled by the wiring of its nervous system, this bird attempts to incubate an oversize "egg" (a fishing float).

exchanges incubation duties with its mate. Yet after two weeks of repeated opportunities to learn about its eggs, a parent gull is unable to choose between a clutch of its olive-green eggs and a second nest of, say, blue eggs. The gull is born knowing all it will ever know about these highly predictable objects: they will be rounded (cubical models are rejected) and speckled—the larger, rounder, and more speckled the better. In experiments, parent gulls will ignore their own clutch in favor of supernormal eggs several times larger and with bigger speckles than the humdrum sort produced by real gulls.

Many species do learn about eggs, however—penguins, orioles, and gannets, to name but three. Birds of these species either live so close together that there is a real possibility of mixing up clutches or are parasitized by species, such as the cuckoo, that lay their eggs in other birds' nests. In short, a learning program for egg recognition has evolved only in the species that need one.

A more complex but revealing case of innately guided learning is evident in the enemy recognition system of birds. There are two general classes of threat faced by nesting birds: predators like hawks, which can catch and kill adults, and nest robbers such as crows, which steal eggs and chicks. In the face of the former, birds hide or dive for cover; when a bird spots a nest predator, however, all the birds in the neighborhood cooperate to attack and drive it off. The attacks are prompted by the mobbing call, a signal produced and recognized innately. But how does a bird know whom to mob and whom to ignore? Are birds born with an innate field guide to possible predators, or do they learn from personal experience, noting which species eat their eggs and chicks (a very inefficient approach); or are they perhaps neophobic, attacking anything unfamiliar?

Above, the paired eyes of owls are a sign stimulus for danger to many species. Below, moths take advantage of the natural aversion to paired eyes by flashing eye spots when discovered.

In fact, none of these possible answers is correct. There are two systems, one based on innate recognition, the other on programmed learning. In the first, birds respond automatically to a sign stimulus provided inadvertently by many predators: a pair of forward-looking eyes. If you think about it, animals with front-mounted eyes—owls, cats, dogs, humans, and so on—are hunters, and use the binocular vision this arrangement provides to judge their distance to prey. Potential victims (rabbits and songbirds, for instance), tend instead to have eyes mounted on the sides of their heads, which allows them to watch as much of their surroundings as possible, ever on the alert for predators. Prey animals generally react innately to paired eyes by fleeing or by feigning death. So powerful is this sign stimulus that a pair of sticks with marbles at the end will send a young chicken into an apparent coma, and many species of moth scare off hunting birds by spreading their wings to reveal eye spots.

But most nest predators, the animals that take eggs and young chicks, lack forward-looking eyes, making some other means of recognition essential. In fact, birds learn which species belong on their enemies list by observing what their colleagues mob. Eberhard Curio provided a convincing demonstration of this by allowing caged blackbirds to view separate quadrants of a rotatable box. Cages of birds were stationed on opposite sides of the box so that one group of birds could see into only one part of it while the other viewed a different section. This setup made it possible to present different models to the two groups simultaneously.

The first step in the experiment was to show that there is no innate response to innocuous species, and Curio chose a stuffed nectar-feeding bird from Australia; when this bird was rotated into view, the blackbirds ignored it. Next one group was shown a stuffed owl, the other the nectar guide; the group viewing the owl went crazy, and broadcasted the mobbing call while they attempted to get through the cage walls to attack the inanimate owl. The other group quickly became upset by the mobbing signal, and attempted to get at the nectar guide. Whenever the nectar guide appeared again, this group tried to mob it. They taught their misplaced aversion to other cages of birds, even different species, through seven generations, though no bird had ever suffered at the hands of a nectar guide. To see just how far this programmed-prejudice system could take the birds, Curio substituted a bottle of laundry detergent, which now elicits a full attack whenever it appears.

The enemy-learning program of birds works because, as with flower learning in bees, the situation is predictably unpredictable: there will be nest predators to attack, but their appearance cannot be known in advance; the only reliable cue is the mobbing call, and that is the trigger for learning. Birds with a readiness to learn from the mobbing of others will

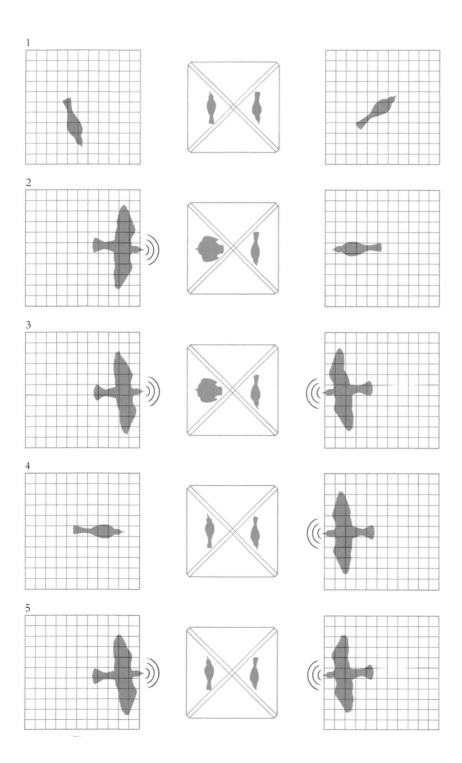

Cultural transmission of enemy recognition was demonstrated by presenting objects to caged birds by means of a box that prevented the occupants of one cage from seeing what the other cage was viewing. A stuffed nectar guide evoked no reaction initially (1), but after one cage of birds attempted to mob a stuffed owl while another group could only see the nectar guide (2), mobbing of the nectar-feeding bird began (3), and the habit was passed from cage to cage (4 and 5).

be favored by natural selection, even at the risk of perpetuating an occasional silly tradition; for nesting birds (and the many species of mammals that share this system), it is better to be safe than sorry.

LABORATORY ANOMALIES

Can it be that these powerful inborn biases, found in virtually every species of animal whose learning has been studied by ethologists, just happen to be absent from the rats and pigeons of laboratory fame, or have psychologists managed to somehow overlook these sorts of inflexibility? In fact, rats and pigeons do well in the artificial environments imposed on them because they are such extreme generalists that they have relatively few biases. In addition, the philosophical underpinnings of psychology in the first half of this century excluded the possibility of innate control of learning—for many behaviorists, indeed, instinct itself was illusion. John B. Watson, the founder of Behaviorism, which was the dominant psychological school until the early 1960s, went so far as to say that the concept of instinct was totally unnecessary, and that even breathing and the circulation of the blood resulted from conditioning. Nevertheless, the learning biases of rats and pigeons were well known to those in the field, though the tendency was to work around them instead of investigating these troublesome irregularities.

The stimulus that changed the attitude of many psychologists and finally brought recognition to that minority of workers investigating the many "anomalies" in laboratory studies, was the discovery by John Garcia that rats could learn in one trial to avoid a food that made them ill. To be more precise, they would learn to avoid anything that tasted like whatever they ate before becoming sick, even though the illness might have been induced separately by injection or radiation. Not only was the delay between the CS (the taste) and the US (illness) incredibly long (hours, rather than the seconds required by Pavlovian dogma), but the rats focused on the taste cues, virtually ignoring visual and auditory stimuli that were just as predictive of danger. This bias is not the result of any general sensory deficit, since rats readily learn sights and sounds when they predict palatable food. Worse yet, when others tried the same experiment with quail, these birds remembered the *color* of the food that later made them ill, but ignored sound and taste.

In general, it is possible to divide learning studies into those that use food as a reward, sickness as a punishment, or the avoidance of physical discomfort (usually shock) as a goal. Also, in general, rats and pigeons learn different things in these different contexts: pigeons, for instance, will attend to sound when shock is the punishment, but not when food is the reward. All of these biases in classical conditioning make sense in retrospect: how often do pigeons need to remember the sound their food (seeds) makes? Selection will have favored pigeons that ignore what are sure to be spurious acoustic correlations with food, but that attend to auditory cues of danger, such as predators or threatening fellow pigeons. Like bees, even rats and pigeons are prepared to make the appropriate associations in each kind of situation, and the natural history of the animal governs the sort of biases favored by natural selection.

The same pattern of prejudices is evident in operant learning as well. Although the operant is supposed to be a novel behavior discovered through trial and error, animals seem to have adaptive preconceptions about what sorts of experiments are most likely to pay off in different contexts. It is fairly easy to teach a rat to press a lever with its forepaws to obtain food, but hard to teach it to jump or run to the other end of a corridor for a meal. When avoiding shock is the goal, however, they can learn running and jumping readily, but it is virtually impossible to condition lever pressing under these conditions. Pigeons learn pecking for a food reward easily, but not treadle hopping. For avoiding danger, the opposite is true.

These laboratory behaviors clearly reflect behaviors in the wild: rats normally manipulate food with the forepaws, and pigeons peck for their seeds; both rats and pigeons run away from danger. Animals biased toward solving problems with the appropriate body parts have been favored by selection. In fact, some of these theoretically impossible operant biases are so strong that under laboratory conditions they can lead to starvation. A pigeon, for instance, that learns to approach a food hopper when a light comes on to receive a food reward will begin to peck at the light spontaneously whenever it is illuminated; the pigeon seems to think that it *must* peck something to get food. If we rewire the apparatus so that pecking at the light extinguishes it, and *prevents* the seed from being dumped into the hopper, the bird will nevertheless continue pecking. It cannot learn *not* to peck at the light when it has been associated with a food reward. If, however, we switch the wiring again so that its pecking now pays off by preventing the pigeon from being shocked, the bird *stops* pecking. It is unable to learn to peck to avoid danger.

The inflexibility of operant learning by pigeons is by no means unique. The best documented saga of the trials and tribulations of attempting to condition behavior comes from Keller and Marian Breland, who established a commercial enterprise to train animals for exhibitions and advertisements. Our favorite example is the raccoon that had been taught by painstaking degrees to take a large artificial coin and deposit it in a piggy bank, for which it was rewarded with food. This part went pretty well, but when the teachers added a stack of coins (so that the

Animals in "Skinner boxes" are trained to perform a behavior to obtain food or escape punishment.

Raccoons spontaneously wash food before eating it.

behavior could go on unattended), everything fell apart: the raccoon would take two coins, hustle off away from the bank, and rub them together in a miserly manner, never putting them into the bank. The problem, of course, was that raccoons are driven to wash and rub their food together. The coins were, to the animals, somehow the source of the food they received near the bank when the training involved only a single coin. So strong is the desire to rub and wash, even without water, that the raccoon was willing to forego the edible reward and would probably have starved if the trainers had not returned to single coins.

SONG AND LANGUAGE

The intriguing pattern of biases that honey bees first alerted us to proves to be widespread in the animal kingdom. If our investigations were to stop here, we could convince ourselves that they are restricted to the simple but critical matters of finding food and avoiding danger. We could rest secure in the comfortable conviction that the flexibility and self-direction we intuitively expect from learning is evident only in more demanding behavioral contexts, in the sort of situations that higher animals face and which have shaped the reasoning creature *Homo sapiens*. A brief overview of research on complex learning, however, reveals that even such sophisticated systems as verbal communication rely on inborn controls.

The best understood cases of complex learning in the wild involve communication in birds and primates, and they have the added advantage that each relates to that most impressive of all behavioral accomplishments, human language acquisition. Not all birds learn their songs; the mating calls of mourning doves and cuckoos, for instance, are innate. Even in the species that do learn, most of the vocal signals—begging calls, mobbing calls, and a score of others—are inborn; only the courtship song is learned. Though these birds learn their songs, however, most can learn *only* the song of their own species.

The most studied songbird is the white-crowned sparrow, a species that can be hatched and reared in isolation in a laboratory. Researchers play medleys of songs of different species to each chick and then, when singing begins, see what tune the bird produces. From these manipulations, we know that there is only a restricted period during which learning takes place, and that the chick can unerringly pick out the song of its own species. If the medley omits the white crown's own song, or if it hears nothing during its learning window, the bird grows up singing only a simple innate melody. Tests with artificially rearranged songs reveal that particular cues—sign stimuli—in the parental song trigger

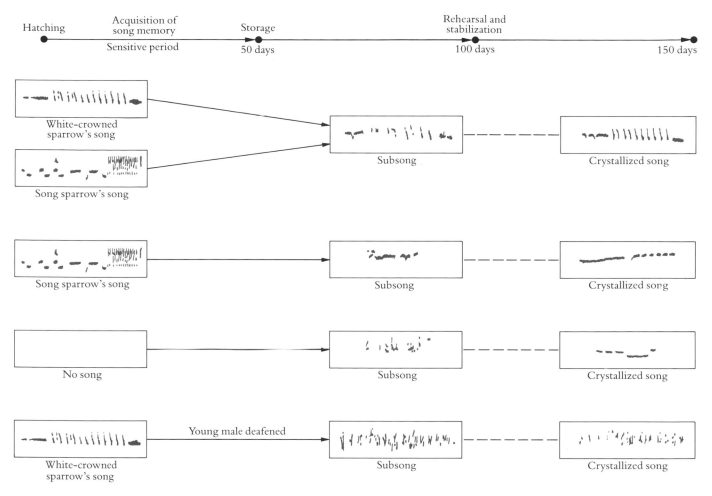

There is a critical period for song learning early in the life of a white-crowned sparrow. During this interval he must hear his species song, and can pick it out of a medley of calls. If the song is not heard, or heard only outside the critical period, then the bird will sing only a simple innate tune when he matures. Even to do this, the bird must be able to hear himself; deafening before rehearsal begins leaves the bird unable to sing anything melodic.

memorization. Though there is considerable variation between the songs of different birds of the same species—indeed, variation is the basis of individual recognition in their social system—all songs contain the essential sign stimuli.

Though song recognition and learning are manifestations of programmed classical conditioning, operant conditioning is also involved.

The birds learn how to produce a good (but not perfect) match of the memorized song through trial and error, a phase in every bird's life known technically as subsong. As a result, a bird deafened after its critical period for memorizing song can never sing normally, because it cannot monitor its own vocal experiments and learn to match the mental tape it has recorded in its brain; birds deafened *after* full song is perfected, however, continue to sing normally. The operant becomes so automatic that feedback is no longer necessary.

When researchers looked closely at how birds match the memorized song by trial and error, they discovered that no matter what version of the species' song had been heard (or even if the chick had been exposed to none), the variety of simple notes produced during early subsong was the same. In other words, the notes themselves are innate motor programs. For birds, operant learning consists of listening to these many snippets of sound, selecting the ones heard in the parental song, arranging this subset in the proper order, and then committing this pattern of vocal muscle movements to memory. At least in birds, operant learning involves selecting from an innate array of predetermined alternatives, just like the flower-recognition learning of bees; it has probably been favored by natural selection for just the same reasons. Whether the operant learning of honey bees and other animals is organized in the same way remains to be discovered.

The flexibility of song learning, then, is largely an illusion: the animal innately recognizes what it is to learn, and then constructs the desired product out of the limited selection of innate acoustic building blocks. The scoring (or "grammar") of the song is also innate: even if the sounds the young bird hears are mixed up or arranged into patterns suitable for other species, the chick will extract and memorize the proper elements, rescoring them according to its own species' arrangement. Again, this is analogous to the predictably unpredictable goals discovered in honey bee learning: the essential features of the song can be predicted in advance, but not its details. The details must be learned, but the range of options is limited to a small subset of the constellation of possibilities, a narrowing of choice that must increase the speed and reliability of the learning.

What has this to do with human language acquisition? Different as we might think song and language are, there are eerie parallels between the learning processes. For example, human infants have a babbling phase at a species-typical age, just as birds do, during which they experiment with a predictable set of sounds. And just as in birds, this phase begins and ends on schedule even if a child is congenitally deaf. Another parallel is that if deafness develops *after* language has been acquired, the affected individual can usually continue to speak more or less normally; the motor programs associated with the different syllable sounds that make up the native language have been committed to memory as effectively as the other operants we learn and never forget—tying shoes, swimming, bicycle riding, and so forth.

But the most powerful parallel of all is that human speech is composed of innately recognized acoustic sign stimuli—sounds we know as consonants. Languages the world over use the same basic set of about 40 consonants; Standard English employs about two dozen. We distinguish consonants on the basis of subtle acoustic cues embedded in the sounds. For example, try saying "ba" and "pa" slowly; both are made with the same "plosive" burst of air from the lips, but they sound different because the vowel "ah" associated with these two simple syllables has a different timing in each. The vowel is made with the vocal cords in the throat; in "ba," the plosive lip gesture occurs at about the same time as the vowel, whereas in "pa" there is a fractional delay—typically about a twentieth of a second, though even an exaggerated one-second interval still sounds like "pa." There are also consonants in which vowel sounds *precede* their accompanying lip gestures, as in "ma."

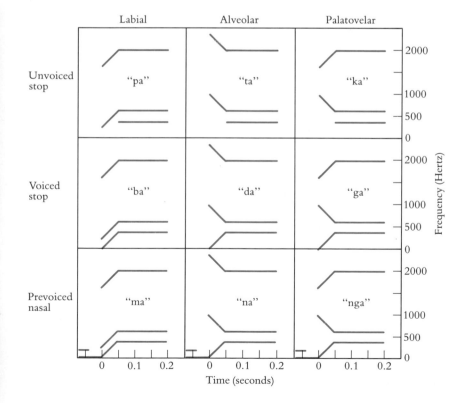

The consonants of human language are acoustic sign stimuli, innately recognized (and probably innately produced). Many differ in the position of the mouth parts during the vocal gesture as well as the relative timing of the gesture and the sounding of the vowel in the throat.

There is a similar set of consonants in which the gesture is made with the tongue against the alveolar ridge just behind the upper front teeth. "Da" is the one we hear when the burst of air and the vowel sound are nearly simultaneous; "ta" is heard when there is a delay of the vowel by a twentieth of a second or more; "na" is what we hear when a vowel precedes the release. Farther back in the mouth, "ga" is produced with a strong release of air from the roof of the mouth and a nearly simultaneous vowel; "ka" has the vowel delay. Other consonants involve similar combinations of tongue/mouth/lip gestures and relative vowel timings.

The evidence for some innate system of language recognition in humans comes from infants that are exposed to tapes of artificially synthesized consonants—recordings in which the interval between the lip-tongue gesture and the vowel can be varied at will. Newborns require constant change to keep their attention: repetitions of the same stimulus quickly bore them. When a series of "ba" sounds comes from a speaker an infant will stare at the speaker, but then lose interest with repetition; if the sound is switched to "pa," however, the child's gaze returns. Using this method, researchers have mapped the boundaries of these distinctions in the newborn mind and found them to be the same the world over. Even in cultures whose languages lack the consonants the experiments map, infants respond to the same exact distinctions. This unlikely phenomenon eliminates the possibility that consonants might be learned *in utero* as the mother talks. We must conclude, therefore, that what we call consonants, the elements out of which our vocal language is built, are innately recognized sign stimuli, similar in design and use to the elements out of which birds build their learned songs.

Less well established but more intriguing are the widespread suggestions that even basic grammar might be innate. It has been known for decades that the neural circuitry for language is reliably localized in certain small parts of the brain, and that one area seems to encode and decode thoughts while another handles the grammatical details. Damage to one of these centers can leave a person just able to arrange words in an order that clearly reflects understanding of what has been said and an attempt to respond logically. But so many of the modifiers and essentially all of those little words that grease the wheels of communication— the articles ("a," "the," and so on), prepositions ("of," "on," and so on) and conjunctions (like "and" and "but") are missing, that it is difficult to follow the train of thought. Damage to the other speech area, on the other hand, leaves the victim able to talk glib nonsense with perfect fluidity and impeccable grammar.

More recently, eminent linguists have argued that the process of language learning does not require correction or explicit reference to rules; they argue instead that it is basically a process of *calibration:* our brains must discover which of the two major linguistic systems is in use locally—whether inflected or word-order—and the nature of its quirks. After that, vocabulary drill completes the lesson. Other specialists believe there is only one system. The various "pidgin" dialects are impoverished hybrids of their immigrant speakers' native and adopted languages, but the children of pidgin speakers generate their own distinctive Creoles which, though vastly different from each other, contain universal grammatical elements not found in the models these children hear. Though debate on these ideas is intense, they can help explain three startling facts. The first is that congenitally deaf people who learn a standard sign language do so with the area of the brain normally involved with vocal language. Second, deaf children *not* taught a sign language invent their own, which, when analyzed, uses its own nouns, verbs, modifiers, and shares the basic grammar of "official" ones. The drive to learn a language is so strong that one is invented, and innate guidelines apparently lead to a system that mirrors the ones we normally learn by example. Finally, it helps to account for the effortlessness of language learning: everyone not seriously disabled—even the severely retarded—learns language, and does so without the need for formal training and reinforcement. But when it comes to learning how to add, subtract, and multiply, a task trivial compared to the gargantuan feat of language acquisition, children need constant correction, encouragement, and reward; "math facts" must be laboriously drilled and memorized, probably because we are not innately prepared to learn them.

But despite their common bases in innate sign stimuli, motor programs, and (probably) grammar, human languages have a feature that the bees' dance language and bird song both lack—an almost limitless open-endedness. Both bees and birds have variety and flexibility in their communication systems because they can use the innate elements in a vast range of combinations; but both are limited because the message has only one general context (advertising location or attracting mates) and a limited length. In human language, consonants are used like building blocks, prefabricated units that can be used to generate almost any kind of structure (words and sentences) from poetry to legalese, to serve almost any communicative need. These acoustic sign stimuli must once have had innately recognized meanings, as do the species-specific consonant-like sounds used by most higher primates, but through evolution they were gradually freed from their original uses. What pressures led to this linguistic liberation remain a mystery, but in animals with complex, innately organized signalling systems we see a kind of behavioral fossil, the precursors from which human speech gradually evolved.

CHAPTER *10*

Insight and Intelligence

Honey bees are well suited to their niche: their physiology and behavior are optimized for their occupation as perennial, highly social, temperate-zone foragers of nectar and pollen. Their communication and navigation are the most complex known among invertebrates and, excepting humans, quite likely among vertebrates as well. Yet all is innate. Even their flower learning, impressive as it is, is preordained to solve predictably unpredictable problems. In all that bees do, and in the way their behavioral systems are organized, we have found strategies that turn out to underlie vertebrate behavior as well, and yet we feel quite certain that higher vertebrates—ourselves, certainly—are more than programmed robots solving the same problems generation after generation. We sense that the flexibility of higher vertebrates *is* real, that there is insight and true intelligence among at least some mammals and birds. Does this criterion define a real gap that separates the insects from higher verte-

A bee studying a flower.

brates? Are insight and intelligence, like the complex behavioral programs that look like flexible learning in birds and bees, an illusion? Or
could it be that insight and thought are real, but that bees have them too?
It seems appropriate to end this discussion of the ever-surprising honey
bee by looking for its ultimate intellectual limits.

WHAT CRITERIA?

To seek intelligence, we must either define the term or decide what behavior will convince us that a creature can think for itself. Definitions are
hard: it is difficult to find a description that is neither too strict, excluding
our own behavior, nor too lax, allowing personal computers and pocket
calculators into the ranks of the intellectual elite; moreover, we know
from experience how difficult it is to get any two scientists to agree on
one definition. The alternative—deciding what evidence is actually appropriate—is equally problematical. By its nature, the mind is a private
organ; inferring what goes on inside the brain is tricky at best. Very
often, introspection finds a behavior to be a convincing demonstration of
insight or thinking, but inspection reveals it to be just a well-
programmed response. Our approach here will be to explore some criteria that are frequently invoked, and to work toward a definition of intelligence by a process of elimination.

Adaptiveness One of the most striking aspects of animal behavior is
how well suited it is for the task at hand, and this adaptiveness is frequently offered as evidence for some degree of thought or problem solving or self-awareness. Early naturalists romanticized the behavior of animals so shamelessly that every organism down to the paramecium was
imagined to have an intellect. The first ethologists, however, were made
of tougher stuff. Consider what may be the most significant experiment
in the history of the field, which revealed how geese roll eggs. Geese
build their nests on the ground; they roll their eggs several times a day to
prevent damage to the embryo, and occasionally cover the nest with
weeds on warm days to go off and feed. During the rolling or, more
often, when the camouflage is being removed after an outing, an egg
may roll out of the nest. After the goose settles back down on the clutch
she may notice the errant egg; if so, she will stare at it, then rise, step
toward it, put her bill gently on the far side of the egg and carefully roll it
back into the nest.

At first sight this looks like a thoughtful piece of behavior: the goose
has realized that there is a problem, formulated a plan for solving it with

The egg-rolling behavior of geese.

the materials at hand, and then successfully executed her design. But when Konrad Lorenz and Niko Tinbergen experimented with the situation, the true sequence of events became clear. First, almost any rounded object would elicit the same behavior—a tennis ball, light bulb, grapefruit, or beer bottle. Obviously, egg rolling is triggered by a sign stimulus. Second, once the goose had begun the behavior, she would finish it regardless: if the egg were removed in plain view of the goose while she reached for it, she would nevertheless continue her painstaking rolling of the nonexistent object back into the nest. Clearly, egg rolling is a motor program. The entire sequence is just a piece of clockwork—elegant and adaptive, to be sure, but just gears and wheels. Mere adaptiveness, then, cannot be a sufficient criterion for distinguishing between the creative intelligence of an individual animal and the blind, pragmatic "intelligence" of natural selection.

Variability If innate behavior is operated by clockwork, then perhaps we should look for intelligence in telltale signs of variability, evidence that different individuals solve a problem in different ways; if a behavior is innate, it seems likely that it will be stereotyped and predictable. Though some instinctive behavior is indeed rigid and unvarying, however, investigation shows that this need not be the case. For example, in territorial conflicts it pays an animal *not* to be predictable; if he were, his opponent would know precisely what he was going to do, and how long he would contest a particular resource before giving up.

Innate honey bee behavior offers several examples of important variability. One is the adaptive "noise" in the dance that serves to spread recruits out around the target. Another instance is the spontaneous preference of recruits: searching bees prefer to land on more complex shapes, for example, but this preference is probabilistic rather than absolute. As a result, a recruit might land five times as often on a ten-petal shape versus a simple circle, but she will try the circle sooner or later. A bee with an absolute preference would never discover the rare flowers with low spatial frequencies—morning glories, for instance. In all such cases, the variability is as adaptive as it is innate; clearly variability is not a sure sign of thought.

Complexity If adaptiveness and variability are untrustworthy guides to the existence of intelligence, what about complexity? Surely there are behaviors too complex to be innately encoded. The trouble with this potential criterion is that far and away the most complex animal behaviors we know of usually *are* innate. Take the nest building of birds, for example. Weaverbirds gather (or make) long strips of material with which they weave the most elaborate nests of all. They tie thousands of knots to create a hanging nest with an egg chamber, a waterproof roof, and a long entrance tube to keep out snakes. Some species even build an additional false entrance and chamber, concealing the true opening (with a door that is invisible when shut) to the nest. Yet a weaverbird hatched in an incubator and reared with no chance to see a nest of its own species will, when the time is right, proceed to gather the correct materials and build its species-specific nest.

Surely the webs of orb-weaving spiders, constructed in total darkness using whatever supports happen to be at hand, are, for the size of the builder, even more complex. And yet web building is wholly instinctive. In our opinion, selection has operated to make complex behavior innate for the simple reason that, if it were not, animals could not hope to discover it by trial and error or to learn it by observation in time to be able to perform it. In the end, then, complexity of behavior is one of the worst guides of all to intelligence.

Learning The most commonly offered criterion of the elusive quality we know as intelligence is learning. It seems reasonable that, if an animal is not to fill its head with all sorts of useless rubbish, it must exercise strict selectivity in what it commits to memory. Believing, as we do, that we always consciously decide what to learn, it would seem that animals, too, need to comprehend what is worth remembering and what is not. But we have seen that the apparent flexibility of learning is largely an illusion where animals are concerned, and that the same pattern probably holds for human infants. Selection has operated to focus learning innately, basing it on species-specific cues rather than counting on the good judgment of the creatures themselves.

The realization that programmed learning dominates the animal world was retarded by the last century's tendency to assign intelligence to essentially every creature, to see conscious thought behind every behavior. The celebrated "thinking" horse Clever Hans provided a cautionary lesson that put an end to that credulousness for decades. Hans

The nest of an Indian weaverbird.

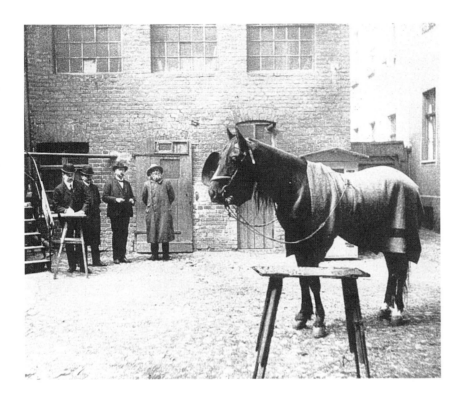

Mr. von Osten (in long coat, center) and Clever Hans.

was the pet of a retired teacher who had made it his goal to instruct Hans in mathematics. Sure enough, in time Hans came to be able to answer simple problems of addition and subtraction with the appropriate number of hoof scrapes or by pointing his nose. Soon Hans proved himself to be conversant with much more sophisticated concepts, including geometry, music, and foreign languages.

The proud teacher invited scientists to come and study his pupil, allowing them to question and test Hans, and all were convinced—all, that is, except Oskar Pfungst. After months of intensive study, Pfungst finally discovered the real cleverness of Hans: as the horse's hoof taps approached the correct number or his nose got near the correct answer on the blackboard, any observers would make slight, involuntary movements. Without being aware of it, they would tense their muscles, catch their breath, or raise an expectant eyebrow, and it was these subtle signs, movements unnoticed by the observers themselves, that Hans used as cues.

After Clever Hans, studies of learning were adapted to the rigidly controlled environment of the psychology laboratory, and questions of thinking, insight, planning, and other mental processes were relegated to romantic fiction. Observations and experiments on learning in the uncontrolled chaos of nature were considered beyond the pale of legitimate science. We are only now recovering from this instance of scientific overkill.

Concepts One of the most crippling legacies of the Clever Hans fiasco was that the analysis of learning was limited to simple S-R (stimulus-response) associations; hypothesizing the existence of higher-level cognitive activities in animals was scrupulously avoided. It was not until the 1960s and 1970s that psychologists and ethologists began to break free of this taboo.

The first of the higher-level mental capacities of animals to be investigated was their formation of cognitive maps. We have touched on the surprising cognitive maps of bees in the discussion of dance evolution, and we will take up the topic again in this chapter. The other major class of complex mental process to be investigated in animals has been concept formation.

Concepts are generalizations. "Tree" is a concept: it is a category of objects that are individually different, and yet basically similar. Until recently, the usual view of a concept was that there is an ideal exemplar of each category—an archetypal tree, for instance, of which all real trees are imperfect approximations. This perspective, which dates from Plato, implies that there is a necessary and sufficient set of characteristics that define a category. Animals could then learn about categories by simple classical conditioning, with the essential characters serving as the CSs; the variable features, lacking predictive value, would be ignored. Novel objects, then, would either be categorized as trees or nontrees according to whether or not they possessed the essential features.

More recently, it has become obvious that there is no set of crucial features. Any requirement we might imagine for "tree" is violated by at least one species that we take automatically to be a tree. For instance, we cannot insist that they have leaves, since pines have needles. We cannot say they must be green, since we recognize trees in autumn foliage and the leafless skeletons of deciduous trees in winter as trees; we cannot say that they must have a central trunk and a circular crown of leaves, since birches have multiple trunks and some poplars are essentially vertical cylinders. In the end, we must conclude that a tree is an object that *usually* has a particular set of characteristics, some of which are more predictive than others, but none of which is absolutely essential. Identification, therefore, is probabilistic, so that a deficit in one highly diagnostic feature must be made up by the presence of several less essential characteristics. Sorting all this out seems pretty complex.

The first good evidence that animals can form categories came from studies of pigeons. The birds were taught that pecking when a slide was projected with a tree in it would cause food to be dispensed, whereas pecking for slides without trees produced nothing. The slides used were selected from personal collections—vacation pictures and the like—so that the trees, when there were any, could be anywhere in the frame, of any apparent size, entirely visible or partly hidden, of any species, bare or fully leafed. From 40 exemplars (and 40 slides without trees), the laboratory-reared pigeons, without having experienced a real tree in their lives, quickly became adept at identifying the training slides with this class of objects. But they might simply have memorized which 40 slides were being reinforced, and have formed no actual idea of trees. To check for whether a real concept had been formed, a new set of slides was presented with no reward for pecking; the pigeons were extremely good at responding to the slides with trees. There were two kinds of "errors": in one sort, the slides were found on closer inspection really to have trees in them, but they were so small or hidden that the experimenters had not noticed them; in the other class, the slides showed television antennas and telephone poles, which might really be considered modern cultural trees.

In later experiments, pigeons successfully acquired concepts of fish, people, particular individuals, leaves in general, oak or maple leaves, and so on. The speed of their learning suggests that this is something pigeons regularly do in nature, and the selective value of forming concepts about food (these slides were CSs for food, after all) is obvious: the pigeon is thereby enabled to make better guesses about unfamiliar objects. Being able to categorize the appearance of food would help a bird avoid pecking at gravel and broken glass, but still allow it to be open-minded enough to test popcorn and bread crumbs.

Do honey bees form concepts? A general concept of "flower" might be useful to a bee, and a concept that allows for a limited range of variation in one kind of blossom would be even more so. You may recall that in one early experiment on visual memory in bees, foragers failed to generalize (form a concept) about triangles; but then, since there was no unrewarded alternative pattern to force them to pay close attention, the bees may have been simply being lazy. In another experiment, a German worker taught bees to prefer either a solid-colored square or a bicolored one, regardless of the precise colors. He did this by presenting both a reinforced and unreinforced alternative simultaneously on each visit, changing the color or color combination of each between visits. He concluded that bees could form a concept of "bicolor," but it is still possible that the higher spatial frequency of the two-colored target (which was a checkerboard of four small squares) was what the bees remembered.

Experiments on concept learning in bees. Training begins with uncluttered panels, and "B" is rewarded regardless of its color, location, or font; later, distracting shapes are added.

   Some of the least ambiguous work on concept formation has been done with letters. These objects are sufficiently unnatural that we need not worry too much about innate preparation for learning or preexisting categories. It is easy for humans to recognize a capital A, say, regardless of size or even font. With the possible exception of gothic script, even a child just learning the alphabet generalizes from one form of type to another. Pigeons have been shown to make the same discriminations, and this is probably the way to ask bees if they form concepts. We have begun to ask this question, using the letter B as the reinforced stimulus, carefully varying its orientation, color, size, location, and font so that only the concept (as opposed to any of its component characteristics that bees so readily learn) is predictive. Some bees can get this far. Next, we begin to add irrelevant, distracting backgrounds, simple at first, but then more complex.

To date, only one bee has been able to identify the letter in novel fonts when embedded (and often partly hidden by) visual "noise" in the form of abstract shapes. Either bees are not very good at forming concepts, or we are incompetent at teaching them; from long experience, we take the latter alternative very seriously. At present, then, we regard the question of whether bees are capable of concept formation as unanswered. Even if the answer is yes, the question still remains whether concept formation involves any intelligence. After all, if pigeons are so adept, it cannot require much mental sophistication. Perhaps concept formation is an innate and automatic process, requiring no comprehension on the part of the animal.

Insight Although much of learning and even concept formation may be innately guided, intuition tells us that animals must sometimes escape from their programming, especially when they must plan responses to contingencies their programming could not anticipate. Here, surely, we must be getting close to real thinking.

During the First World War, the German psychologist Wolfgang Köhler worked on an island off the coast of Africa. He provided a group of chimps in a large enclosure with some "toys"—boxes, poles, and so forth. Like all good primates, these otherwise bored animals played with the materials until they had worn out their possibilities. Next, Köhler hung a clump of bananas out of reach and left the chimps to their own devices. At first the animals made hopeless jumps at the fruit, and then stalked away and sulked. But then a chimp began to look at the boxes, then the bananas, then back at the boxes, then at the bananas again, then at the boxes; finally it rushed over to the boxes and began piling them up. The stacking was fairly incompetent—the chimp did not seem to understand about center of gravity—but in the end the pile grew high enough, and the animal got the bananas.

This looks like a case of *cognitive* trial and error: instead of experimenting with its physical behavior, the animal formulated a plan in its mind and then set about to execute it. This is about as close as we can get to a reliable behavioral assay for insight and thought, and it is this approach that we will explore.

Judging whether a creature's behavior involves insight requires some knowledge of the natural history of the creature. For instance, the "tradi-

Köhler's chimpanzees solving the problem of how to reach food high overhead.

Blue tits stealing cream from milk bottles by peeling back the foil top.

tion" among chimpanzees of using sticks and grass blades to fish for termites is an oft-cited instance of intelligence; especially memorable are pictures of youngsters watching their elders capture tasty insects by inserting what is inevitably referred to as a "tool" into the termite hole. Yet all chimpanzees engage in this behavior; in labs, domestically reared chimps spontaneously take pencils and coathangers and poke them into holes—electrical outlets, in particular. This poking behavior that looks so much like intelligent tool use could result from an innate program.

In discussions of intelligence, nearly every behavior textbook relates how blue tits in England discovered a method for stealing the cream at the top of bottles of home-delivered milk. The birds would peel back the foil tops before the householder fetched the milk from the front step, and the practice spread across the country. But blue tits make their living in the wild by peeling back tree bark to search for insect larvae, and so strong is this drive to peel that hand-reared blue tits compulsively peel the wallpaper off their keepers' walls. So the cleverness, if any, in getting cream is certainly not in the peeling behavior.

To be considered seriously as insightful, a behavior should be something outside the normal repertoire of the species, a response that could not reasonably have evolved in advance. Do honey bees ever behave in this way? In fact, several possibilities have been suggested.

INSIGHT IN BEES?

Alfalfa is normally pollinated by bumble bees, but modern agricultural practices have, through the elimination of hedgerows, greatly reduced the habitat of these robust insects. For honey bees, the spring-loaded anther of the alfalfa blossom is a positive hazard: not only does it deliver an unpleasant blow, but it can even trap the bee's proboscis. As a result, honey bees avoid alfalfa. But a hive placed in the middle of miles of this crop is faced with the grim prospect of starvation, and in time the bees *do* begin to forage the flowers. The interesting fact is that they do so without tripping the anthers. Some bees come to recognize tripped from untripped blossoms (a subtle distinction, given their poor vision) and frequent only the latter; others land on the back of the flower and feed from the side, or even chew through a petal to get at the nectar.

These subterfuges strike us as pretty clever, but perhaps we are too easily impressed. Distinguishing tripped from untripped blossoms, for instance, could simply be a matter of pushing shape memory to its limit. Feeding from the side might be a contingency behavior that forms part of the bees' innate repertoire. In fact, bees regularly feed from the sides of flowers or chew through when the morphology of a flower is such that the bee's tongue will not reach the nectar (usually because the flower has coevolved with a long-tongued pollinator such as hawk moths). Honey bees may simply try this programmed alternative on alfalfa, discover that it works, and stick with it. It may take a certain amount of intelligence to think of trying this ruse, but we cannot tell from the behavior.

Another example is less easy to dismiss. As von Frisch first pointed out, there comes a point in the training procedure at which at least some of the foragers begin to catch on to the timing and pattern of the experimenter's movements. As we described in an earlier chapter, we train bees by setting a dish of sugar solution at the hive entrance, then moving it progressively farther away as bees begin to visit it. Each step in the process is in some more-or-less fixed proportion of the previous distance (25 percent farther, typically), and some of the bees begin to anticipate our movements. Characteristically we notice this rather eerie phenomenon when we foolishly delay moving the station while waiting for a tardy bee to return—we say foolish because the trained forager may have been killed, or gotten lost, or have begun dancing in the hive. What happens in these cases is that some foragers fly on past the training station and wait at the spot we are aiming for on the next move. There is certainly nothing in the behavior of natural flowers that is likely to have led to the evolution of circuitry dedicated to guessing where a plant will move next. To us, this looks genuinely clever.

Another observation also suggests that bees may be able to think or imagine. Once, we trained a group of foragers to a feeder in a rowboat. The boat was moved systematically farther and farther out into a lake, and a second group of bees from the same hive was trained to a food source at the same distance, but along the shoreline. When the quality of the food was increased, both groups of foragers danced, but recruits arrived almost exclusively at the shore station; in fact, the bees that had attended the lake-station dances did not even seem to leave the hive. We thought that perhaps the odor of the lake water might be carried back by the lake-station foragers and serve to discourage recruits, since Lindauer had once shown a reluctance on the part of bees to fly over a lake. But when we moved the boat near the far shore of the lake, recruitment picked up enormously, though there was just as much water around the boat as ever.

Given what we now know about the cognitive maps of bees, one possible explanation of the behavior is that recruits decode the dances in the hive and then, from the distance and direction coordinates, place the location on their mental maps. Recruits attending lake-station dances would discover that the advertised spot lay in a lake and so was implausible, whereas those attending shore-station dances would "picture" a more believable location and act on the information. When the boat was rowed near the far shore, recruits would have been able to interpret the dances as reporting food in a plausible spot, and so now these foragers would begin to attract recruits.

Though this is an interesting hypothesis, we cannot be sure that this is actually what went on—particularly since it requires bees to be able to have something very like an imagination. The test we have devised is to try to trick the recruits into "imagining" the wrong terrain. We begin by setting up the hive at the same lake and training two groups of foragers, one to a scow in the lake and another to an identical vessel at the same distance along the shore. After a week or two, every flying bee should know enough about the locale to understand that there is a shoreline running from the northeast to the southwest, with a lake on the southeast side and forest on the northwest.

Instead of simply increasing the sugar concentration (to encourage dancing) and seeing who goes where, we first move the hive overnight

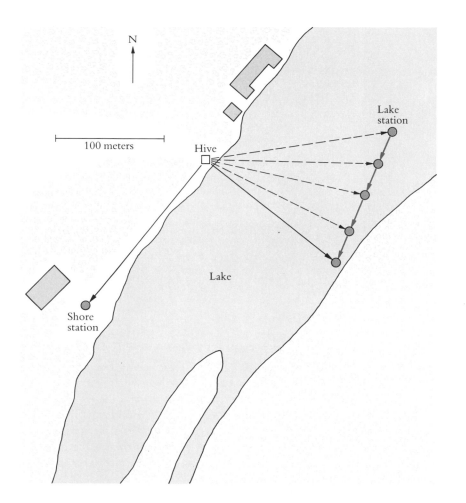

In the original lake experiment, one group of foragers was trained to a boat in the lake while another was trained to a feeder along the near shore. Dances to the lake site produced no recruits until the boat was moved near the far shore.

to a field whose forest/field boundary has the same orientation as the forest/lake boundary. Next we move the boats and set them out in the field and along the forest edge in the same relative locations as at the lake. As the morning begins, the trained foragers fly out to the boats, not noticing (or perhaps not caring) that the lake has dried up overnight, and begin regular round trips to collect food. *Now* we increase the food quality and see what happens. If the recruits believe there is still a lake where there is now a field, they should discount the dances to the field station and only respond to the forest-edge feeder, even though there are no hypothetical lake smells to warn attenders off.

The lake experiment. Foragers were trained to boats either at the lake site or an equivalent shoreline site; the hive was moved overnight and the behavior of recruited bees observed.

The ruse cannot be perfect, since bees available as recruits may well have been out foraging elsewhere before the experiment begins (though we do start pretty early), and so have noticed the switch. As the experiment goes on, too, more and more recruits will have had a chance to venture out and discover the change. Still, there should be a strong preference for the forest-edge feeder. In fact, the first time we managed to stage this tedious and demanding test, 80 recruits turned up at the edge station but only 27 appeared in the field, even though the dancing to the two locations was equally intense.

To be convincing, we need to leave the hive at the field site for a week or two, so that all potential recruits know that there is a field outside. Meanwhile, we must continue to train foragers to the two boats. Then we must move the hives and boats back to the lake overnight and run the experiment again. If, after this move, recruits favor the lake station nearly as much as the shore feeder, and if a series of essential control experiments demonstrate that the sites have no other asymmetries, we will have to take the idea of bee "imagination" more seriously.

Most researchers take the existence of cognitive maps as evidence of a certain degree of imagination and planning, but we have had some second thoughts about what maps really mean. Our perspective on cognitive maps changed after our son got a chess-playing computer. By its nature, chess is a game with far too many possible combinations of piece positions to allow a specific prewired response to each contingency. But chess is predictably unpredictable: although the location of the pieces is highly variable, the object of the game, the size of the board, and the capacities of each piece are fixed. The chess program works by evaluating various alternative moves and selecting the one that maximizes certain offensive and defensive goals—and it does so with surprising speed and alarming skill. Consider how similar a game bees must play when they plan a route: the object (the patch of flowers) and its location are known in advance, as is the gameboard (the locale with its many landmarks). Surely calculating the optimum route is child's play compared with chess. In short, it is not obvious to us that the "planning" that animals engage in with the aid of their mental maps requires any personal intelligence or comprehension. On the other hand, an ability to imagine a location based on dance coordinates or to grasp how a feeder is moving, assuming that these behaviors are what they appear to be, seems far more challenging.

THE FUTURE

When we first began working on bees, we thought we would exhaust our store of questions in a few years, at most; and yet the questions multiply—the more we know, the more we know we do not know. As Karl von Frisch put it, "The life of the bee is like a magic well: the more you draw from it, the more there is to draw." But this is the nature of all science, with questions begetting experiments, which (with luck) yield answers, which beget new questions. The worry, then, is not that we will run out of questions, but that we will fail to imagine the full range of possible answers—hypotheses—to test, or be unable to dream up clever ways to perform critical experiments without investing an inordinate amount of time or money in the effort. And yet, mistaken hypotheses can be as eye-opening as correct ones: very often we ask one question and answer another—that is, the animals do something wholly unexpected, indicating that there is a serious gap in our understanding, a major capacity that we have overlooked and that has resulted in our failure to predict this possible outcome. These anomalies are the golden opportunities of science, and the sophisticated programming and capacities of the honey bee have provided a series of these pleasant shocks unequalled by any other nonhuman species. It remains to be seen whether, in the end, our increasing understanding of the mind of the bee will turn out to have been crucial to our comprehension—if it ever comes—of how human learning, language, and thought operate (and go awry). In any case, for us it is a continuing joy to study these clever creatures with whom it is our undeserved good fortune to share this planet.

Selected Readings

ETHOLOGY

Gould, J. L. *Ethology: The Mechanisms and Evolution of Behavior*. New York: Norton, 1982.

Lorenz, K. Z. *King Solomon's Ring*. London: Methuen, 1952.

Tinbergen, N. *The Study of Instinct*. Oxford: Oxford University Press, 1951.

LEARNING

Gould, J. L. *Ethology: The Mechanisms and Evolution of Behavior*. New York: Norton, 1982.

Schwartz, B. *Psychology of Learning and Behavior*. New York: Norton, 1985.

SOCIAL INSECTS

Michener, C. D. *The Social Behavior of the Bees.* Cambridge, Mass.: Harvard University Press, 1974.

Wilson, E. O. *The Insect Societies.* Cambridge, Mass.: Harvard University Press, 1971.

THINKING AND COGNITION

Griffin, D. R. *Animal Thinking.* Cambridge, Mass.: Harvard University Press, 1985.

CHAPTER 1: BEEKEEPING

Crane, E. *The Archaeology of Beekeeping.* Ithaca, N.Y.: Cornell University Press, 1983.

Dadant and Sons, ed. *The Hive and the Honey Bee.* Hamilton, Ill. Dadant & Sons, 1975.

Fraser, H. M. *Beekeeping in Antiquity.* London: University of London Press, 1951.

CHAPTER 2: THE LIFE OF THE BEE

Free, J. B. *The Social Organization of Honey Bees.* London: Edward Arnold, 1977.

Frisch, K. v. *Bees: Their Vision, Chemical Senses, and Language.* Ithaca, N.Y.: Cornell University Press, 1971.

Gould, J. L. *Ethology: The Mechanisms and Evolution of Behavior.* New York: Norton, 1982.

Menzel, R., and A. Mercer. *Neurobiology and Behavior of Honey Bees.* Berlin: Springer-Verlag, 1987.

Morse, R. A. "Environmental control in a beehive." *Scientific American* 226 (4), 92–98 (1972).

Ribbands, C. R. *Social Life of Honey Bees.* London: Bee Research Association, 1953.

Seeley, T. D. "The ecology of temperate and tropical honey bee societies." *American Scientist* 71, 264–272 (1983).

Snodgrass, R. E. *Anatomy of the Honey Bee.* Ithaca, N.Y.: Cornell University Press, 1956.

Winston, M. *The Biology of the Honey Bee.* Cambridge, Mass.: Harvard University Press, 1987.

CHAPTER 3: COMMUNICATION

Adler, J. "Chcmotaxis behavior of bacteria. "*Scientific American* 234 (4), 40–47 (1976).

Frisch, K. v. "Dialects in the language of the bee." *Scientific American* 207 (2), 78–87 (1962).

Frisch, K. v. *The Dance Language and Orientation of Bees.* Cambridge, Mass.: Harvard University Press, 1967.

Frisch, K. v. "Decoding the language of the bee." *Science* 185, 663–668 (1974).

Gould, J. L. *Ethology: The Mechanisms and Evolution of Behavior.* New York: Norton, 1982.

Lindauer, M. *Communication among Social Bees.* Cambridge, Mass.: Harvard University Press, 1978.

Seeley, T. D. "How honey bees find a home." *Scientific American* 247 (4), 158–168 (1982).

Wenner, A. M. "Sound communication in honey bees." *Scientific American* 210 (4), 116–124 (1964).

Wilson, E. O. "Pheromones." *Scientific American* 208 (5), 100–114 (1963).

CHAPTER 4: THE DANCE–LANGUAGE CONTROVERSY

Gould, J. L. "Honey bee recruitment." *Science* 189, 685–693 (1975).

Gould, J. L. "The honey bee dance-language controversy." *Quarterly Review of Biology* 51, 211–244 (1976).

Gould, J. L., M. Henerey, & M. C. MacLeod. "Communication of direction by the honey bee." *Science* 169, 544–554 (1970).

Wenner, A. M. *The Bee Language Controversy.* Boulder, Col.: Educational Programs Improvement Corp., 1971.

CHAPTER 5: DANCE ECONOMICS

Frisch, K. v. *The Dance Language and Orientation of Bees.* Cambridge, Mass.: Harvard University Press, 1967.

Seeley, T. D. "How honey bees find a home." *Scientific American* 247 (4), 158–168 (1982).

Seeley, T. D. *Honey Bee Ecology*. Princeton: Princeton University Press, 1985.

CHAPTER 6: DANCE EVOLUTION

Esch, H. "Evolution of bee language." *Scientific American* 216 (4), 96–105 (1967).

Frisch, K. v. *The Dance Language and Orientation of Bees*. Cambridge, Mass.: Harvard University Press, 1967.

Gould, J. L., and W. F. Towne. "Evolution of the dance language of honey bees." *American Naturalist* 130, 317–338 (1987).

CHAPTER 7: NAVIGATION

Dyer, F. C., and J. L. Gould. "Honey bee navigation." *American Scientist* 71, 587–597 (1983).

Frisch, K. v. *The Dance Language and Orientation of Bees*. Cambridge, Mass.: Harvard University Press, 1967.

Gould, J. L. "The case for magnetic-field sensitivity in birds and bees (such as it is)." *American Scientist* 68, 256–267 (1980).

Wehner, R. "Polarized-light navigation by insects." *Scientific American* 235 (1), 106–115 (1976).

CHAPTER 8: FLOWER LEARNING

Bornstein, M. H., C. G. Gross, and J. Z. Wolf. "Perceptual similarity of mirror images in infancy." *Cognition* 6, 89–116 (1978).

Gould, J. L. "Natural history of honey bee learning." In *The Biology of Learning* (ed. P. Marler and H. S. Terrace), pp. 149–180. Berlin: Springer-Verlag, 1984.

Gould, J. L., and W. F. Towne. "Honey bee learning." *Advances in Insect Physiology* 20, 55–75 (1987).

Menzel, R., and J. Erber. "Learning and memory in honey bees." *Scientific American* 239, (1), 102–111 (1978).

CHAPTER 9: PROGRAMMED LEARNING

Eimas, P. "The perception of speech in early infancy." *Scientific American* 252 (1), 46–52, (1985).

Geschwind, N. "Specializations of the human brain." *Scientific American* 252 (1), 180–199 (1985).

Gould, J. L. *Ethology: The Mechanisms and Evolution of Behavior.* New York: Norton, 1982.

Gould, J. L., and P. Marler. "Ethology and natural history of learning." In *The Biology of Learning* (ed. P. Marler and H. S. Terrace), pp. 47–74. Berlin: Springer-Verlag, 1984.

Gould, J. L., and P. Marler. "Learning by instinct." *Scientific American* 255 (1), 74–85 (1987).

Hailman, J. "How an instinct is 'learned.'" *Scientific American* 221 (6), 98–108 (1969).

Hubel, D. H. "The visual cortex of the brain." *Scientific American* 209 (5), 54–63 (1963).

Margolis, R. L., S. K. Mariscal, J. D. Gordon, J. Dollinger, and J. L. Gould. "The ontogeny of the pecking response of laughing gull chicks." *Animal Behaviour* 35, 191–202 (1987).

Michael, C. R. "Retinal processing of visual images." *Scientific American* 220 (5), 104–114 (1969).

Stevens, C. F. "The neuron." *Scientific American* 241 (3), 54–65 (1979).

CHAPTER 10: INSIGHT AND INTELLIGENCE

Bonner, J. T. *The Evolution of Culture in Animals.* Princeton: Princeton University Press, 1980.

Gould, J. L. and C. G. Gould. "The insect mind: physics or metaphysics?" In *Animal Mind–Human Mind* (ed. D. R. Griffin), pp. 269–298. Berlin: Springer-Verlag, 1981.

Sources of Illustrations

Drawings by Gabor Kiss. Bees and other animals drawn by John Hatzakis

Chapter 1 opener
Mädchen bei der Bienen, Curt Liebich, Augustinermuseum, Freiburg. Photo, Hans Peter Vieser

Page 2
E. Hernandez-Pancheco. From Eva Crane, *The Archaeology of Beekeeping,* Cornell University Press, Ithaca, N.Y., 1983

Page 3
Harald Pager. From Eva Crane, *The Archaeology of Beekeeping*

Page 4
left, Kenneth Lorenzen

Page 4
right, Harald Pager. Adapted from Eva Crane, *The Archaeology of Beekeeping*

Page 5
Egyptian National Museum catalogue. From Eva Crane, *The Archaeology of Beekeeping*

Page 6
left, Metropolitan Museum of Art, New York

Page 6
right, John Free

Page 7
John Free

Page 10
From J. G. Krunitz, *Das Wesentlichste der Bienen-Geschichte und Bienen-Zucht,* Joachim Pauli, 1744

Page 11
Bildarchiv Preussischer Kulturbesitz, Berlin

Page 12
Giraudon/Art Resource

Page 13
top left and right, Hereford City Library

Page 13
bottom left, From A. Neighbour, *The Apiary; or, Bees, Bee-hives and Bee Culture . . . ,* 2d ed., Kent & Neighbour, London, 1878

Page 13
bottom right, International Bee Research Association Collection B54/57

Page 14
left, John Free

Page 14
right, woodcut by Johann Grüninger from Sebastian Brant, *Georgica,* Strassburg., 1502. From Eva Crane, *The Archaeology of Beekeeping.*

Page 15
left, from Sir George Wheler, *A Journey into Greece,* T. Cademan, London, 1682

Page 15
right, from F. Huber, *Nouvelles observations sur les abeilles,* Barde, Manget, Geneva, 1792

Page 16
right, from L. L. Langstroth, *A Practical Treatise on the Hive and Honey-bee,* 2d ed., C. M. Saxton & Co., New York, 1857. From Eva Crane, *The Archaeology of Beekeeping*

Page 18
Edward Ross

Page 21
Thomas Seeley

Page 24
Thomas Seeley

Page 25
left, Kenneth Lorenzen

Page 25
right, Stephen Dalton/NHPA

Page 26
left top, center, and bottom, Stephen Dalton/NHPA

Page 26
right top, John Free

Page 27
right, adapted with permission from E. P. Jeffree, *Journal of Economic Entomology* 48, © 1955 by Entomological Society of America

Page 28
Stephen Dalton/NHPA

Page 29
John Free

Page 30
Adapted from M. Lindauer, *Zeitschrift für vergleichende Physiologie* 34 (1952)

Page 32
top, Kenneth Lorenzen

Page 32
middle, John Free

Page 32
bottom, John Free

Page 34
left, adapted from H. A. Dade, *Anatomy and Dissection of the Honey Bee,* International Bee Research Association, London, 1978

Page 34
right, John Free

Page 35
Stephen Dalton/NHPA

Page 37
John Free

Page 40
Stephen Dalton/NHPA

Page 42
left, adapted from K. v. Frisch, *Tanzsprache und Orientierung der Bienen,* Springer-Verlag, Berlin, 1965

Page 42
right, Randolf Menzel

Page 43
James Gould

Page 44
Heather Angel/Biofotos

Page 45
Friedrich Barth

Page 46
Kenneth Lorenzen

Page 48
From Lynn Margulis and Karlene V. Schwartz, *Five Kingdoms,* 2d ed., W. H. Freeman and Co., New York, 1988, page 59. Photo by D. Chase

Page 51
Norman Gary

Page 53
Kenneth Lorenzen

Page 54
A. M. Wenner, *Science* 138, © 1962 by AAAS

Pages 57–60
Adapted from K. v. Frisch, *Tanzsprache und Orientierung der Bienen*

Pages 62–64
Redrawn from K. v. Frisch, *Tanzsprache und Orientierung der Bienen*

Page 66
Adapted from M. Lindauer, *Zeitschrift für vergleichende Physiologie* 37 (1955)

Page 67
Kenneth Lorenzen

Page 68
Kenneth Lorenzen

Page 71
John Shaw

Page 75
Adapted from K. v. Frisch, *Tanzsprache und Orientierung der Bienen*

Page 77
James Gould

Page 84
John Shaw

Page 86
Adapted from M. Lindauer, *Zeitschrift für vergleichende Physiologie* 31 (1948)

Pages 88–89
Adapted from P. K. Visscher and T. D. Seeley, *Ecology* 63, © 1982 by Ecological Society of America

Page 89
right, Kenneth Lorenzen

Page 95
James Gould

Page 96
Adapted from R. Boch, *Zeitschrift für vergleichende Physiologie* 38 (1956)

Page 97
Adapted from K. v. Frisch, *Tanzsprache und Orientierung der Bienen*

Page 98
Adapted from M. Lindauer, *Zeitschrift für vergleichende Physiologie* 36 (1954)

Page 99
Kenneth Lorenzen

Page 100
William Towne

Page 102
Larry Spear

Page 103
William Towne

Page 117
James Gould

Page 124
Stephen Dalton/NHPA

Page 126
Adapted from M. Lindauer, *Naturwissenschaften* 44 (1957)

Page 129
Adapted E. Meder, *Zeitschrift für vergleichende Physiologie* 40 (1958)

Page 130
left, Dennis di Cicco

Page 130
right, adapted from I. Biling, *Zeitschrift für vergleichende Physiologie* 9 (1929)

Page 136
Adapted from M. Lindauer, *Ergebnisse der Biologie* 26 (1963)

Page 138
From Karl von Frisch, *The Dance Language and Orientation of Bees,* Harvard University Press, Cambridge, Mass., 1967

Page 141
James Gould

Page 149
Adapted from K. v. Frisch, *Tanzsprache und Orientierung der Bienen*

Page 152
above, M. Lindauer and H. Martin, *Animal Orientation and Navigation* (ed. S. R. Galler et al.), U.S. Government Printing Office, Washington, D.C., 1972
below, U. Jacobs-Jessen, *Zeitschrift für vergleichende Physiologie* 41 (1959)

Page 153
Adapted from H. Martin and M. Lindauer, *Journal of Comparative Physiology* 122 (1977)

Page 154
From Karl von Frisch, *Dance Language*

Page 156
James Gould

Pages 160–162
Adapted from R. Menzel et al.,

Experimental Analysis of Insect Behavior (ed. L. B. Browne), Springer-Verlag, Berlin, 1974

Page 166
Adapted from B. Schnetter, *Zeitschrift für vergleichende Physiologie* 59 (1968)

Page 167
Redrawn from A. Anderson, *Information Processing in the Visual Systems of Arthropods* (ed. R. Wehner), Springer-Verlag, Berlin, 1972

Page 169
Redrawn from K. v. Frisch, *Tanzsprache und Orientierung der Bienen*

Page 171
James Gould

Page 174
top, James Gould

Page 174
bottom, John Shaw

Page 176
top, John Shaw

Page 176
bottom, Edward Ross

Page 177
top and bottom, James Gould

Pages 180–181
James Gould

Page 184
Larry Spear

Page 188
James Gould

Page 194
Redrawn from J. Kien and R. Menzel, *Journal of Comparative Physiology* 113 (1977)

Page 195
Kenneth Lorenzen

Page 197
John Sparks, BBC Natural History Unit

Page 199
Frans Lanting

Page 200
James Gould

Page 205
Susan Hogoe/Anthro-Photo

Page 204
John Shaw

Page 207
Adapted from W. Strange and J. J. Jenkins, *Perception and Experience* (ed. R. D. Walk and H. L. Pick), Plenum, New York, 1978

Page 210
Dwight Kuhn

Page 214
Kathleen Monahan

Page 215
Karl Krall, *Denkende Tiere,* F. Engelmann, 1912

Page 218
James Gould

Page 219
From Wolfgang Köhler, *The Mentality of Apes,* Harcourt, Brace, New York, 1927

Page 220
R. Thompson/Bruce Coleman

Page 224
James Gould

Index

Other books in the Scientific American Library Series

POWERS OF TEN
by Philip and Phylis Morrison and
the Office of Charles and Ray Eames

HUMAN DIVERSITY
by Richard Lewontin

THE DISCOVERY OF
SUBATOMIC PARTICLES
by Steven Weinberg

THE SCIENCE OF MUSICAL SOUND
by John R. Pierce

FOSSILS AND THE HISTORY OF LIFE
by George Gaylord Simpson

THE SOLAR SYSTEM
by Roman Smoluchowski

ON SIZE AND LIFE
by Thomas A. McMahon and John Tyler Bonner

PERCEPTION
by Irvin Rock

CONSTRUCTING THE UNIVERSE
by David Layzer

THE SECOND LAW
by P. W. Atkins

THE LIVING CELL, VOLUMES I AND II
by Christian de Duve

MATHEMATICS AND OPTIMAL FORM
by Stefan Hildebrandt and Antony Tromba

FIRE
by John W. Lyons

SUN AND EARTH
by Herbert Friedman

EINSTEIN'S LEGACY
by Julian Schwinger

ISLANDS
by H. William Menard

DRUGS AND THE BRAIN
by Solomon H. Snyder

THE TIMING OF BIOLOGICAL CLOCKS
by Arthur T. Winfree

EXTINCTION
by Steven M. Stanley

MOLECULES
by P. W. Atkins

EYE, BRAIN, AND VISION
by David H. Hubel

THE SCIENCE OF STRUCTURES AND MATERIALS
by J. E. Gordon

SAND
by Raymond Siever